Evidence for Truth: Archaeology

From: The Right Reverend Bishop Michael Marshall
Lambeth Palace, London SE1 7JU

I heard Prebendary Pearce lecture the Christian Broadcasting Council at the end of last year and was most struck by the importance of what he is saying. There is no doubt in my mind that there is a kind of 'academic mafia' around Biblical scholarship which resists and resents any traditional and radical reappraisal of Biblical scholarship. Prebendary Pearce is a glorious exception by his singularity. He is a scholar of amazing and substantial ability and experience and needs to be taken seriously in this whole quest for the recovery of our scriptural nerve for the Decade of Evangelism.

From: the late Dr John W. Wenham
Vice-principal, Trinity College, Bristol
Warden of Latimer House, Oxford
Co-founder of Tyndale House, Cambridge

Victor Pearce has a great breadth of knowledge in theology and science and has great courage in relating them to one another. His particular strength is in anthropology, a subject about which few Christians are well informed, but one in which he has specialised. He does not indulge in cranky or unsubstantiated scientific ideas, but sorts out the sound scientific conclusions from the notions based on secularist philosophies. He works from an unashamed acceptance of Scripture as God's Word (in the way that Jesus himself did) and robustly and straightforwardly relates secular knowledge to this basic truth.

Evidence for Truth: Archaeology

Victor Pearce

Series Editor: David Page

eagle

Guildford, Surrey

Books in this series by Dr. Victor Pearce:
B.Sc.(Hons), Dip.Anth(Oxon), ALCD, MRE, DEd., FRAI, CF(founder/director)

Vol. 1 Science
Vol. 2 Archaeology
Vol. 3 Preophecy
Vol. 4 Miracles and Angels
Vol. 5 The Origin and Destiny of Life

Other titles by the same author:

Who Was Adam?
Origin of Man
The Science of Man and Genesis
Advent or Atom?

Copyright © Victor Pearce 1993,1998 and 2003
First edition published by Evidence Programmes, Eastbourne, 1993
Second edition first published 2000
Revised and reprinted 2003, © Eagle Publishing Ltd.

British Library Cataloguing in Publication Data. A catalogue record for this book is available from the British Library.

Published by Eagle Publishing Ltd., 6 Kestrel House, Mill Street, Trowbridge, Wilts. BA14 8BE

Scripture quotations: unless specified, Bible quotations are the author's own translation from the Greek or Hebrew text.

Typeset by GCS
Printed by CPD Wales
ISBN No: 0 86347 577 9

CONTENTS

LIST OF ILLUSTRATIONS

THE PRINCIPLES BEHIND THIS SERIES

WE HAVE MORE EVIDENCE TODAY that the Bible is true and accurate than ever before, but the facts have been denied to the public and even to many church people. Evidence and the Bible text have convinced Dr Pearce that the Bible is true from the beginning. It is his purpose to reveal all the undeniable facts:

1. That the Creator of the world is also the Author of the Word. He fully inspired all the 41 writers of the Bible who contributed to the sacred Scriptures over a span of 1,500 years. This is the only explanation of the accuracy and cohesion of the Bible.
2. That the message in the Bible concerning spiritual truth is true, as is also its history, prophecy and science. All are completely true, reliable and factual. This has been confirmed by research.
3. That those who doubt, do so because they do not have the facts, or do not wish to have them or believe them.

Those who have attended the author's lectures have included atheists and agnostics who thought that they had explained everything without God, but as the result of his teaching, have become convinced and converted and blessed.

Dr Pearce has found it is possible to explain science, archaeology and prophecy in simple ways which thrill the student.

Psalm 119:160 'Your Word is true from the beginning.'
Psalm 119:18 'Open my eyes that I may see wonderful things out of your law.'
Psalm 119:42 'Then I shall have an answer for him who taunts me.'
1 Peter 3:15 'Be ready to give an answer to everyone who asks you for a reason for the hope that is in you'.

The Creator is seen in his works and has spoken in his Word.

ABOUT THE AUTHOR

DR VICTOR PEARCE had factory experience as an apprentice and later as a personnel officer and so knows the type of discussion typical of the factory floor and in the office. His experience as a teacher in comprehensive and grammar schools, also his training and lecturing in universities, gives him additional insight to academic views on science, archaeology, theology, anthropology and philosophy. He became an honours graduate of London University in anthropology, through University College, and specialised at Oxford in prehistoric archaeology. He travelled for archaeological digs and research around the Mediterranean including Turkey and the Levant and also in the USA. He read theology at the London College of Divinity; is a Prebendary of Lichfield Cathedral; was Rector of one of the largest Anglican parishes in England; has had 25 curates, built two churches and several halls (one by voluntary labour). He was a member of the Diocesan Synod; was chairman of an ad hoc committee of the Education Council for a new religious syllabus and a visiting lecturer in two Bible colleges. Because this combination of skills with geology and fieldwork is unusual, Victor Pearce is able to offer a unique ministry. He has been much used of God in the conversion of atheists and agnostics who become surprised and fascinated by the facts which previously had been denied them.

He is author of *Who was Adam?*, *Origin of Man*, *The Science of Man and Genesis* and a contributor to the Dictionary of the Church and writes in various periodicals. He has lectured on evidences for biblical truth in university unions and schools. He was a broadcaster for Hour of Revival Association and Transworld Radio for 18 years and for a decade since then for United Christian Broadcasters. His main subject is the accuracy of the Bible as corroborated by the science of man (anthropology) and archaeology. His organisation is inter-church and the staff includes people from most denominations.

PREFACE TO THE FIRST EDITION
WHAT THIS COULD DO FOR YOU

LET ME ASSURE YOU from the outset that there is abundant evidence available which can establish you in a triumphant faith in God and help you to convey it to others.

There is much background information in the Bible which can be accounted for only if the Author of the Bible is the Creator of the universe. In Volume 1 of this series, I gave many examples where science has confirmed and added to our knowledge of the Bible and the origins of life.

Likewise, in Volume 2, I set out to demonstrate how archaeology has confirmed that all the written history in the Bible is true, accurate and factual. Tablets, mounds and pottery dug up from past civilisations confirm this, especially when the Bible dates for events are accepted.

Above all, the Bible contains the prophecies by God of future history right from the beginning. God foretells to the prophets, at each stage, all that is to happen and why, thus all that will happen. In this way, God proves that he is unfolding a remarkable plan for the future happiness of the world and for you. This plan could have unfolded without suffering had not mankind rebelled against God, but now, even by suffering, especially that of Jesus Christ, those purposes will be fulfilled. This is covered in Volume 3.

The evidence for truth which will be brought before you can give you a firm, practical faith to face life and to convince friends.

Victor Pearce
Kidsgrove, England, 1993

PREFACE TO THE SECOND EDITION

SINCE THE FIRST EDITION, there has been a slight improvement in the secular world of publishing towards allowing evidence for Bible truth and accuracy to be presented through the media.

On television, David Rohl has questioned the reliability of some Egyptian records instead of always doubting the Bible's statements. (David Rohl, *A Test of Time: The Bible from Myth to History*, Century Books, 1995.)

Also, to the credit of the press, the Daily Mail and the Daily Express have published articles correcting some attacks on the Bible and The Times published the remarkable evidence found by Dr Thiede which indicates that Matthew wrote his Gospel from notes taken down while Jesus was actually teaching. This confirms the statement by Papius who knew the apostles. It also highlights recent information that **it was customary for rabbis of Christ's time to be followed by disciples with scribing pads to note down the teaching**. Christ himself was recognised as a rabbi because of this very practice. Dr Thiede is saying that some of the New Testament writers heard the Sermon on the Mount in person, stood by the grave of Lazarus, climbed the hill of Calvary and witnessed Christ in his resurrection. He is in fact saying what the New Testament itself claims when the apostle John, for example, wrote of seeing, speaking to and knowing Christ; or the apostle Peter who wrote of being on the Mount of Transfiguration in person as stated in 2 Peter 1:16–18 and in Mark's Gospel (which is really Peter's gospel). All this shows the contemporary nature of the received text. This much we should of course expect, since God has given many prophecies down the ages of the coming of his Son: it would be strange if he had not made provision for accurate records during their fulfilment.

What has influenced the media to adopt a more open view of biblical analysis? Is it the realisation that the breakdown of society, the increase in vandalism, and other appalling symptoms might be the result of widespread unbelief in God's revelation? Perhaps journalists are sensing the growing expectancy within the Church of revival and End Times as we approach the new millenium.

Negative forces are still busy, however, so the facts given in this volume are as necessary as ever.

Victor Pearce
Kidsgrove, May 1998

FOREWORDS

From: Donald J. Wiseman
Professor Emeritus of Assyriology
University of London

Dr Pearce has here brought his wide experience to bear on many of the aspects of the Bible including some which are commonly criticised or attacked. Among these are the Exodus, Exile and the life of Jesus Christ, which are essential to the Christian faith.

Archaeology, the handmaid of history, has much to tell us that illustrates, explains and confirms the biblical narrative and its text. Moreover it often acts as a corrective to false theories and evaluations. As a fast-moving discipline with its use of all available scientific methods, it is important to keep up to date with the evidence. Inevitably various authors may differ over some interpretations, but it has been my long experience that when the Bible is rightly understood and interpreted it is never contradicted by archaeological and historical evidence when that too has been subjected to strict scrutiny.

Dr Pearce touches on many matters in which he is an able and judicious guide. A book like this should encourage you in your study and to look for further evidence and in this you will not be disappointed. I commend to you these pages as worthy of careful study.

From: Kenneth Kitchen
Professor of Egyptology in the School of Archaeology
and Oriental Studies, University of Liverpool

It gives me great pleasure to commend to you these writings of Dr Victor Pearce. I share his concern that scientific and archaeological research is not getting through to young people in schools and colleges – particularly all the evidence supporting the reliability of the Bible.

In some circles there even seems to be a deliberate withholding of such information, yet, it is the fruit of leading scholars. The late F. F. Bruce was internationally acclaimed as a fair-minded scholar of the first rank and president of leading learned societies. Professor D. Wiseman is an Assyriologist and Semitist of international standing; likewise such colleagues as Professor Alan Millard and Dr Terence Mitchell, formerly of the British Museum. These men are known for their restrained, moderate, factual presentation of their researches, as indeed Victor himself is in his books and lectures among us. Victor has brought his own special area of research to bear upon the Bible accounts, namely anthropology and prehistoric archaeology.

Victor refers to me in his works. For myself, I have gone for facts not party opinions. Consequently, as does Victor, I have gone for source material and translated from tablets written thousands of years even before Christ: Hittite, Elamite, Sumerian, Aramaic, Egyptian, Ugaritic, Akkadian and Eblaite.

Yet many critics ignore most of this evidence which establishes the accuracy of the Bible text and sadly it is neglected in many certificate courses sanctioned by some of the mainstream churches. Victor has given us the fruit of his own researches which have taken him into universities, museums, laboratories and archaeological sites in many parts of the world. This has enabled him to contribute original source material himself.

I encourage you to read thoroughly every page which has flowed from his pen – a distillation of years of work in this field. Do not discount the simpler bits nor balk at the technical pieces: allow this work to purge out the deceits and suppositions that may have settled in your mind over the years regarding the world's view of fundamentals. While there is room for more than one opinion at various points, the overall trend is clear.

1 ROLLS-ROYCE TRANSPORT – 2000 BC
EVIDENCE OF ADVANCED LIFESTYLE IN ABRAHAM'S ERA

When archaeology was first launched in the nineteenth century, the discoveries which were made helped both the public and the scholars to see that the amazing Bible stories were factual and not folklore.

Scholars like Dr Layard in 1851, Conder in 1887 and Professor Sayce in 1906, all thought at first that the Bible, though fascinating, was mythological. They thought the wonderful stories never really happened; but when they left their comfortable studies and theories and excavated the actual places described in the Bible, they became convinced that the Scriptures were accurate to the finest detail. Even the very ancient times of the Old Testament were described accurately; and when Sir William Ramsay went out in unbelief to follow St Paul's journeys, he, too, was in for a big surprise. He found that Luke's accounts of the incidents around the Mediterranean matched the highest calibre of precision. Still later, in 1940, Dr W. F. Albright, Director of the American School of Oriental Research, had to keep rewriting his books as he found more and more evidence which refuted the unbelief of the Bible critics.

Sadly, there has risen a generation or more which seems to have lost the advantage of all these discoveries and the misguided assumptions on TV and in the press have gone largely uncorrected. Consequently, even churchgoers who tune in to what they think is a religious programme, find their faith undermined. One programme declared 'The walls of Jericho never tumbled down!' Even a church paper repeated this.

Recently I received a letter from Germany which said:

I am enclosing a clipping from our weekly church paper, showing a picture of the pillars of a palace in Jericho. According to science, it has been proved long ago that the people of Israel found Jericho already in complete ruins when they arrived. The Bible gives a detailed account of how this city was captured. How can you explain this? My problem is that I can either believe everything in the Bible or nothing.

Tactics with Archaeology

The explanation is that a wrong date for the Exodus is given and also for the fall of Jericho when Israel entered the Promised Land. The date given is about 200 years later than the Bible says and so they say that Jericho had already fallen, according to archaeology. Then they go on to accuse the Bible of having mythological stories which never happened. But the Bible quite clearly gives a date for the Exodus and the entry in 1 Kings 6:1 and in Judges 11:13–26. It puts the Exodus earlier in 1440 BC. I shall give you the evidence for this later.

When that Bible date is accepted, all the archaeology of the Middle East falls into place as a beautiful testimony to the accuracy of every event in the Bible. Jericho's collapse is then dated at 1400 BC. When the Bible date is ignored and placed 200 years or so later, of course they can say Jericho was already fallen. They say this repeatedly in television programme after programme.

As no reply was allowed in this particular case either by me or any others trained in archaeology, I replied through the various series in our radio programmes and also in Christian magazines. The biblical series of dates are given to you in Chapter 21, so that you can see what kind of answer to make when people question you. As the general public see the programmes which are repeated at intervals, you will see how to answer them.

Also, when we accept the length of life attributed to Abraham and accept that the length of Israel's stay in Egypt was about 400 years as foretold by God to Abraham, we find that this places Abraham's birth at 2161 BC. At that time, Abraham would be schooled in an advanced civilisation. He would be taught column addition maths, algebra and square roots. Also, he had become a highly organised businessman who later mortgaged his property to follow God's call. These are significant pointers to confirming biblical truth, as we shall see.

The Bible's date for the Exodus also enables us to date Abraham's life at about 2000 BC in the Middle Bronze 1 period.

ABRAHAM COMES ALIVE

Although Abraham lived so long ago, we have some very interesting archaeological finds about his time. There is much that we can learn that shows us that Abraham was a very different kind of man than many often imagine. Professor W. F. Albright, the renowned archaeologist, wrote:

> Dossin and Jean are editing the thousands of tablets from Mari; every new publication of theirs helps us better to understand the life and times of the Hebrew Patriarchs. Abraham, Isaac, and Jacob no longer seem isolated

figures, much less reflections of later Israelite history; they now appear as true children of their age, bearing the same names, moving about over the same territory, visiting the same towns (especially Haran and Nahor), practising the same customs as their contemporaries. In other words, the patriarchal narratives have a historical nucleus throughout.

Abraham's Private Army

Here is one such instance of interesting biblical detail: did you know Abraham had a private army? Of course, the Bible said this all along, but many wrote it off as a fanciful embellishment to make Abraham seem more important than he really was. But now we have found some tablets which shed a surprising light on that rather strange story in Genesis 14. It tells how Abraham had a private army of 318 men. With them he pursued an enemy who had captured his nephew Lot, and rescued him. The army travelled with him all the way from Ur of the Chaldees, and the younger men would be those born to the older members of his private army. The tablets reveal this to be a story true to the facts.

Q But what was Abraham doing with a private army?

Well, these tablets which have been found are called the Execration Texts. First they throw light on the meaning of a word in Genesis – *hanikim*. Men of influence had them; they were retainers or private soldiers. They would have regular inspections. Professor Albright further wrote:

> The strange word for 'retainers', used in verse 14, which occurs nowhere else in the Bible, is now known to be an Egyptian word employed in the Execration Texts of the late nineteenth century BC of the retainers of Palestinian chieftains . . . The enigmatic fourteenth chapter of Genesis, describes the triumph of Abraham over the Mesopotamian kings headed by Chedorlaomer of Elam. A generation ago, most critical scholars regarded this chapter as very late and as quite unhistorical. Now we cannot accept such an easy way out of the difficulties which the chapter presents, since some of its allusions are exceedingly early, carrying us directly back into the Middle Bronze Age.

One tablet records an inspection of private armies which took place in the city of Ur, which was Abraham's city. This was in 2000 BC – the time of Abraham. The tablet shows that others had small private armies too and gives a list of them. The smallest was 40 soldiers and the largest was 600. So that means that Abraham's army of 318 was about average in size.

The tablets reveal that this inspection took place in the third dynasty, Abraham's time. The private armies were all lined up and reviewed by the Commissioner of Ur. All the merchant princes had armies and their numbers were listed for the official records. They were trained to fight.

Genesis 14 shows that Abraham was a good strategist. He defeated four armies, all much larger than his own. He did it by dividing his force in two and making a surprise attack by night.

Notice how far that forced march took him – up north to Dan and then on into Syria and Damascus (Genesis 14:14–16). In the early part of that chapter, it is the war of four kings against five. Critics used to think it was a fairy story, but again that battle was recorded on monuments which have been found. The five kings of Sodom and Gomorrah were defeated because they were trapped in slimy tar pits. Later, that area was invaded by the Dead Sea flowing southwards, but on an occasion when the Dead Sea was low, I walked into the water and picked up bitumen – and had tar on my feet. The enemy kings took the women captive as well as the men, and that included Lot and his wife.

The King of Sodom was grateful for the rescue. He told Abraham to keep all the spoil and goods he had recovered, but Abraham said he wouldn't touch it, not even a thread or a shoelace. All he would keep was the food his soldiers had eaten, he said he wasn't going to make them cough that up! Abraham refused the offer of the spoil and goods because he realised how sinful those cities were getting. There was shameless homosexuality. God was giving them time to repent, but they didn't, and later fire and sulphur and salt rained down from the sky (see next chapter). Jesus said, 'As it was in the days of Lot, so it will be in the days when I, the Son of Man shall come.' So don't let it take you unawares. Homosexuality is a feature today all right! The Bible tells us to turn to God for deliverance.

Abraham's Mysterious Visitor

Fortunately, there is a beautiful end to the story of Abraham's private army. A mysterious person came to him and blessed him. Abraham gave him a tenth of all his possessions.

Tithing had actually started earlier on in history. We know from archaeology that tithing – that is, giving a tenth of one's income or profits back to God – was already being practised in the temples. These temples were built soon after the Flood. In fact, the early forms of writing were invented in order to record these gifts to God. We have some of these tablets in the Oxford Ashmolean library. Archaeologists date tithing at 3400 BC – that is, 1,400 years before Abraham. That is as long before Abraham as Moses was before Christ.

Coming back to this mysterious person: his name was

Melchizedek, the priest of the Most High God. The letter to the Hebrews is all about him! He represents the one whose sacrifice for all sins was sufficient for the forgiveness of every sinner who repents. This priesthood is better than the Levite kind of priesthood. The Levites had to offer a sacrifice every day. That proved that their sacrifices were not effective, otherwise they would not have been repeated each day.

So Melchizedek represented the Lord Jesus Christ, because his offering did not need to be repeated. Jesus' sacrifice on the cross was sufficient for the forgiveness of every sinner who repented – it did not need to be repeated. Anybody who accepts Christ's sacrifice for their sin is saved for ever.

Now there are some remarkable things about this mysterious person whom Abraham met. He was, we are told, the King of Peace. That is what the word *salem* means. And there is another remarkable thing. He brought bread and wine to Abraham. The bread would represent the Lord's body and the wine his blood, which would be poured out for sinners. That was a symbol of what Jesus was going to do; but when we take the Lord's Supper, it is a sign of what he has already done. So the bread and wine given to Abraham looked *forward to the cross* and the bread and wine given to us believers looks *back to the cross* and reminds us of what the precious Lord Jesus has done to save us.

Melchizedek is mentioned only once more in the Old Testament. That is in what God said to David 1,000 years later and 1,000 years before the cross and what he said was remarkable. It is in Psalm 110. It says that God will say to the Lord Jesus, 'Sit at my right hand, after the resurrection, until you return to judge the world. You are a priest like Melchizedek.'

So the comment in the New Testament is this, 'When Christ had offered for all time a single sacrifice for sins, he sat down at the right hand of God . . . for by one offering only on the cross, he has made complete salvation for ever, for those who are washed through trusting in the precious blood of Christ.'

Evidence for Abraham's Lifestyle

Q Why would Abraham require such a private army as described in Genesis chapter 14?

Archaeology has opened up a whole new vista of Abraham's culture. He and his family maintained a commercial trade route from Mesopotamia (Iraq), through Haran in North Syria and down to Palestine. They needed an army to protect their caravans travelling in an arc of over a thousand miles along the edge of that fertile crescent.

Abraham would regard himself as a modern, educated man of his day. The idea that some had of Abraham as a primitive Bedouin chief with a few sheep and goats nibbling at his tent pegs has been changed by archaeological discovery. Thousands of tablets have now been deciphered which give us a very full picture of life 2,000 years BC. We have more detailed knowledge of those times than we have even of medieval England!

Thirty thousand Akkadian and Sumerian tablets describe children's education, their mathematics, spelling tablets and work schedules, and nearly 2,000 children's 'text books' have been found in the form of tablets written by the children. History, religion and mathematics were taught.

Advanced systems of calculation included adding up in columns of 60. This value column system made our modern calculators possible, and the figure 60 persists on our watches still, giving us 60 seconds to the minute and 60 minutes to the hour. The circle was divided up into 360 degrees at this time. This also came from the Sumerians who appear to have got it from Noah. Why? Because the timing of Noah's Flood was based upon a year of 360 days, 12 months of 30 days each (see *Volume 1: Science,* Chapter 13). Algebra and square roots were also taught. Who would have imagined that Abraham must have learnt algebra at school in the city of Ur in Mesopotamia 4,000 years ago!

All this was brought to light by Sir Leonard Woolley in 1929 and brought up to date by Dr P.R.S. Moorey at Oxford in 1982. In his book, *Ur of the Chaldees* (Pelican, 1952), Woolley reported:

We had expected to find very modest dwellings one storey high and built of mud brick consisting of three or four rooms opening on to a court. Instead of this, we discovered that in Abraham's time, men lived in houses built with walls of burnt brick below, rising in mud brick above, with plaster and whitewash hiding the change in material, two storeys high, and containing as many as thirteen or fourteen rooms round a central paved court which supplied light and air to the house. The streets were narrow, winding, and unpaved, with on either side, blank walls unbroken by any windows – streets such as one sees in any native town even today, impossible for wheeled traffic. Against one house, a mounting-block showed that donkeys would be used for riding or for freight, and the corners of the narrow lanes were carefully rounded off to prevent injury to goods or riders.

Through the front door of a house one passed into a tiny lobby with a drain in its floor where the visitor might wash his hands or feet, and from that into the central court. On one side rose the brick stairs leading to the upper floor, and behind the stairs was a lavatory with its terra-cotta drain; then came the kitchen, distinguished by its fireplace and the stone grinders left on the ground; a reception room with two doors or one door unusually wide was for guests, another room might be for the servants, and yet

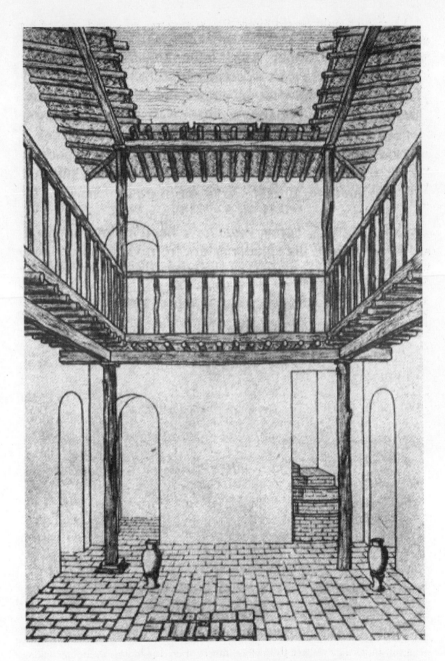

Figure 1.1. Restoration of a house of the time of Abraham in the town of Ur, 4,000 years ago. This demonstrates the advanced development of civilisation and habitation with bathrooms, drainage (linked to town drains) and second storeys for servant accommodation.

Courtesy: Sir Leonard Woolley, Ur of the Chaldees, *Pelican Books, 1952* another the domestic chapel.

We must revise considerably our ideas of the Hebrew patriarch when we learn that his earlier years were spent in such sophisticated surroundings; he was the citizen of a great city and inherited the tradition of ancient and highly-organised civilisation. The houses themselves bespoke comfort and even luxury. Apart from the actual fabric, there was little left to throw light on the daily life of the inhabitants, but one or two stores of tablets did bear witness to their intellectual interests. We found copies of the hymns which were used in the service of the temples, and with them mathematical tables ranging from plain sums in addition to formulae for the extraction of square and cube roots, and other texts.

The Sumerians were essentially business-like, and no transaction was recognised in law unless it was witnessed to by a written document, and so for all incomings, the priests drew up formal receipts of which copies were filed in the temple archives.

Figure 1.2. Ladies' fashions in the town of Ur.
Royal finery from Abraham's city. Recovered from a deathpit in the royal cemetery at Ur, this headdress belonged to Queen Shub-ad, buried, amidst the bodies of her maids of honour, more than a 1,000 years before Abraham lived. One of the oldest specimens known of the goldsmith's art, it is also an example of the astonishing height of achievement already reached by the forerunners of craftsmen who were contemporary with the Patriarch. It may be seen today in the British Museum.

Courtesy: Sir Leonard Woolley 'Ur of the Chaldees' Pelican Books, 1952

ABRAHAM, A HIGHLY SUCCESSFUL BUSINESSMAN

'It appears,' says Dr Leslie Dent in his lecture notes, 'that Abraham was a highly successful businessman who ran caravan trains throughout the Middle East.' He lived in the mid-Bronze Age, dated 2100 to 1900 BC. In that period, new trade routes were opening up.

Abraham's father, Terah, developed the family business by moving to Haran. The name Haran is significant. It means 'crossroads'. It was the northern crossroads at the apex of the trade route which stretched from Iraq in the south-east and down to Canaan and Kadesh-Barnea in the south-west and on to Egypt. These were all international roads. One is sometimes referred to in Scripture as 'The King's Highway'.

Terah must have been an international businessman. So he moved his headquarters from Ur to Haran, says Dr Dent. Genesis 11:31 says:

> And Terah took Abraham his son and Lot the son of Haran his grandson, and Sarai his daughter-in-law, who was his son Abraham's wife, and they moved out with them from Ur of the Chaldees to go into the land of Canaan, but when they reached Haran, they settled there.

So Terah was keeping pace with modern progress in ancient times. His business logo could well have proclaimed, 'Terah and Sons International Transport Supervisors'.

Abraham was soon to move farther on down the trade route, for the Lord said to Abraham, 'Get out from your country and from your relatives and from your father's house and go to a land I will show you.'

This was a call of God of great importance for the whole world, Genesis 14:3 implies, for it would be in the land of Canaan that the Saviour of the world would come as a descendant through Isaac.

On the route south from 'Crossroads', however, was the city of Damascus in what is now called Syria. This was an important banking centre, thus it would seem that to obey the call, Abraham had to mortgage his business to a financier called Eliezer. According to the laws of the time, it was to him that all his inheritance would go if Abraham had no heir (Genesis 15:2), and being childless at the age of 75, God's promise of many decendants took some believing. God's assurance was, 'Fear not, Abraham, I am your shield and your exceedingly great reward.'

Donkeys and 'Rolls-Royce' Camel Transport

I have told you about Abraham's private army, which protected his transport business. What were these caravans like and how were supplies maintained?

The size, numbers and system are surprising. Dr Dent says, 'There are Syrian records of caravan trains with 3,000 donkeys! There was an elaborate maintenance system. Grass was planted along the trails to feed the pack animals. People were employed to make specially ter-raced fields. They had to fetch water and lived in beehive-shaped hous-es along the routes. The caravan donkey was a particular breed. It could travel for two or three days without water while carrying a pack weighing 150–200 lb. One man would control five donkeys and walk behind their charges, but the leader would ride on a donkey.'

Camels were also in use in Abraham's time. The Bible critics did not know this and their out-of-date accusations that the association of camels with Abraham was an anachronism – as has been portrayed on television – is wrong. Some theologians are still teaching it though.

Bones of domesticated camels 2000 BC have now been found, but the camel was a prestige symbol, ridden only by the general manager. It was his Rolls-Royce. When Abraham's steward journeyed north to 'Crossroads', to find a suitable bride for his master's son, Isaac, it was his master's 'Rolls-Royce' camels he took. He would have donkeys only for himself. 'The servant took ten camels, of the camels *of his master,* and he departed' (Genesis 24:10).

The Shady Transactions of a Wily Father-in-Law

Thank God for fathers-in-law and, of course, for splendid mothers-in-law. Unfortunately, however, some family disputes grow out of wills and inheritance.

Jacob, Abraham's grandson, who lived 18 centuries BC, had a father-in-law named Laban. This father-in-law employed Jacob, but kept breaking his contract. Worse still, he sold his two daughters to Jacob for wives. This was a very unfair dowry system and the two daughters complained that their father was even squandering the money Jacob had paid him. This, they said, squandered their inheri-tance. They would have no money for their children, so they decided with Jacob to run away from their father's house and go to live in Jacob's home.

Now Rachel, the younger daughter, did something very puzzling, until archaeology threw light upon the affair. She packed her family doll, called a teraphim, into her camel's saddle bag (Genesis 31:34). Now, I ask you, what would a grown woman want with a doll?

The father chased after them in fury. He also was very angry that the family doll had disappeared. He searched Rachel's tent, but didn't find the doll because Rachel was sitting on the camel saddle and refused to move.

Quaint Evidence for Truth in Archaeology

Why all this fuss about a doll? What on earth was the father doing searching desperately for it? Archaeology has found that, on the back of these teraphim dolls, there was inscribed the rights of inheritance. So when Rachel carried off the doll, she was taking her title deeds with her! It was her right to the inheritance.

Now the point is this. To be so accurate in such quaint customs as this is a quite definite proof that the Bible story was contemporary. It was not written 1,000 years or so later!

Why do I say that? Because, in the last century, some said that people such as Abraham and Moses could not have written the first five books of the Bible. They insisted that these were put together 1,000 years later.

We now know this is impossible. Why? Because the laws of inheritance and legal methods change down the centuries and nobody living 1,000 years later could have got such details right.

The evidence of the Bible getting it right is found in the first five books of the Bible. We now know that they must have been written 14 centuries BC, because all five of Moses' books are drawn up on the Hittite legal method of that time. A document had to contain six major sections and procedures set out in separate legal styles. These procedures are accurately given in Exodus to Deuteronomy. Some, not knowing this, have said that it must have been written 1,000 years later, but we can now safely say that it must have been set out in the time of Moses. Scribes in later times would not have got the proceedings correct.

Q Why do legal enactments take place at a law 'court'?

The word 'court' means a courtyard. In Abraham's time, 2000 BC, legal agreements were enacted in the court by the city gate. We read of a transaction between Abraham and a Hittite in Genesis chapter 23. Abraham was purchasing a burial cave for his beloved wife Sarah who had just died.

Now the details given in Genesis show just how accurate the early chapters of the Bible are. They must have been recorded at the time because a later generation would not know the Hittite legal procedure. This procedure has been unearthed by the discovery of ancient tablets. It proves that, when we read such passages as Genesis 23, we are reading something which was recorded at the time of the events.

And to think that, until recently, many denied that the Hittites had ever existed and tried to discredit the Bible for mentioning them!

Archaeologists have dug up many tablets written in those times. Here is an extract from one which mentions the court. The writer says he will take the offenders to court:

> I am sending you this tablet of mine to warn you that nobody must come near the house of the woman dream interpreter. I have bought that house with all its bricks. If anyone so much as touches a brick of it, I will go to the gate court against all of you.

Here is another tablet dug up from Abraham's time:

> Your sister Akatija sends the following message. For three years the field has not been thirsting for water . . . the field is now full of barley. Now I am raising a boy, telling myself, 'let him grow up, so that there will be somebody to bury me'. But the merchant demands, 'Hand over the deeds now'.

Now let me read the transaction between Abraham and the Hittite, from Genesis chapter 23, to show how accurately it recaptures that background:

> Abraham rose and bowed to the people of the land . . . Ephron the Hittite answered Abraham in the hearing of all at the gate court of his city, saying, 'Hear me, I give you the field and I give you the cave that is in it, in the presence of witnesses – bury your dead wife.' Abraham bowed and said, 'My lord, a piece of land worth 400 shekels of silver – what is that between me and you?' Abraham weighed out 400 shekels of silver at the standard rate . . . and it was witnessed in the gate court of the city.

This transaction in the Bible accurately reflects the culture of Abraham's time. The Bible is always accurate even in circumstantial details like that.

THE DEVELOPMENT OF THE ALPHABET

While we are on the subject of the Genesis account, it used to be frequently said that Moses could not have written the Torah (first five books) because writing had not yet developed in his time. This position may have been understandable 100 years ago, but it has now become untenable. Yet we still find some trying to make us believe that the Torah was written 1,000 years after Moses.

Dr W. F. Albright was Director of the American School of Oriental Research, and a member of the British Society for Old Testament Study. In his Pelican paperback, *Archaeology of Palestine* (1957), he says, 'It is, accordingly, sheer hypercriticism to deny the substantially Mosaic character of the Pentateuchal tradition'.

We need not dwell on this matter, for we have already made mention of the vast amount of tablets which have been discovered from periods going way back before Abraham, and even back to what may have been Noah's log book.

Figure 1.3. Evidence of writing established before Abraham.
Another 'Flood' record. Written in cuneiform script, near Ur, when Abraham was actually alive, the Blundell prism (above) affords evidence of the current traditional belief concerning the period of the Deluge. The catastrophe was held to have happened long before the Patriarch's time. It gives a long list of rulers who lived before the Flood, then says 'The flood came up' and speaks of those who ruled after the Flood.

Courtesy: Ashmolean Museum, Oxford

The spectacular finds at Ebla show that, as early as 2300 BC, major city states were using cuneiform script and the Sumerian language for a wide variety of documents. But, in Syria and Palestine, from c.1500 BC, a still more important script came into use: the alphabet.

The development of writing was such that Sir Charles Marston, in *The Bible Comes Alive*, sums up by saying:

The Israelites had, from the time of Moses onwards, at least three alphabetical scripts. First, what is known as the Sinai Hebrew; next, what is known as Phoenician Hebrew; and lastly, after the captivity in Babylon, what is known as Assyrian Hebrew. Those facts entirely change the whole literary problem. Oral transmission becomes inadmissible.

SUMMARY

'ROLLS-ROYCE CAMELS', 2000 BC

1. The Bible dates make harmony with history:
Some critics give dates 200 years later than Bible dates and then accuse the Bible of not matching history.

2. Tablets tally with Bible truth, e.g.
- Abraham's private army parade (Ur).
- Abraham's business (Haran).
- Abraham's mortgage risk (Eliezer), Gen 15:2.
- Abraham's family international transport company.
- The 'Battle of the Four Kings against Five' is recorded on archaeological tablets.
- Deeds on the doll for Rachel. (Legal knowledge lost later.)
- Court cases held at city gates.

3. Abraham's advanced civilisation 2000 BC.
- Algebra and arithmetic for Abram (Abraham) at Ur.
- The proof: 60 sec; 60 min on our watches.
- 360 degrees and compasses come from Ur.

4. Camels were the 'Rolls-Royce' of the bosses.
Only donkeys for employees.

2 GOD IS A GEOLOGIST

EVIDENCE OF INCIDENTAL KNOWLEDGE IN SCRIPTURE

God is a geologist! We have seen in *Volume 1: Science*, how he made earth and there is plenty of evidence of this in the Bible: the Creator has left his genetic fingerprints in his written Word as well as in his material creation. But there are remarkable indications in various passages of the Bible of a geological knowledge of the structure of the continents and earth movements.

THE DEAD SEA RIFT VALLEY

A convincing instance is the geological history of Sodom and Gomorrah, past, present and future. The first reference to Sodom comes early in Scripture. Turn to it in Genesis 10:19. It refers to Sodom and the cities of this deep Dead Sea valley as the area of prime beauty and productivity which was inhabited by the descendants of Noah's son, Ham. In this verse there is no hint of the destruction to come in the days of Abraham. We can therefore reasonably conclude that the source of this information is prior even to Abraham himself.

That this area was beautiful and fertile at the time of Abraham is confirmed in chapter 13, verse 10: 'Lot looked up and scrutinised all the plain of Jordan and saw that it was well watered everywhere, before the Lord destroyed Sodom and Gomorrah. It was like the garden of the Lord, like the land of Egypt as you come to Zoar.'

Lot and his wife and their two daughters went down into that valley to live in Sodom. The area was 1,200 feet below sea level and consequently had a tropical climate. But there was a danger Lot did not know of – it was a classical deep rift valley. The land had sunk into a valley because it had collapsed downwards when the rift had opened up. The rift was caused through two continental margins drawing away from each other, so that an area which had perhaps previously been 3,000 feet above sea level had sunk to well below sea level, as in the case of Sodom. At various times, such a rift valley can shift and sink again (see Fig 2.1).

The Testimony of the Dead Sea: Past, Present and Future

The extraordinary thing is this. The experience of this rift valley is featured throughout Scripture past, present and future, from prehistory in

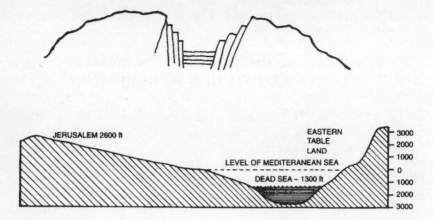

Figure 2.1. The cross-section of a typical rift valley and the rift of the Jordan Valley to scale.

Genesis to historic times in Ezekiel, and to the last days in Revelation. God knows beforehand when these geological events are going to happen!

First, we have a description of its beauty long before Moses. Where did this information come from? Perhaps it was handed down from Abraham. Archaeology has found evidence which confirms that the area was extremely fertile before the overthrow of Sodom and Gomorrah. Beneath the barren sterile soft soils of the surface there is a thick layer of rich soil.

There is evidence all around the Dead Sea of the overthrow of the wicked cities as described in Genesis chapter 19. Salt-encrusted mountain peaks and salt-coated fossil trees are there. The account also describes sulphur raining down on the cities from the sky, ignited by volcanic fires.

One can pick up lumps of this sulphur around the Dead Sea. Bitumen is also present. If you paddle round the edge of the sea where it is shallow, you can scoop up lots of black muddy tar. In fact, the ladies smear it over their bodies as a beauty treatment for healthy skin!

The Bible foretells another eruption through a further sinking of the rift valley floor in the last days when anti-Semitic armies will invade Israel and perish in the overthrow. 'As it was in the days of Sodom and Gomorrah, so will it be when the Son of Man shall come,' said the Lord Jesus (Luke 17:26). This will be in more ways than one, for God described to Ezekiel the overthrow of invading armies at the second coming of Christ (which we shall deal with in *Volume 3: Prophecy*):

I will rain upon him and upon his military divisions and the multitudes of people with him, an overflowing rain of great hailstones, fire and sulphur. Thus will I magnify myself. I will be known in the vision of many nations, and they will know that I am the Lord (Ezekiel 38:22).

There are more events described which extend this knowledge of geology far beyond the land of Palestine. This great rift valley extends from Jordan down to the Red Sea, which is part of it, on into the great rift valley of Africa. I'm sure you will have seen pictures of it on TV nature programmes.

In Africa, the rift valley is 60 miles wide. It is flat and the edges of the rifted continent rise up on both sides; it stretches southwards until it comes out opposite Madagascar. There are long narrow lakes in the valley to mark its progress.

The movement of continents against each other is all part of the tectonic plate movements throughout the world. This causes earthquakes all around the world, especially along what are called the New Fold mountains. Most earthquakes have occurred along these mountains and the Lord Jesus said they would increase as the time of his second coming drew near (Matthew 24).

The Mount of Olives Split in Two?

Q How can we say the rift valley will erupt again?

It is because God told the prophets that when Jesus descended to the Mount of Olives on the east side of Jerusalem, the mountain would split in two from east to west and join up the Mediterranean with the Dead Sea rift by a very wide new valley. The description of the new environment created is all that of a new rift valley. Zechariah 14:4: 'The Mount of Olives will cleave in the middle from east to west and there will be a very great valley. Half of the mountain will move northwards and half of it towards the south.'

What geological movement would cause this? It is the movement of the continent of Africa at its junction with Europe and Asia. That junction is in the Middle East. The huge continent of Africa would swivel as on an apex. That has already caused what is called the Great Rift Valley. An Oxford geologist told me that one day, Africa would split off from Asia somewhere in the Middle East. He did not know where and when, but three places in the Bible tell you. It will be when Christ descends from heaven, and it will be at the Mount of Olives.

I have personally observed a major fault which runs throughout the middle of the Mount of Olives. So here, the Creator geologist knows and controls the time and place of that tremendous event.

Jerusalem-on-Sea?

Verse 8 of Zechariah 14 indicates that this rift valley will join up the Mediterranean Sea on the west with the 'eastern sea' (Indian Ocean?) and the Lord will become King over all the earth. Jerusalem could become the shipping centre of the world! It is to Ezekiel that God gives more details, in Ezekiel 47. Verse 10 describes how the fish of the Mediterranean Sea will swim throughout this new inter-continental channel. They will come into the Jordan Valley which will fill up to sea level. The Dead Sea will no longer be dead with salt concentrates, but all kinds of fish will swim in it. In fact, Scripture says, 'Fishermen will stand beside the sea from En-gedi to En-eglaim'. That will be at the new sea level. At present, the Dead Sea is 1,300 feet below sea level.

Q How did the Bible know where sea level was in inland areas?

The way to measure sea level is a modern science. The Bible knows only because God the marine geologist told Ezekiel. God also told the prophet Joel eight centuries BC about this sea level and the rift valley. He said that sea level will be at the Valley of Shittim.

Fresh Water for Jerusalem

To all those three prophets, God also spoke about fresh water flowing from 'the house of the Lord in Jerusalem'. To Joel, he says in chapter 3 verse 18, 'A fountain will come forth from the house of the Lord'.

To Zechariah (14:8) God said, 'On that day' (that is the day that Christ returns), 'living waters will flow from Jerusalem . . . throughout summer and winter'. In other words, it will never dry up. To Ezekiel, he gave a very full description in chapter 47 verses 1–9:

> Then he brought me back to the door of the temple and behold, water was issuing from below the threshold of the temple toward the east (for the temple faced east), and the water was flowing down from below the south end of the threshold of the temple, south of the altar. Then he brought me out by way of the north gate and led me round on the outside to the outer gate that faces toward the east and the water was coming out on the south side. Going on eastward with a line in his hand, the man measured a thousand cubits and then led me through the water and it was ankle-deep. Again, he measured a thousand and led me through the water and it was knee-deep. Again he measured a thousand and led me through the water and it was up to the loins. Again he measured a thousand and it was a river that I could not pass through for the water had risen, it was deep enough to swim in, a river that could not be passed through. And he said to me, 'Son of man, have you seen this?' Then he led me back along the bank of the river. As I went back, I saw upon the bank of the river, very many trees

on the one side and on the other. And he said to me, 'This water flows toward the eastern region and goes down in the Arabah, and when it enters the stagnant waters of the sea, the water will become fresh. And wherever the river goes, every living creature which swarms will live, and there will be very many fish because this water goes there; so the waters [of the Dead Sea] will become fresh, and everything will live where the river goes.'

Q Where will all this fresh water come from?

I asked the Lord to show me and he did. I came upon a hydrological survey of the Land of Palestine by the Government. This survey revealed that underneath Palestine from Mount Carmel in the north to Beersheba in the south, was a great artesian basin of water – thousands and thousands of gallons of water. Then I read the words, 'There is enough water in this limestone basin to supply the whole of Palestine for three-and-a-half years, even if not a single drop of rain fell.'

Then I read the words in this survey. 'If a fracture occurred in the rock at Jerusalem, perpetual fresh water would flow.' Why? Because the middle part of this natural water basin reaches its deepest part under Jerusalem.

I said, 'Praise the Lord for showing me!' That is why God told Zechariah that it would flow even in the hot dry summer. Yes, God knows his earth! He is an expert geologist and hydrologist. You ought to have God on your Water Board. By the way, how much water rate do you pay to God?!

Of course, this has a spiritual lesson also. The water – the fresh water of life – flows out from the temple of God. But that does not mean this will not literally happen at Christ's coming. The accounts are written as facts of future history with scientific accuracy by the God of geology.

St John, in the last chapter of the Book of Revelation, gives a spiritual application. He wrote, 'The angel showed me the river of life, bright and clear as crystal, flowing from the throne of God and of the Lamb . . . The Spirit and the Bride say, "Come, let him who is thirsty come, let him who desires take the water of life without payment".'

THE INCREASE OF EARTHQUAKES

Q What connection has this with the increase of earthquakes around the world?

During the last 100 years, that increase has been calculated. It is an increase of 300 per cent. They occur mostly in the New Fold mountains. This linear range is where all the continents and sub-continents pushed or pulled on each other in the continental drift, called the tectonic plate movement. They pushed up the Alps, they pushed up the Everest range, they raised the range which encircles the Pacific Ocean.

God's Geology Preparing for Christ's Return

So why are the earthquakes increasing? It is because God's geology is preparing for the return of Christ to Olivet. The continents are getting ready for when the feet of their Creator touch down upon Olivet. The continental tensions will snap and the rift valley will break through to the Mediterranean.

Now here is an effective answer to someone who asks, 'Why does God allow earthquakes?' Instead of apologising for God, we can show them that prophecy is being fulfilled, that Christ is coming and that they need to get ready in this age of increased sodomy.

The Lord Jesus himself said that one of the signs of Christ's imminent return would be earthquakes. Earthquakes have been recorded by some as increasing tenfold. Yes, the whole earth is preparing for the return of Christ. Every earthquake – tragic though it may be – should tell you that the descent of Christ to Olivet is near. When his feet touch Olivet, the apex of the stress of the African continent will pull away from Asia and Europe.

Let's look at the accuracy of the description of that rift valley which will open up between the Mediterranean and the Jordan Valley. It is what God told Zechariah 500 years BC recorded in Zechariah 14:4: 'On that day the Lord's feet shall stand on the Mount of Olives which is by Jerusalem on its east side. And the Mount of Olives will split in two and will run from east to west by a very wide valley.' Stop there for a minute. How wide will it be? Well the rift valley in Jordan is about ten miles wide, but becomes wider as it goes south into Africa. There it is 60 miles wide. So this could be a tremendous movement of the earth. The text goes on to say, '. . . a very wide valley, so that one half of the mountain will withdraw northward and the other half southward'. Imagine the terror of the godless armies which will be attacking Jerusalem at that time. God says, 'You will run away in panic as you fled from the earthquake in the days of King Uzziah.'

Geological Consequences – Did Jesus Know?

Somebody asked me, 'Did Jesus know that the earth was round?' I think he did. I think he showed this when he spoke of his second coming. He showed that at that moment some would be asleep in bed, some would be doing the morning cooking and some would be at work later in the day. See Luke 17:34,35; Matthew 24:40–42.

Did Jesus know about the geological consequences of his second coming? I think he did. I think also that Jesus knew about the rift valley consequences of his second coming. Why? Because he refers to it as being like the overthrow of Sodom and Gomorrah. That terrible hail of fire and sulphur from the sky was caused by the rift valley in Lot's day subsiding a bit further. That rain of melting and molten salt which rained down and encrusted Lot's wife in salt was a partial rift valley subsidence.

Sodom: City of the Dead Sea

Remember that the Lord punished Sodom for its homosexuality by making fire and sulphur rain down from the sky. As I have said, if you go down to the Dead Sea, you can see evidence for the destruction of that city of Sodom. If you walk round the southern end, you can pick up lumps of sulphur even today and the salt which rained down and engulfed Lot's wife can be seen around on the peaks and rocks. They are encrusted with salt!

There is a salt mountain with a 150-foot thick stratum of salt. The earthquake ruptured this and the fierce volcanic fire would melt it as it shot up into the air and rained down its terrible death upon those who disbelieved God's warning.

You can also see the bitumen if you paddle in the Dead Sea at some spots. This tar, melted by volcanic heat, rained down all aflame.

Sodom and the Jordan Valley were at the northern end of that great rift valley which runs south down into Africa. In that same rift valley in Africa, there are lakes of tar. A lot of our roads are made from it.

Lot's Wife

You will remember the fate of Lot's wife. She looked back. Jesus says she went back. Yes, first the look and then the backsliding. She walked back and got caught in that frightening horrific rain of volcanic minerals. She became a pillar of salt. There are tree stumps which have become pillars of salt at the southern end of the Dead Sea. Wouldn't it be startling if you chipped away at one of those salt stumps and found Lot's wife inside! I wonder what your reaction would be! Can you imagine yourself finding a body standing upright, fully preserved from decay in the salt which had rained down, melted by fire and then cooled and solidified around that body! You can see the crusts of salt on the hill peaks and on the fossilised tree trunks. Could any one of those tree trunks be Lot's wife? Would you remember the Lord's words to those living in these last days? 'Remember Lot's wife.' They were kindly said to backsliders in the last days.

Jesus urged us elsewhere to have salt of a different kind within ourselves. Have your trials made you a bit irritable and complaining or are you the salt which is saving your family from corrupting? Do you bring the sweetness of Jesus into your home? Forgive me for asking, but I am sure you have found, as I have, that we can easily let the wholesome sweetness drain away from our character if we don't have salt within ourselves. Perhaps, like Lot's wife, you looked back upon your possessions and took your eyes off Jesus. Have salt within yourself, seek not to be comforted, so much as to comfort others with the peace and love and cheerfulness of Jesus.

'Beware!' said Jesus. 'Be ready for my coming! Don't be caught unawares like Lot's wife!' Jesus makes it clear that Mrs Lot actually went back. He says, 'Don't you go back to rescue worldly goods.' Are you tempted to go back from following Christ, lured by worldly gain? Are you backsliding? Jesus said that the love of many for him would grow cold because wickedness would increase just before he came to judge the world.

Armageddon

You have heard of the Battle of Armageddon, haven't you? It is often mentioned on the news. It is the Bible's Last War of the Age. Do you see that fire and sulphur will rain down upon the armies attacking Jerusalem, as prophesied in Ezekiel 38:22? Yes, the rift valley experience will happen again in the last war of the age when Christ returns. He comes to stop it. He is the only hope for this world – this age in which certain tyrant rulers are finding out how to produce the nuclear bomb and warheads.

Fortunately, I believe Christ will rescue the saved before this by their resurrection. St Paul calls them those 'who belong to Christ'.

SODOM AND GOMORRAH CONFIRMED

A television writer says that the story of Sodom and Gomorrah is a myth! There was no city called Sodom, he said. As if in answer, a report has come from the newly discovered tablets at Ebla, Syria, dated 2300 BC, which is 300 years before the biblical overthrow. Archaeologists have just translated a tablet which is a merchant's invoice addressed to Sodom. Material goods are not made out to a mythical city!

The reason that the remains of Sodom have not been discovered is that shallow waters of the Dead Sea, only 50 feet deep, cover the site. The area sank after the earth movements (Fig 2.2).

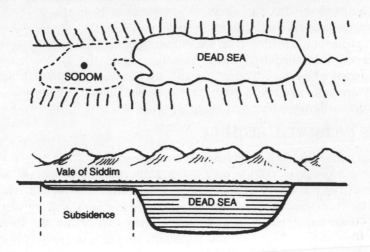

Figure 2.2. The Dead Sea before and after the overthrow of Sodom and Gomorrah, 2000 BC. Most archaeologists believe that Sodom and Gomorrah were in the region of the subsidence shown because all local ancient roads lead to this area.

Threefold Confirmation of the Bible

There are three sources of information which tell us this. Josephus, writing AD 75, records that the Vale of Siddim called 'Slime Pits', because of its tar and asphalt, 'became Lake Asphaltites (Dead Sea) upon the destruction of the city of Sodom'.

Also, an ancient Phoenician priest writes, 'The Vale of Siddim sank and became a lake'. This explains the remark in Genesis 14:3 that 'Siddim is now the Dead Sea'.

There is a great amount of salt in the area which volcanic fires would melt. The Salt Mountain nearby contains a stratum of salt 150 feet thick and 6 miles long. The Arabs still call it Jebel-U-Sodum.

Excavators found a layer of fossil fertile soil and growth covered by later deposits, which showed how productive this area was before the catastrophe, and Dr N. Glueck found that before 2000 BC this was an area of high population and prosperity which quickly became abandoned and desolate. This bears out Genesis 13:10 that it was 'like the garden of the Lord . . . before the Lord destroyed Sodom and Gomorrah'.

We can thus form a picture of what happened. Suddenly there was an explosion of the natural gases in the sub-strata of this rift valley. The volcanic heat melted the salt and ignited the tar and sulphur which shot up into the sky. Then these burning chemicals rained down death upon the evil cities.

Formerly, the Dead Sea reached no farther south than the el-Lisan peninsula, but the floor of the valley then sank to let those leaden waters flow south for another 15 miles.

When the sun shines on the sea in the right direction, one can see sunken salt-encrusted tree trunks shimmering in the green depths, gaunt ghosts of an ungodly past. A startling legend is that these pillars of salt are not broken-off tree trunks as supposed, but crowds of Sodomites who were trying to escape.

GOD'S INCIDENTAL GEOLOGY

You can often tell if a person has greater knowledge behind what he is saying, even if he is talking on another subject. He will tend to add snippets from his source of knowledge during the course of conversation.

We have examples of this 'incidental knowledge' in the Bible. Isaiah 40 is one in which God is bringing the message of comfort to his people who have been devastated by events. To illustrate his ability to reverse the situation, he draws upon a geological example which has been discovered only by modern geology. It is this: 'Every valley shall be exalted and every mountain and hill will be made low' (Isaiah 40:4; Luke 3:4).

Syncline Uplift

Did you know that the highest mountains in Wales were once valleys? Cader Idris and Mount Snowdon were once valleys! The original mountains rose up higher above them but they were worn down quicker because their height exposed them to the elements.

We have proof of this in the curve of the strata or rock layers. On the top of those mountains, they curve upwards in a 'U' shape. In geological language, the synclines are now elevated (see Fig 2.3). In other words, 'Every valley has been exalted'.

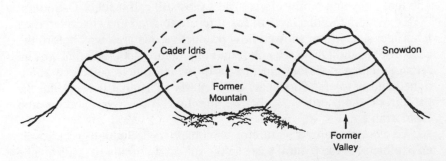

Figure 2.3. Cader Idris and Snowdon in North Wales showing mountain-top 'valleys' in cross-section.

Some of the world's highest mountains have been the result of what is called a syncline uplift or upthrust. Valleys have become mountains in a different way from erosion. The tops of some mountains were once valleys at the bottom of the sea. Did you know that the Mount Everest range and the Alps were once sea-covered synclines? How then did they get pushed up from the sea bed into mountain tops? It was the result of continental movements. They put pressure on the sea troughs between them. The continental edges closed in on one another, with the sea bed between them caught in an inexorable vice.

Isostasy

Another piece of God's 'incidental geology' is in verse 12 of Isaiah 40 where God says he 'weighed the mountains in scales and the hills in a balance'. This is called 'isostasy'. The height of the hills and mountains is counterbalanced by the depth of the 'root' of the elevated area. The 'root' goes down deeper into the sima of the plastic crust and remains balanced by its weight (see Fig 2.4).

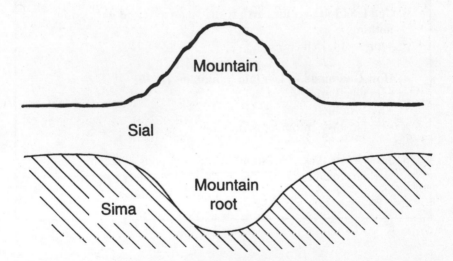

Figure 2.4. An example of isostasy in which the upthrust of a mountain is counterbalanced by a 'root' protruding into the sima.

So God is a geologist as well as a scientist. In *Volume 1: Science* we have seen that the Bible indicates that life is created by God's words, the DNA code, and how Psalm 139 refers to the genetic Book of Man. Also, we have seen God's explanation to Job (Chapter 12) of what makes the sun rise, namely by the earth turning on an axis described in the Bible as like a Babylonian clay cylinder on a spindle (see Fig 12.5, *Volume 1*).

Jesus also used the word 'uranium' for nuclear fission as a sign of his coming; Peter spoke of the elements of matter; Paul referred to atomic change in connection with the resurrection – but more of that later.

SUMMARY

GOD IS A GEOLOGIST

1. **Gen 1 gives right order of events.**
   • Supported from astrophysics and fossils.

2. **God tells three prophets of rift valley events to come.**
   • Joel, Ezekiel, Zechariah.

3. **God tells Job that the earth turns on an axis and hangs on nothing.**
   • Job 38:14; Heb 26:7

4. **How God made valleys into mountains (Is 40)**
   • by weathering;
   • by synclines;
   • by isostasy 'mountains in balance'.

5. **Jesus knew that at his second coming** in parts of the world it would be night, other parts morning, other parts afternoon (showing knowledge of Earth as a globe).

3 CRITICS MAKE UP THEIR OWN EXODUS
EVIDENCE ABOUT MOSES AND HIS WRITINGS

One of the things that was said in the TV series *Testament* was that there was no evidence that Israel came out of Egypt in the year 1250 BC. That's the event that we call the Exodus. It was claimed that the whole story is fictional; that it never happened.

Of course it didn't. Not in 1250 BC anyway. You see, the Bible says it happened 200 years earlier. If people don't take the Bible's dates to guide them, they are bound to get things wrong. The Bible says it took place in 1440 BC. If you accept the Bible date, you will find that all the events of Exodus in the Bible slot into the framework of Egyptian history marvellously.

This is the kind of circular argument which is typical of Bible sceptics. They manufacture their own contradictions and then accuse the Bible of error.

Professor D. Wiseman, a leading archaeologist of London University, says critics have ignored evidence which supports biblical facts, and suggests that the BBC should present a balance of reasonable views.

Q Where in the Bible does it say that the Exodus happened in 1440 BC?

Well, there are two or three places; 1 Kings 6:1 is one place. It says that Solomon started to build the temple 480 years after the Israelites escaped from Egypt. Now the date of Solomon's temple was 960 BC. Even sceptics agree with that date. So, add 480 to 960 BC and that gives you the date of the Exodus as 1440 BC. Now if we start with the Bible date, we find that Egyptian history not only fits in, it explains why Moses ran away from Egypt at the age of 40, why he returned 40 years later, who the Pharaohs were, and that the archaeology slots into the whole framework. The whole list of dates and events in the Bible harmonises perfectly.

THE BIBLE HELPS TO PUT HISTORY STRAIGHT

Ah, you may say, you have said a lot, but you have quoted only one verse. You said that there were two or three places. Can you give more detail about this?

We had better start with how the Israelites came to be slaves in Egypt. They went to get food during a terrible drought because one of the Israelites, Joseph, had become Prime Minister there. Exodus is the second book in the Bible and it starts by saying that a pharaoh arose who did not know Joseph. This fits in with the eighteenth dynasty in 1580 BC when the native Egyptian king drove out the foreign pharaoh. It was this foreign regime which made Joseph, the Israelite, a prime minister. We know that there were foreign 'shepherd kings' which we read about in ancient Egyptian history.

So no wonder the new dynasty was very suspicious of the Israelites, especially when their birth-rate was higher than the Egyptians; so they made slaves of them. What was worse, they made the Israelites throw their baby boys to the crocodiles in the Nile.

We all know that story from the Bible. The baby Moses was put into the Nile, but in a small reed boat so that he floated safely, and that would be in 1520 BC when Moses was born. The monuments of Egypt show paintings of those reed boats.

Well, as everybody knows, the princess came to bathe in the river and found the baby and went on to adopt him. By following the Bible dates, we can know who that was. It was Princess Hatshepsut. She would have been 17 years old at that time. We have found this out by following the Bible clue. So this isn't just a fairy story. We actually know it was this 17-year-old princess. She became the most powerful queen in Egypt. One reason was that she was of royal blood by both parents. She was a masterly woman. Even her father, Thotmes I (Thutmose I), was dominated by her, at about the time Moses was born ,and she continued to be the real ruler even during the reign of Thotmes II (Thutmose II) and for the first 16 years of Thotmes III (Thutmose III). So why was Moses protected only for the first 16 years of the reign of Thotmes III? Because Queen Hatshepsut died – in 1485 BC.

Moses, the Commander of Queen Hatshepsut

Q But what has all this got to do with Moses?

It was five years after her death that Moses ran from the palace into hiding in the desert. Pharaoh had found out that Moses had killed an Egyptian slave-driver for cruelty. He no longer had his powerful

Figure 3.1. Pharaoh's daughter. In 1 Kings 6:1 and Judges 11:13–26, the Bible says that the correct date of the Exodus is 1440 BC. Thus the princess who discovered the infant Moses 'by the river's brink' was Hatshepsut, the most celebrated woman in Egyptian history.

Courtesy: Metropolitan Museum, New York

Figure 3.2. Queen Hatshepsut's column at Karnak, Southern Egypt. According to the Bible dates, this would be the princess who rescued Moses from the bulrushes and brought him up in the royal palace. Hatshepsut was the most powerful queen in all the history of Egypt, ranking in equivalence to pharaoh. Only the most powerful pharaohs could erect an obelisk to themselves.

Queen Mother to protect him and Thotmes III hated her.

How do we know that? We have discovered that he tried to erase her name from all the monuments of Egypt, but was not thorough enough and left some evidence that was not fully erased. He then became one of Egypt's greatest conquerors.

Now here comes an important question. Why didn't he go out and make great conquests under Queen Hatshepsut? The answer is that the Queen herself did them. She sent fleets of ships up the Nile to conquer Central Africa. All this sounds a bit like Queen Boadicea in England.

But it is strange. Why did she go herself? Why didn't she send Thotmes III as her commander of the army? That's an interesting question. Josephus, the historian, says that she made Prince Moses her commander, and he led the military force up to the junction of the White Nile with the Blue Nile and captured Merrow. He also captured and married the Ethiopian princess.

You are probably thinking, I can't believe that. You are making this into a love story! Well, there might be something in what Josephus says because, in Numbers 12, we read that Miriam and Aaron tried to alienate support from Moses because he had married an Ethiopian. Anyway, Thotmes must have regarded him as a serious rival, as Acts 27:2 says, 'Moses was instructed in all the wisdom of Egypt and was powerful in words and works'.

So then, the Bible says that Moses went into hiding in the desert for 40 years. But does this slot into Egyptian history as well? We see that it was then that God told Moses that the Pharaoh had died and that he must go back to deliver the slaves. So Thotmes III had died and Amenhetep II was now on the throne.

A Drowned Mummy

Some people have said to me, 'So you're saying then that Amenhetep II was the Pharaoh of the Exodus. But that can't be. The Pharaoh and his army were drowned in the Red Sea according to the Bible, but Amenhetep's tomb is still around with his mummified body in it. That's just not possible if he drowned!'

There are some strange circumstances about that tomb. It was only half finished as if they were not expecting his death.

Even so, if the Bible says he drowned, but his body is supposed to be in the tomb, how did it get there? If you read the scripture carefully, you will see that it does not specifically say that Pharaoh himself ,went into the sea but it was his chariots and horses and army that went in and were drowned. In any case, the Bible says the soldiers' bodies were washed up on the shore and, if Pharaoh was among them, they would soon identify his body and royal armour. It is possible he was

Figure 3.3. Statue of Thutmose III. Though forced for twenty years to submit to the will of Hatshepsut, his aunt and co-regent, he came to be one of the greatest of the pharaohs. Victor in many campaigns, he showed a streak of littleness by masking the inscribed bases of Hatshepsut's obelisks with brick walls and obliterating, so far as possible, her name and memory from the rolls of history.

Courtesy: Story of the Bible, *Fleetway House, London*

drowned, because his mummy was obviously very hastily prepared and they didn't bother to finish his tomb once he was dead; that was very unusual for pharaohs.

THE TESTIMONY OF THE SPHINX TO THE TENTH PLAGUE

But what about his son and heir? He was supposed to have been killed as well. According to the Bible, he was killed in the slaying of the first-born. It is in the book of Exodus, chapter 12:

> At midnight the Lord struck down all the first-born in Egypt, from the first-born of Pharaoh who sat on the throne, to the first-born of the prisoner who was in the dungeon and the first-born of all the livestock as well. Pharaoh and all his officials and all the Egyptians got up during the night and there was loud wailing in Egypt for there was not a house without someone dead.

Now some readers immediately jump on this. To their minds, the Bible must be cleared of all supernatural acts of God and this is one of them. So, they reason, it just couldn't have happened – it's all too far-fetched for the minds of those who have written God off before considering the evidence. Yet, there is evidence for this great event of God's judgment on Egypt.

A Slab of Evidence

Have you heard of the astonishing evidence which has been discovered at the Sphinx? I mean the Sphinx that is just outside Cairo – that great statue of a lion carved out of the rock – the lion with a pharaoh's head.

Yes, but what has that got to do with the Bible? Well, when the sand was cleared away from between the paws, what do you think they found? A great red granite memorial stone to say that Pharaoh's eldest son did not come to the throne. His younger brother did instead (see Fig 3.4).

Some things seem impossible don't they, but when they happen, we call them miracles. Does it seem a momentous miracle to you, the story of the slaying of the first-born – the first-born of every house where the blood of the lamb had not been applied? Perhaps that is why God instructed Pharaoh to erect that red granite slab at the Sphinx in testimony that it actually happened.

The other plagues of Egypt have been described as natural calamities, but which had been intensified by God, then made to happen one after the other in a most unnatural way and almost all at once. Normally such calamities would happen rarely and over a long period of time, but for them to be intensified by perhaps ten times, and all to happen within a year or so, would bring the exclamation even from Egyptian magicians, 'This is the hand of God!'

Figure 3.4. Egypt's famous Sphinx showing between its paws the memorial slab of Thotmes IV, who came to the throne unexpectedly because his elder brother, the heir, died in the slaying of the first-born, recorded in Exodus 12.

Sometimes God does explain how he accomplished a dramatic event. For instance, he said that the way through the Red Sea would be by sending a terrific east gale to blow all the night through (Exodus 14:21).

In this materialistic age many find it difficult to believe unless they are given a physical explanation. They do not realise that this limits proof to their five or six senses of detection. The NASA space probe reveals that 99 per cent of things that exist in the universe are not detectable by the six senses of man.

This means that to reduce what we believe to what is humanly comprehensible is to reduce God to our own level and size. This attitude is called reductionism.

In what way is the slaying of the first-born explainable? To postulate an epidemic seems inadequate because how could germs choose only the houses where there was no blood of the lamb smeared upon the door frame? Also how could all the deaths occur precisely at the hour of midnight so that 'from the heir to the throne the first-born of Pharaoh who sat upon the throne even to the first-born of the prisoner in the dungeon' all the first-born died suddenly? So that 'there was a great cry throughout Egypt for there was not one house where there was not one dead'.

In such a case, which is beyond scientific explanation, people are inclined to call this a miracle. For evidence of its factuality, science cannot help us, so we turn to archaeology, not to explain but to witness that it really did happen; and what an unexpected source of witness was provided for this age of doubting Thomases – the Sphinx!

It also corrects the fashionable theology that God is too soft to judge. The Egyptians had been given chance after chance to respond to their Creator's instruction. They had degenerated from belief in one God into a multiplicity of gods. The plagues of Egypt were actually aimed at those gods they venerated as displayed in the murals of their monuments. Only a terrific shock to a deeply entrenched monarchy could bring the desired result. It not only delivered Israel and founded the Passover, it also brought reformation through Pharaoh Akhnaton who introduced monotheism – but was called a heretic for doing so.

The Sphinx Full Text

When the sand which hid the tablet was cleared away, it was found that Pharaoh's second son had done the same as in Moses' time and been told to record an unexpected event.

As I have said, the Bible date for the correct time of the Exodus is 1440 BC. When we accept that, we find that the Pharaoh who succeeded to the throne was Thotmes IV (Thutmose IV). It was he who placed that vast slab of red rose granite. He placed it at the chest of the Sphinx between the front legs. This stood 14 feet (4 metres) high. It was covered by sand until 1936 and was revealed only when the sand was cleared away between the paws down to the brick pavement.

Thotmes IV was told by the sun-god to erect this slab when he unexpectedly came to the throne. He did so and recorded on the slab how it came about. He tells how, long before his father's death, he had been hunting in the desert above Memphis and got very tired, so he lay down to sleep in the very shadow of the Sphinx. The Sphinx represented the sun-god and, in his sleep, the god spoke to him. He promised Thotmes that one day he would come to the throne and that when he became king, he must venerate the God who foretold his succession. He must clear away the piles of sand which had begun to cover the Sphinx and record the fulfilment of the prophecy.

Now it was clear that he was not the next heir to the throne. His elder brother was not only the eldest son of Amenhetep II, but also the son of a royal princess. Thotmes, on the other hand, had a mother who was not of royal birth, so the younger son was only of semi-royal birth.

This certainly throws new light on the Bible story, but there are some other instances when Egyptian history ties in with the account of the Exodus in the Bible. In fact, there are dozens of others. For instance, Hatshepsut's temple was built for Moses; the next Pharaoh after the ten plagues reformed religion to worship one God; tablets were also discovered reporting Israel's invasion of Palestine. I'll

Figure 3.5. Memorial Slab of Thotmes IV. The translation reads: 'I shall bequeath my kingdom which is upon earth upon thee. I shall place thee at the head of the living, and thou shalt wear the white crown [of southern Egypt] and the red crown [of northern Egypt] on the throne of Pharaoh . . . so approach and do what I desire . . . remove the sand from around the limbs [of the Sphinx].' The tablet goes on to say that when he came to the throne unexpectedly, he was to erect this tablet, to record its fulfilment.

enlarge on all this, but first a question springs to mind.

THE FLAWED ARGUMENTS OVER ISRAEL IN EGYPT

Why, after all the evidence which is available, does a critic on television declare that Israel had never been in Egypt? He quotes an Egyptian record which shows that Israel was in Palestine in 1207 BC. But of course they were there then, because the Bible dates show that they had left Egypt 200 years earlier. Critics ignore the Bible date and then accuse the Bible of being wrong. This argument which is given in reality proves that the Bible date is right and that Israel had successfully entered the Promised Land long before.

I have shown from 1 Kings 6:1 that we can determine the date of the Exodus as 1440 BC. Judges 11:26 makes it clear, too. The evidence shows that the Bible ties in perfectly with Egyptian history. If you observe the Bible's guidelines, you always get the facts right – 1440 BC is the time fixed by the Bible.

Some were misled by a reference to the cities which the Hebrew slaves were forced to build. In Exodus 1:11, they are referred to as Pithom and Rameses. Rameses II did not reign until 1290, but there are two explanations for his name being applied to the city. One is that its more modern name was appended in the same way that we now call Mesopotamia 'Iraq'. The other is that it is known that Rameses was a fraud and erased the name of the original Pharaoh to claim the credit for himself.

Small difficulties should not negate Scripture's plain statements about dates. You will see how it all harmonises with records of the unexpected death of the heir to the Egyptian throne, the reformation in Egypt which followed to institute a type of monotheism, the letters to Pharaoh from Canaanite kings for help against the Hebrew invasion and the fall of Jericho. There are many other remarkable correlations and insights into the personalities involved on the Egyptian monuments.

No Slaves in Egypt?

Undaunted, the critic says that the Egyptians didn't look down on foreigners and didn't make slaves of foreigners so Israel couldn't have been slaves in Egypt.

The Bible confirms that Egypt was friendly to foreigners. Abraham was welcomed with courtesy; Joseph became Prime Minister and Israel was welcomed. It was only when the new regime felt threatened that they subjected them to slavery.

But the critics do not give up easily! They say that there was no evidence, not even wall paintings or anything, to show that there were ever any slaves in Egypt. Well, I beg to differ here. Egyptologists have found depicted taskmasters who are declaring to the slaves 'you are idle, you are lazy'. (See Figure 3.6.) These are the very words in the Bible. Exodus 5:8 says that for this reason Pharaoh made their tasks harder and said they would have to find their own straw for their bricks. There is evidence for this. At this period, we have found that there were bricks made without straw. Exodus 5:7–8 (AV) states:

> Ye shall no more give the people straw to make brick, as heretofore: let them go and gather straw for themselves. And the tale of the bricks, which they did make heretofore, ye shall lay upon them; ye shall not diminish ought thereof, for they be idle: therefore they cry, saying, Let us go and sacrifice to our God.

Straw was used as binding material in the brick and the Bible goes on to say that the Israelites scattered to find straw and could only collect stubble. These bricks containing stubble have actually been found.

THE IMPACT OF ISRAEL ON EGYPT AND CANAAN

Critics claim that there are no monuments either in Egypt or Palestine that refer to Israel. But this is not valid. It should be realised that none of the Egyptian monuments ever refer to a defeat. Consequently, the escape of the slaves is sarcastically recorded as the 'escape of the lepers'. Moreover, the entry into Palestine is recorded on the Tel Amarna tablets. The Canaanites had been appealing for help from Pharaoh Akhnaton. The tablets ask for help to stop the Israelite invasion. They say that if he doesn't, 'the whole of the land will be overrun'. A loyal soldier called Abdkhiba writes about Jerusalem to Egypt. He wrote to this Pharaoh Akhnaton:

> The king's whole land will be lost. Behold the territory of Seir as far as Carmel, its princes are wholly lost and hostility prevails against me. [He has appealed apparently several times, for he goes on.] If no troops come this year, the whole territory of my lord the king will perish. [Then he appeals that the king will at least send forces to ensure the retreat of himself and his men doesn't happen, and in a postscript he adds to Akhnaton's secretary:] Bring these words plainly before my lord the king. The whole land of my lord the king is going to ruin.

The tablets say that the Hebrews were invading from Seir and Edom and the Bible says that that is where the Israelites launched their early invasion. You find the details in Deuteronomy 2.

Q Did Pharaoh Akhnaton actually send his army to help the Canaanites?

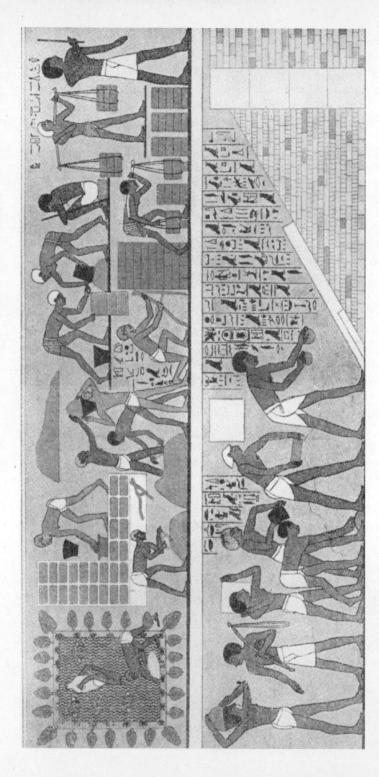

Figure 3.6. Evidence of the Hebrew slaves in Egypt. Egyptian mural of Moses' time contains the words: 'You are idle! You are idle!' In Exodus 5:8 and 17, these words are spoken by Pharaoh about the Hebrew brickmakers, and when telling the slavedrivers to be more severe.

Courtesy: 'Story of the Bible' Fleetway House, London

Figure 3.7. Evidence of Israel in Egypt. The so-called Cleopatra's Needles – one of which is now in New York and the other, viewed above, in London, on the Thames Embankment – are a pair of obelisks once set up by Thotmes III, about 1500 BC, at Heliopolis, the biblical city of On. According to biblical dating, he is identified with the pharaoh of the oppression of the Israelites. **Note:** In the modern pedestal was placed a jar which contains copies of the Bible in four languages and John 3:16 in 215 languages: 'For God so loved the world, that he gave his only begotten Son, that whosoever believeth on him should not perish, but have everlasting life.'

No, he didn't, and there is a good reason why he didn't. He knew by then that the pharaohs could not fight against God. The ten plagues and the crossing of the Red Sea and the miraculous drying-up of the River Jordan had proved that. God said to Moses in Exodus 9:13:

> Then the Lord said to Moses, rise up early in the morning and stand before Pharaoh and say to him 'Thus saith the Lord, the God of the Hebrews, let my people go that they may serve me for this time. I will send all my plagues to your heart and upon your servants and your people that you may know that there is none like me in all the earth, for by now I could have put forth my hand and struck you and your people with pestilence and you would have been cut off from the earth, but for this purpose have I let you live to show you my power so that my name may be declared throughout all the earth.'

Now many find it hard to believe that Pharaoh actually came to believe in Jehovah, the God of the Israelites. Egypt had so many different gods. But he did believe in God. He brought about a reformation. Akhnaton's reformation is well known. In fact, later, the Egyptians called him a heretic. He introduced monotheism, the belief in one supreme God.

So you see another instance here in which the Bible harmonises, if only you will accept the Bible dates.

No Lack of Evidence of the Conquest of Canaan

But there is another problem here that some find difficult. Apart from Jericho, there is no sign of any of the towns in Palestine having been destroyed by the Israelites. This shows how easy it is to read the Bible without observing the details correctly. You have to read the Bible carefully. In several scriptures, God says that the Israelites will be able to occupy houses without destroying them and cities without building them. Look at Deuteronomy 6:10, for example. Moses says, 'The Lord your God will bring you into a land which he promised to Abraham, to occupy cities which you did not build and houses full of good things.' So, if the cities weren't destroyed, then there is not going to be any evidence for the conquest!

What about Jericho? The Bible says that Jericho was destroyed and not rebuilt, yet there is Jericho mentioned in the New Testament and in fact we even hear about it on the news every so often.

The modern Jericho is in a different place, alongside the old Jericho. If you go there, you can see the ancient city mound and there has been no rebuilding of Jericho since it was destroyed, just as the Bible says. (See next chapter.) Actually, in the days of King Ahab, Hiel tried to start a little building, beginning with the sacrifice of his eldest son and ending with the sacrifice of his youngest son. He never completed the rebuilding. The reason is to be found in what the Bible said long before, in Joshua 6:26:

> And Joshua adjured them at that time, saying, 'Cursed be the man before the Lord, that riseth up and buildeth this city Jericho: he shall lay the foundation thereof in his first-born, and in his youngest son shall he set up the gates of it.'

This was fulfilled in 1 Kings 16:34, 'In his days did Hiel the Bethelite build Jericho: he laid the foundation thereof in Abiram his first-born and set up the gates thereof in his youngest son Segub, according to the word of the Lord, which he spake by Joshua the son of Nun.'

So the Jericho that is mentioned in the New Testament, where Jesus visited, is the Jericho nearby. It is the city of the palm trees, very lush with vegetation; there is also a more modern Jericho, but neither are on the old archaeological site.

Thus the Bible was right and the arguments of Bible critics fall flat, like Jericho's walls.

MOSES IN AND OUT OF EGYPT

Temple Built by Queen Hatshepsut for Moses

Many more contentions are raised in an effort to find fault with the Bible. To start with, it is said that Moses got his religious ideas from the various Egyptian gods. But there is another discovery which corrects that idea. I refer to the temple which Queen Hatshepsut built for Moses. It shows that the worship God revealed to Moses was quite different from that which the Egyptians allowed.

This temple was built in the desert, three days' journey away in the wilderness. Why so far away? Why not actually in the royal city of Egypt? The reason is significant. It is because the Hebrew ritual was distasteful to the Egyptians. The Hebrews sacrificed the cows that were sacred to the Egyptians who worshipped the cow and the bull, but the Hebrew Israelites burnt them as sin offerings to God. The Egyptians would not tolerate this. Queen Hatshepsut therefore provided this temple (see Fig 3.8) far away so that her adopted son Moses could worship in this way which would otherwise be offensive to Egyptians.

> Archaeology has made a fascinating find about the temple. A tablet found in the temple was deciphered by Professor Grime of Munster University. It reads, 'I, Manasseh, Captain of the Mines, Chief of the Temple, offer thanks to the Pharaohonic Queen Hatshepsut because she drew me out of the Nile and advanced me to high honours.'

Figure 3.8. Ruins of Queen Hatshepsut's temple at Serabit. Built for Israelite sacrifices three days' journey into the desert because such sacrifices were not allowed in Egypt.

Courtesy: Charles Marston, Eyre & Spottiswoode

Now, from what the Bible says, it was Moses whom Queen Hatshepsut drew out of the water. And do you know what the name Moses means? It means 'drawn out'. Exodus 2:10 says, 'She brought him to Pharaoh's daughter and he became her son and she named him Moses for she said, "because I drew him out of the water".' So this inscription at Queen Hatshepsut's temple was made by Moses because it says, 'she drew me out of the Nile'.

But the person's name was Manasseh, not Moses! Manasseh was a Hebrew name. The word Moses is an Egyptian word and that was his Egyptian name given to him when he was adopted. It was not the name his real mother gave him. Judges 18:30 uses his Egyptian name (NIV footnote). It was actually Manasseh – the name on the tablet.

Moses Flees for His Life: Thotmes III Fulfils God's Plans

After the death of his protectoress, Hatshepsut, Moses had to flee from Thotmes III to the land of Midian, following the incident recorded in Exodus 2:11–15. There he spent the second forty years of his life (see Exodus 7:7; Acts 7:30).

Q Why then did God call Moses to return to Egypt?

Well, it is towards the end of the 40-year period spent in Midian that we read in Exodus 2:23, 'During that long period, the king of Egypt died'. There is confirmation of this in the chronological record which shows that this corresponds with the death of Thotmes III in 1447 BC, which was probably about 38 years after Moses had fled to Midian.

Again we see the Bible story tying in with the findings of archaeology and chronology. But, during Moses' time in the land of Midian, where he was safe from the vengeance of the pharaoh, God had been working out his plan for the future.

Thotmes III had made a series of conquests in Palestine and Syria, carrying out 17 expeditions in all, capturing their cities and breaking down their defences. The Egyptian hieroglyphics record his great battle of Megiddo, in 1479 BC, in which he captured 900 chariots and 2,200 horses.

Q How was Thotmes lll playing into God's plans?

Thotmes III was effectively carrying out a softening-up process which would make the Israelite conquest of the land much easier later on, under Joshua's leadership. This was the scarab, or sacred beetle, symbol of Egypt, which God told Moses he was sending on before Israel arrived, as we shall see later on.

THE CALL OF MOSES AND HIS PLEA TO PHARAOH

So it was a few years after the death of Thotmes III that Moses received his vision of the Burning Bush (Exodus chapter 3), and God's call to return to Egypt. He and Aaron then appeared before Thotmes' successor, Amenhetep II, and put God's request that the Israelites be allowed to go, 'that they may hold a festival to me in the desert' (Exodus 5:1).

Now this is an interesting request. Moses did not ask Pharaoh to let him take the people of Israel to the land of Canaan. He asked for permission to hold a worship festival in the desert. A further clue to his intention is given in verse 3: 'The God of the Hebrews has met with us. Now let us take a three-day journey into the desert to offer sacrifices to the Lord our God, or he may strike us with plagues or with the sword.'

Now what is the significance of Moses' request for a three-day journey into the wilderness? Although the Temple of Serabit which Queen Hatshepsut had built for Moses in the desert is not mentioned in the Bible, this must surely be a reference to a right which was granted the Israelites during her reign. The temple was three-days' journey into the Sinai Desert, and it seems that pilgrimages were allowed there for the Hebrews to offer sacrifice.

Amenhetep II increased the oppression of the Israelites and these pilgrimages had probably long since ceased. But, by requesting permission for this three-day pilgrimage, Moses was only seeking the

Unger's List of Biblical Dates

The harmonisation of Bible dates with Egyptian and Canaanite history from Terah to Solomon

Date	Events in Biblical History	Events in Contemporary History
c.2250-2200 BC	Terah born	First Intermediate Period or Dark Age in Egypt (c.2200-1989).
c.2161 BC	Birth of Abraham.	Gutian Rule in Babylonia (c.2180-2070). Sumerian revival under Third Dynasty of Ur (c.2070-1960).
c.2086 BC	**Abraham's entrance into Canaan.**	Ur-Nammu, Dungi, Bur-Sin, Gimil-Sin and Ibi-Sin rule in power at Ur, Abraham's birthplace.
c.2075 BC	Invasion of Mesopotamian kings (**Gen. 14**).	Amraphel (Hammurabi) of Babylon raids Palestine.
c.2050 BC	Destruction of Sodom and Gomorrah.	
c.1950 BC	Isaac.	Fall of Ur (c.1960). Elamite princes in Isin and Larsa in lower Babylonia. Small Amorite and Elamite states in Babylonia.
c.1871 BC	**Israel's entrance into Egypt.** **Joseph's Viceroyship.**	**Strong Middle Kingdom** in Egypt (Dynasty XII). **Amenemes I-IV**, Senwosret I-III (c.1989-1776 BC).
c.1780 BC	Israel in Egypt.	First Dynasty of Babylon (c.1850-1550). Hammurabi (c.1728-1689). Mari Age. **Hyksos Period** of foreign domination in Egypt (c.1720-1570).
c.1520 BC	**Moses born.**	**New Empire**, Dynasty XVIII (c.1570-1150), Kamose, Thutmose I, II, **Queen Hatshepsut** (c.1570-1482).
c.1485 BC	Final phase of Israelite oppression.	Thutmose III (c.1482-1450).
c.1441 BC	**Exodus** from Egypt.	Amenhotep II (c.1450-1425).

c.1441 BC	Israel in Wilderness.	Thutmose IV (c.1425-1412).
c.1405 BC	2½ tribes occupy Arnon	East Bank of Jordan cf. Jepthah 1105 BC
c.1401 BC	**Fall of Jericho.**	Amenhotep III (c.1412-1387). Amarna Period.
c.1400-1361 BC	**Conquest of Canaan.** Period of Joshua and Elders.	**Invasion of Palestine by Hebrews.** Amenhotep III (Ikhnaton) (c.1387-1366). Advance of Hittites.
c.1361 BC	Oppression of Cushan-Rishathaim.	**Tutankamun** in Egypt (c.1366-1357).
c.1353 BC	Othneil's Deliverance – forty years peace.	Harmhab – decline of Egyptian influence in Palestine.
c.1313 BC	Oppression by Eglon of Moab.	Seti I, pharaoh (c.1314-1290).
c.1295 BC	Ehud's Deliverance.	**Raamses II** (c.1290-1224) – brilliant reign.
c.1295 BC	Peace for 80 years.	Hittite advance into Syria. Merneptah's Stele **mentions Israel in Palestine.**
c.1215 BC	Jabin's Oppression.	Weak kinglets on throne of Egypt – Amenmose, Siptah, Seti II.
c.1195-1155 BC	Deborah's Exploit. Forty-year peace.	Raamses III (c.1198-1167). Invasion of Sea Peoples repulsed. Greek History: **The Trojan War** (c.1200).
c.1155 BC	Midianite Oppression.	Decline of Egyptian power – weak reign of Raamses IV and V.
c.1148 BC	Gideon's Victory and Judgeship.	Egypt power in Palestine practically nil.
c.1148	40-year peace after Gideon.	
c.1108 BC	Abimelech king at Shechem.	Peleset (Philistines) increase in power.
c.1105 BC	Ammonite Oppression, **Jephthah** judge.	**'about 300 years since' Judges 11:26**
c.1099 BC	Philistine Ascendancy.	
c.1085 BC	Samson is Judge.	
c.1065 BC	Eli is Judge.	
c.1050 BC	Battle of Ebenezer, Philistines take ark.	Great Empires on Tigris-Euphrates, Halys and Nile **decline** leaving Syria-Palestine open for conquests of
c.1020 BC	Saul and beginnings of Monarchy.	**David** (c.1004-965) and the splendor of **Solomon's** reign (c.965-926).
c.1004 BC	David king of Judah.	
c.998 BC	David king of Israel	
c.965 BC	Solomon	
c.960 BC	Solomon's Temple	480 years after Exodus (1 Kings 6:1)

renewal of a privilege which had been exercised before.

The request was refused because Pharaoh suspected it would be used as a means of escape. As the terrible plagues sent by God intensified, Amenhetep II was compelled to let the Israelites go. Pharaoh said, 'All right, you can go if you leave hostages behind.' First it was the cattle, then it was the women and children he wanted left as hostages. But Moses was not accepting any conditions The deadlock was resolved only by the final plague: the death of the first-born.

Weak Faith Flounders while the Bible Shines

Do you see how everything fits neatly into place if we follow the dates and facts given to us in the Bible? Isn't it exciting to see how the Bible's story of Israel in Egypt, Moses and the Exodus all fit in with the chronology of the Egyptian pharaohs, as revealed by archaeology?

Don't falter and lose your way by ignoring the clear statements of the Bible! Take heart – God's Word is faithful and true!

But did Moses actually write the first five books of the Bible? That is the next question which is often raised.

EVIDENCE FOR THE WRITINGS OF MOSES

There is now strong evidence that Moses did write the first five books of the Bible as was originally believed. These books are called the Pentateuch or Torah.

Leading scholars with expertise in the literary methods of the ancient Near East bring evidence which was unknown by those who call themselves the Higher Critics. The Higher Critics commenced their theories against Moses nearly 250 years ago, before Assyriologists and Egyptologists discovered how the ancients actually did record history. The Higher Critics, who lacked scientific information, formed their theories subjectively on wrong assumptions. Their theory assumed that the books of Moses were not finally compiled until 400 BC instead of a thousand years earlier by Moses himself. At first, archaeology was not available to correct these assumptions.

Course Material in Error

The theory was founded by a Frenchman named Astruc. Sadly, most theological courses still teach it, ignoring the findings of archaeology.

Experts have since found that the literary methods evident in the Pentateuch are those of the time of Moses and not of a later date when methods changed. Experts in this practical field are Professor Kenneth Kitchen, Professor of Archaeology and Oriental Studies; Dr D. Wiseman, Professor of Assyriology and a Semitist; and Professor Alan Millard. All have recognised international standing.

Professor Kitchen himself has translated tablets and scripts from treaties in Hittite, Elamite, Sumerian and Aramaic languages as well as Egyptian, Ugaritic, Akkadian, etc.

In a typical course for lay readers in one diocese there was no mention of their scholarly, factual findings, so I have been asked to supply this lack. Neither was any mention made of up-to-date scholars who have taught in theological colleges such as J.A. Motyer; Dr John Wenham; Dr W.J. Martin; Donald Robinson; Professor F.F. Bruce; A. Gibson; Bishop John Robinson; R.T. France and others.

Even the revised book list of the course, for the Old and New Testament units, only added a book by R.K. Harrison, yet none of his material affects the course or is even mentioned.

Without any knowledge of the literary methods of ancient times, the Higher Critics divided up Scripture passages according to the names given to God – names such as Lord (Yah) or God (El) – which gave rise to an incorrect structure to the events recorded by Moses.

Concerning the Old Testament, the course gives detailed examples of text separated into Yah and El segments, in order to make them contradict one another; but no information is given that in the Ebla tablets, of 500 years before Abraham and 1,000 years before Moses, the use of Yah and El appear together on each tablet in a harmonious account, according to Professor A. Gibson.

Professor D. Wiseman, former Professor of Assyriology in the University of London, says the 'JEDP theory' was formed before any of the literary methods of the ancient Near East were known. Also it ignores the Hittite Gattung structure of the different styles current in one legal covenant of Moses' day and which is characteristic of the Pentateuch.

These experts found that ancient tablets and scripts used both divine names in their accounts, sometimes together and sometimes singly according to the subject material. They did not indicate different authorship or sources.

The old-fashioned Higher Critics did not know this, so they divided up the Bible stories according to the name used for God. By doing this, they made the one version into two or three versions, and thus they artificially created contradictory versions.

A classic example of this is their treatment of the story of the Flood. As it stands in Genesis chapters 6 to 9, it is a remarkable record of a flood lasting 371 days. The date it started is given, the date it reached its peak is given and the date it ended is given. Between these dates, various happenings are logged by periods of 7 days, 40 days, 150 days, etc. The whole is a remarkably harmonious record.

By dividing this up into segments, the Higher Critics turned them into conflicting accounts, from supposed different literature sources.

A Diocesan Certificate course swallows the theory whole without question and plunges the students into confusion right near the beginning of the Old Testament studies by asking them, 'How many different sorts of literature can you identify? Make a list', and 'How would you explain the apparent contradictions?'

The course goes on to suggest that 'Genesis comes from various different sources'. Later in the Certificate course, segments are allocated to 'J', other segments to 'E' and others to 'P'. The latter stands for priestly writers who, it is supposed, wrote as late as 400 BC. This theory was to give time for the evolution of priestly religion. The supposed 'P' sources in the Flood account were allocated to the sacrifices and to other precise details.

Notice the questions about trying to detect different literature sources on the assumption that they did not come from Moses. But instead of these sources being 1,000 years after Moses, it is now found that the different styles were the legal way of compiling a covenant in the time of Moses. This method was called the Hittite treaty and was established by the Hittites throughout the ancient Near East of Moses' time. Then it dropped out of use soon after, and was unknown by the time the Higher Critics thought the documents were being pieced together.

UNDERSTANDING THE STYLE OF THE BOOKS OF MOSES

Professor K. Kitchen of Liverpool University School of Archaeology and Oriental Studies, gives some examples showing that the covenant in Exodus to Deuteronomy is set out on the same principles as the Gattung covenant: 'Much information on covenants and treaties in the Near East has come to light. From no less than 25 treaties from the archives of the Hittites, Ugarit, etc., it has been possible to establish the clear pattern.' This is:

(1) The author of the covenant (Jehovah);
(2) Reference to earlier relations (Patriarchs);
(3) Basic stipulations (Ten Commandments) followed by more details (Exodus 21 to Numbers 10);
(4) Arrangement for deposit of the covenant in the vassal's sanctuary (recorded only in Deuteronomy 31:24–25);
(5) Periodic reading of the covenant terms to the people (recorded only in Deuteronomy);
(6) Witnesses (Exodus 24) sealed by sprinkling the blood of the covenant;
(7) Curses for disobedience to the covenant and blessings for keeping it (Leviticus 26 and Deuteronomy 30);
(8) Oath of obedience with solemn ceremony.

This is also fully documented by V. Korosec of Leipzig and G. E. Mendenhall (Oxford Ashmolean Museum).

Critical Fashion Moves On

Moses himself may have used his own sources. Professor K. Kitchen says:

> It never seems to have crossed Astruc's mind, as a Frenchman and European of the 18th century AD, that the literary peculiarities of the OT text might be due to its origin in a distant antiquity and an alien (Near Eastern) culture. Failure to allow for the non-European, non-modern origin of the OT text was a cardinal error of the first magnitude, fatally repeated by practically all his successors in conventional criticism.

The effect of the discovery of Middle East laws and literary methods has been to change the fashion of criticism. Attention now is concentrated on reading the established text in the light of its contemporary environment and culture, rather than fragmenting the text according to subjective Western imagination.

Who Is Telling the Truth?

You will have noticed that the legal system of Moses' day included two items which are contained only in Deuteronomy, one being that the covenant had to be deposited in the sanctuary.

Near the end of Deuteronomy (31:24) we read the statement that Moses, who wrote this scroll, commanded that it should be put in the sanctuary ark:

> When Moses had finished writing the words of this Torah in a scroll to the very end . . . he said 'Take this scroll of the Torah and put it in the side of the ark'. This also gives the clear statement that Moses wrote this Torah scroll of the covenant.

Deuteronomy was written after the defeat of Og recorded in Numbers 21 and Deuteronomy 1:3,4. But documentary theorists are prepared to deny that Moses wrote it then. They contend that Deuteronomy was not written until 632 BC and then found in the temple sanctuary by Hilkiah, the high priest. All this is part of the JEDP theory, the letter 'D' standing for Deuteronomy. The other letters stand for supposed anonymous authors. 'J' stands for Jehovah because it was thought that passages containing Jehovah (or Yahweh) as the divine name were contributed by scribes living about 500 years after Moses. 'E' is for passages using El or Elohim as the divine name. It is supposed that scribes using this name for God wrote about 600 years after Moses. 'P' stands for priestly code. This was thought to be an advanced brand of religion and, as they thought religion had evolved, they deduced these could not have been written until 400 BC.

As Deuteronomy was the last of Moses' five books, this is treated as a separate book. This the Higher Critics dated to King Josiah's reign, also on the theory that religion had evolved. The evolution in this case was that every individual was responsible for his own sins. 'A son should not be punished for the sins of his father.' They ignore the same quotation 200 years earlier in the reign of Amaziah, 2 Kings 14:6. The same book is referred to, namely 'The Torah' or the Book of the Law. This always refers to the Pentateuch, not to Deuteronomy alone.

The theory that religion evolved has long been abandoned by anthropologists. (See my article in *Origin of the Bible* and in Volume 1 of this series.) The theory was formed on the assumption that God did not reveal himself. However, the Bible claims, in many places, that God clearly revealed his truth to the prophets. Concerning Moses, for example, Numbers 12:6,7 states:

> The Lord said 'Hear my words: If there is a prophet among you, I the Lord make myself known to him in a vision; I speak with him in a dream. Not so with my servant Moses; he is entrusted with all my house. With him I will speak mouth to mouth clearly, and not in a dark speech; and he beholds the form of the Lord. Why then were you not afraid to speak against my servant Moses?'

So, to sum up, archaelogy rejects the JEDP theory, and supports that Moses did write Genesis to Deuteronomy. That this was one book or scroll originally before it was divided into five books by the Greek translators in 285 BC. That the statement near the end of Deuteronomy that Moses finished writing this book refers not only to Deuteronomy, but to all his work from Genesis to Deuteronomy.

SUMMARY

CRITICS' EXODUS

1. Three TV programmes ignore information and biblical alignment:

Bible	Egyptian archaeology
Joseph	Foreign shepherd kings
Slavery	Nationals gain throne 18th
Moses adopted	by Princess Hatshepsut
	(Thotmes III)
Moses flees	Hatshepsut had died.
Exodus	Amenhetep II
First-born death	Thotmes IV not the heir
Conquest 1400	Amenhetep III (Akhnaton)
	ignores appeals found on
	Amarna tablets

2. Three-days' journey to Hatshepsut's temple for Moses.
Moses' Hebrew name 'Manasseh' inscribed. 'Drawn out' is meaning of 'Moses' (on tablet).

3. Hasty entombment of Amenhetep II.
   Sphinx slab by Thotmes IV testimony (after Exodus). Critics' wrong reckoning. 'You are idle' on Egyptian mural (cf. Exodus 5:17).

4. Beetle symbol (scarab) = Egypt (as found in British Museum).
Reduces Palestine resistance to Israel's conquest (Exodus 23:28 Deuteronomy 7:20; *scarab* = 'harmful insect', often translated as 'hornet').

5. Amenhetep III (also called Akhnaton) brings monotheism to Egypt after the Exodus.

6. Experts in archaeology reject lack of knowledge of Higher Critics.

4   ■T'S MIRACLE TIME!

MOSES AND JOSHUA SET THE PACE

The archaeological evidence for Moses (Manasseh) in Egypt is plain
for all to see. Why do you think some fail to take the facts at face
value. Is it that if they were to do so, the biblical picture would begin
to come together and they would then have to consider the reality of
God's miracle-working, which some bluntly refuse to do. They would
rather twist the evidence and try to prove that the Israelites were never
in Egypt or that the Exodus happened at a much later date than accept
the biblical statements – corroborated by science – and the miracles
that go with them.

THE TEN PLAGUES OF EGYPT

Pharaoh's reply to Moses and Aaron's request to leave Egypt was to
redouble Israel's labours; he realised he would lose his slaves if he let
them so far out of his sight, and he needed them for his ambitious
building projects.

God's reply came in the form of ten horrific plagues. As we saw in
the previous chapter, these plagues were not merely God's condemna-
tion on the Egyptians: they had an ulterior purpose, '. . . to show you
my power so that my name may be declared throughout all the earth'
(Exodus 9:13–16).

The first nine plagues of Egypt have been shown to be capable of
natural explanation. Weather conditions over Ethiopia and Lake
Victoria (sources of the Blue and White Niles) affect the height of the
annual inundation of Egypt, the colour of the waters and the numbers
of frogs, flies, locusts and other creatures. Dust and hail storms are not
unusual.

What is miraculous about the plagues is their timing and intensity
and their prophetic neutralisation of the associated Egyptian gods.
Contemporary Egyptian records of such disasters were not kept.

The Lamb and Lintel

The tenth plague, however, the death of the first-born, has no possible
natural explanation. God moved in a token judgment against sin, fear-
fully demonstrating what the wages of sin are. For all who would
believe and obey, graciously there was provided a means of escape in

the Passover. In every household there would be one death – either that of the first-born or the divinely-appointed substitute lamb.

In Eastbourne, there is an inn called the 'Lamb Inn'. Somewhere else, I remember one called 'The Lamb and Lintel'. It made me think, 'You must have the two – both lamb and lintel.

Q Why were both lamb and lintel needed to deliver Israel from Egypt?

Look at the lamb first. In how many ways did the lamb foreshadow Christ? First, God said the lamb must be perfect. It must have no blemishes. This depicted Jesus who was without sin or blemish. That is why he could die in the sinner's place.

Second, the lamb must be slain. So the Lord Jesus was killed for us. His blood atoned for our sins, 'Behold the Lamb of God which takes away the sin of the world', said John the Baptist.

'I looked, and lo in heaven, in the middle of the throne stood a Lamb as if it had been slain,' said St John.

'Worthy is the Lamb who was slain for us and has redeemed us by his blood out of every tribe, tongue, family and nation,' said the saved in heaven.

Now, was the lintel also necessary? You know what a lintel is don't you? It is the top of a door frame. The Israelites were not delivered from Egypt because of their nationality. They were delivered because they applied the blood to the lintel. God said that anyone who did not apply the blood was to die when the angel of death passed over the land. If an Israelite did not apply the blood of the sacrificed lamb, he died despite his nationality. Also, any Egyptian who applied the blood would be saved. In fact, there was a mixed host who came out of Egypt with the Israelites. So you see, it was the lamb and the lintel. It was not sufficient for the lamb to be slain, the person had to spread the precious blood onto the lintel post of the door of his house.

ISRAELITES IN THE WILDERNESS

It has been thought impossible that 600,000 Israelite slaves could possibly have survived for 40 years in the desert, but the whole point was that God was able to support them miraculously by sending them quails for meat, blown by the wind and manna for bread. There are, too, various kinds of wilderness. There was also scrub land in the desert. Remember they took sheep and cattle with them and the nomads must be able to graze them. They needed them too for the tabernacle sacrifices.

Remember too, there were water-holes and that God brought water out of the rock. There is an artesian basin underlying the desert, but

God had a purpose while he was keeping them there for the 40 years. He said, 'While you are there, I will send the scarab before you into the Promised Land to subdue the inhabitants.' We now know from Egyptian history that the Pharaoh was conducting military campaigns into Palestine. The *scarab,* or sacred beetle, was the symbol of the Egyptian forces. You can see those huge stone beetles in Egypt today.

The Bible mentions the *scarab* in Exodus 23:28. 'I, the Lord, will send the beetle before you which will drive out the enemy Hivite, the Canaanite and the Hittite before you. I will not drive them out before you in one year, lest the land becomes desolate, but little by little I will drive them out'. (Note that *scarab* literally means 'harmful insect' and is commonly translated 'hornet' by Bible translators who are unaware of the Egyptian beetle symbol.) We know Pharaoh did just as the Lord says here. He subdued Canaan little by little. I draw your attention to how God overrules history. He spoke of what the Egyptians were doing as if he were doing it.

Miracle Times or Ages

It is said that miracles just don't happen in real life, but in time of crisis God does unexpected things. Nor do miracles happen on every page of the Bible history. There are long gaps of centuries when nothing seems to happen. During the 400 years following the events we are talking about, Gideon complained to God, 'Where are all the miracles our fathers told us about. Did not the Lord bring us up out of Egypt; but now the Lord has forsaken us?'

There were also miracles in the time of the prophet Elijah and that was over 600 years after the Exodus. Elijah's day was the next peak crisis time. The false religion of Baal had practically thrown over the Israelite faith. If Israel's faith was to be preserved for the coming of the Saviour, something spectacular had to be done.

The next age of miracles was that of the Lord Jesus Christ himself. That was after a wait of another 900 years and then God testified to his Messiah Son by mighty works. Jesus cured many of their illnesses, diseases, evil spirits and, to the blind, he gave sight. The power of the Lord was present to heal.

God is the God of nature. The Bible is quite frank about how God divided the Red Sea. Exodus 14:21 says that God sent a fierce east wind which blew the whole of the night and by the morning it had blown a pathway through the sea. Now, it actually happened again in 1936. The miracle was in that God timed it so well.

Manners and Manna

There is a short, surprising remark in Joshua 5:12. It says that, when Israel entered the Promised Land and ate corn, the manna stopped.

Two things that Israel learnt in the wilderness were, manners and manna. What was that manna? Manna was the honey-sweet bread which the pilgrims in the desert collected every morning with the dew. Manners, or correct living, was what they learned from following God's guidance and laws and worship.

As the New Testament says, what the pilgrims learnt during their 40 years' probation, pictured our spiritual birth and growth in the Lord. It was not sufficient merely to be saved by the blood of the Passover Lamb. They needed to grow in manners, which make a Christian man or woman.

WAS MOSES THE FIRST HEBREW TO USE AN ALPHABET?

Israel had to learn these rules both in the desert and when they had entered the Promised Land. Joshua wrote them out at Shechem on stone. Also, it would seem likely that a copy of Moses' Torah – the five books of Moses – were also copied out there. There is the surprising possibility that the copy inherited by the Samaritans who lived later at Shechem was that copy.

The biblical tradition that Moses was the first of the Hebrews to use an alphabet is so insistent that it cannot be disregarded. Whatever arguments can be used in favour of Abraham's educational ability, apply tenfold to the great Law-giver. Learned in all the wisdom of the Egyptians, as the Bible tells us (Acts 7:22), Moses would have had at his command not only cuneiform, at that time the international script of the Near East, but Egyptian hieroglyphics or even, as recent discoveries in Sinai and Syria have shown, the much handier invention of a primitive Semitic alphabet! From childhood he would have been familiar not only with inscriptions on clay tablets and stone, but with pen and ink and paper – or papyrus as it was called.

It is now well established that the use of a formal alphabet came in about this time. This was a great advance for literature. They could now use 22 signs in Hebrew, which stood for sounds, instead of having to learn thousands of symbols. Perhaps Moses adapted the finer Syrian cuneiform alphabet of 1400 BC into Hebrew letters.

Moses would have been surrounded by every incentive of precedent, for by that time Egypt was littered with papyrus writings containing historical records, philosophy, psalms, moral treatises and sacred legend.

Figure 4.1. Script Moses may have used. The white letters painted on this red pottery bowl of about 1300 BC, found during the excavations by the Wellcome Archaeological Research Expedition of the biblical city of Lachish, belong to the very old Hebrew alphabetical writing. Read from left to right after inverting the bowl, the inscription was translated by Dr Landon, late Professor of Assyriology at Oxford, as 'His righteousness is my hand (or support)'. He affirmed that the sentence is in archaic Hebrew. It is considered to be evidence that the Pentateuch was written in alphabetic script.

Courtesy: Charles Marston, The Bible Comes Alive, *Eyre & Spottiswoode (1937)*

An Acrostic Shows up True Authorship

There is a mystery about that Samaritan copy of the Torah which seems difficult to explain unless it is true.

An acrostic is worked into the text which says that the Samaritan copy was made by Abishua, the son of Phinehas. Now the name of Phinehas appears at the end of the book of Joshua in an appendix. This indicates that Phinehas the priest was Joshua's scribe, and it would be natural for his son to follow in his footsteps and make the copy of the scroll of the Law, the Torah. Now the name of Abishua is not added to the text. That could be done fraudulently. But no, the letters of Abishua's name can be picked out of the existing text acrostically and says, 'I Abishua, wrote this copy'. This is the copy in very ancient Hebrew which the Samaritans carefully guard today.

This extraordinary find, a complete copy of the Torah – all five books of Moses – is a piece of evidence which, if its legitimacy is corroborated, will show beyond a shadow of doubt that the books of Moses were written by him and were all available to the Hebrews at the time of the conquest of Canaan.

INTO THE PROMISED LAND WITH JOSHUA

On one occasion, when I was going along the Jordan Valley, I took a photo of the place where the River Jordan got blocked off. The Jordan ceased to flow when steep soft banks collapsed, just as Joshua reported.

Joshua, of course, took miracles for granted. He lived in an age of miracles for a special purpose, so he expected God to do miracles for him just as he had done for Moses. But how was God going to stop the Jordan from flowing? God was kind enough to tell him in Joshua 3:13: 'The waters of Jordan will be cut off from the waters that come down from higher up; and they shall stand upon a heap.'

In other words, God was going to make the banks higher up the river to collapse. That would dam up the river above Jericho. The water below the blockage would flow away down to the Dead Sea and that would leave the river bed dry for all Israel to cross.

Now just think about that for a moment. It shows God's control over natural events. God was actually telling Joshua before it happened that the banks would collapse just at the right moment, just as the ark of the covenant was approaching the flood waters. The waters would shrink away just at the speed with which the priests marched forward with the ark.

They walked on dry ground all the way. The timing was perfect, yet it was a natural phenomenon which God made happen.

Later, after victory was won, Joshua would walk upstream to see where it had happened. In his memoirs, he reports (in chapter 3 verse 16), that it happened near the town of Adam, a few miles upstream. When I went to photograph the place, I found that it was still called Adamieh today. I saw how the collapse of the banks certainly could block up the flooded river. At that point, the River Jordan passed through steep banks. The soil was very soft on both sides and, as the fast swirling flood swept past, it would undermine those soft banks which fell in to a great height and stopped the river flowing.

As I stood there, I imagined Joshua also standing there and writing in his report those words in chapter 3 verse16:

> The waters which came down from above stood and rose up upon a heap not far from the city called Adam, that is beside Zaretan, and those waters which came down toward the Dead Sea were cut off.

The same thing happened in 1927! Sir Charles Marston writes in his book, *The Bible Comes Alive*, that an earthquake shook Palestine in 1927. This made those soft banks collapse as they did in Joshua's day, making the Jordan dry up for 22 hours. Such a length of time would give ample time for the armies of Israel to cross over and camp at Gilgal, ready to attack Jericho.

The Fall of Jericho

Before the attack on Jericho, Israel was at Shittim, which is where 24,000 Israelites died in a plague (Numbers 25:9). The famous archaeologist, Kathleen Kenyon, reports hastily-prepared mass burial tombs before the city was destroyed. There were no signs of injury to the bodies; food offerings buried with them proved there was no famine. Kenyon inferred there was a plague shortly before the destruction took place.

F. E. Zeuner studied some of the shafts and chambers of the tombs and found evidence of seismic movement immediately after the burials. Methane had permeated the chambers, preventing deterioration of the corpses and food offerings. Even cooked meat still appeared fresh.

Marston suggests that perhaps the earthquake weakened the walls of Jericho. The Bible does not say so, but this is a very distinct possibility.

Fallacy of Undisclosed Evidence

One commentator in a TV series used to say, 'The Bible says so-and-so but there is no evidence of this'. Against this subtle implication, archaeologists calculate that so far only two per cent of all historical remains have been excavated.

At one time, scholars were saying that there was no evidence that the Hittites, so often spoken of in Scripture, ever existed. Later it was discovered that the Hittites were a great power who invented the Iron Age weapons, as the Bible says.

It is significant that, in the Bible, all references to Stone Age, Bronze Age and Iron Age tools are correct in time and type (see *Volume 1: Science*). These would be confused or lost if they were later myths.

Joshua's Close Encounter

Now it was all very well to overcome one difficulty, but as Joshua surveyed Jericho, another big difficulty was evident. Jericho was a strongly-walled city and Israel had no experience of siege warfare, no battering rams, no stone-throwing engines, no scaling ladders.

So here was Joshua, standing and consciously looking at Jericho. One great difficulty was behind him, Jordan had been crossed; how should the next problem be tackled? He began to draw a sketch of a possible plan. Then suddenly he looked up and with a shock saw in front of him a military commander. He had drawn his sword from the sheath. Was he going to strike Joshua down?

Recovering himself a little, Joshua noted that the commander's sword was not threatening him. It was pointed towards Jericho. What did this mean? Was he an enemy or was he an ally? Joshua went up to him and challenged him. 'Are you for us or for our adversaries?'

'Neither! I am Prince and Chief of the Host of Jehovah.'

Joshua knew he was in the presence of Divinity. It was one of those mysterious pre-incarnation appearances of the Lord Jesus Christ. Joshua fell to his knees and worshipped him. Why did Joshua do that? He knew the instructions to Moses. He must not worship man or idol or any supposed God, only the Lord Jehovah, the Creator.

Was Joshua's reaction misguided? No! Chapter 6 continues the account and calls this mysterious Prince Chief, the Lord. The Lord said to Joshua, 'See, I have given into your hand Jericho and the king and the soldiers.'

Another proof that this Prince Chief was the Lord was the answer he gave to Joshua's question, 'What says my Lord unto me his servant?'

The reply was the same given to Moses at the burning bush: 'Loose your shoe from off your foot for the place upon which you are standing is holy ground.' Joshua obeyed and made that act of reverence.

But there were other things to obey as well. A detailed list of instructions was given to Joshua on how the Lord would enable him to capture Jericho. Here was the answer to Joshua's difficulties. Siege warfare would not be required. Scrap your plans and difficulties!

Then the Lord gave Joshua the strangest and most novel order of battle that anyone has heard before or since. The whole host of Israel was to march around Jericho, once each day, in utter silence, for six days. On the seventh day they were to repeat this six times. Then the trumpets would blow. The whole host would shout, 'Jehovah has given us the city!' The walls would fall down flat and they must rush in and capture the city.

The Empty Mound of Jericho

If you go to the Holy Land, you will be shown the ruined mound of Jericho. It rises up above the plain. As you clamber up its slopes, the dry grey dust rises to your nostrils.

Perhaps you will stop to think, 'How strange! Why has this mound stood empty; empty since the walls fell down in Joshua's time; empty for 3,400 years?'

The answer is, because there is a curse on it. Does that make you shudder? Yes, God placed a curse on anyone who attempted to re-build Jericho. The city was so evil. False gods and Satan worship had even made that cruel people ram their babies into large pots and burn them alive to appease an evil spirit called Moleck.

I'm sorry to mention this horror, but I have to, because it explains why God had to wipe out the inhabitants. God could not stand the cruelty any longer. He had given them chances to change for over 400 years, but they were getting even worse. I won't mention other horrors, but archaeological discovery has revealed them.

So then, a curse was laid on the city, but wicked King Ahab ignored it 500 years later, for 1 Kings 16:33 says:

> Ahab did more to provoke the Lord God to anger than all the kings of Israel that were before him. In his day Hiel the Bethelite started to build Jericho. He laid the foundation of it in his first-born and set up the gates on his youngest son, according to the word of the Lord which he spoke by Joshua.

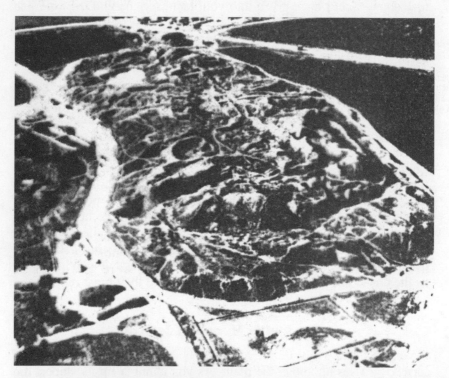

Figure 4.2. Jericho old city mound. The old city mound as Joshua left it. It has not been built on as commanded in Joshua 6:26. Hiel, who made an abortive attempt 600 years later, suffered the curse of 1 Kings 16:34. It is very unusual for ancient city mounds not to be used again and again.

Source unknown

So that curse made in Joshua's day was implemented in Ahab's reign and then the building stopped. But there is another curse which has fallen upon Jericho. It is the curse of unbelief and scepticism.

I have an article here before me in which a critic says that the fall of Jericho, as recorded in the Bible, was a myth. Why? Because he says Jericho was already fallen before Joshua came. I have already explained to you that some sceptics place the time of Joshua's entry into Palestine over 200 years later than the Bible date. I have given you a correlation list which shows that all the history harmonises with the Bible dates, but there are more details now to help you.

You have seen that 1 Kings 6:1 says that Solomon began to build the temple 480 years after the Israelites left Egypt. That dates Joshua's campaign as 1400 BC. There is also another scripture which confirms this. It is Judges 11:26. This dates Jephthah as 300 years after the fall of Jericho. That puts you in the same time period, as Jephthah lived about 180 years before Solomon.

The Bible's dates make everything fit perfectly with all that archaeology has found and all that the history of surrounding nations has recorded.

THE CANAANITES' SOS TO PHARAOH

So Jericho fell in the miraculous manner recorded in Scripture. When the kings in the northern part of the Promised Land heard of Joshua's victory over Jericho and neighbouring Ai, they formed a powerful confederation to stop him. Joshua 9:2 reads, 'They gathered themselves together to fight Joshua with one accord.' Five kings combined their forces. But God encouraged Joshua. He said to him, 'Do not fear them, for I have delivered them into your hand. There shall not a man stand before you.'

So Joshua marched up his men from their base at Gilgal and came upon them suddenly. The surprise attack scattered them.

Now archaeology has revealed something not recorded in Scripture. The alarmed kings in Canaan sent urgent requests for help to Pharaoh of Egypt. Their letters or tablets were found in his record office. They are called 'The Tel el Amarna tablets'. They were found by an old peasant woman in Egypt when she was rummaging in the ruins. They are dated between 1400 and 1360 BC. That time fits in perfectly. The Israelites are called Hebrews, but pronounced 'Habiru'. Notice that Pharaoh knows them as Hebrews in Exodus 7:16.

Here are some of the cries for Pharaoh's help:

1. 'The land of Shechem has gone over to the Hebrews.' Shechem was where Joshua read out the blessings and cursings from Deuteronomy as God instructed.
2. Another extract from the king of Sidon reads: 'Behold all my cities which the Pharaoh has given into my hands have fallen into the hands of the Hebrews.'
3. Another king (of Gebal) wrote: 'He has conquered beyond the land of the Ammonites. The city of Sidon has submitted to the occupation of his allies. The lands are for this Hebrew, so now there is none who is a friend to me.'

These and other letters reported what Joshua chapter 10 tells us. It was the defeat of those kings in northern Palestine. Archaeology also found that the area was arranged on a city states system and each city had its own king. But there is still more indisputable evidence. A letter has been found in Pharaoh's Record Library which actually mentions Joshua: 'As my Lord the King lives, Job is not in Pella. For two months he has been in hiding. Ask why from Benjamin, ask why from Joshua.' You can seek the answers from Joshua by reading his book in the Old Testament.

This Pharaoh never came to their help. We have seen why. By now he knew it was no use fighting against God. They still smarted from the drowning of Pharaoh's crack army in the Red Sea. The drying up of the River Jordan had been reported.

Consequently, Pharaoh Akhnaton reformed his land's religion to a form of monotheism – the belief in one Creator. This fulfilled God's words about Egypt in Exodus 7:5: 'Then shall they know that I am the Lord'. For many years after, Egypt had a new attitude towards Israel. But Pharaoh had had to learn it the hard way.

Does God Condone Utter Devastation?

After such a resounding defeat of the Canaanites by Joshua, other campaigns were mopping-up operations. These Tel el Amarna tablets speak of the utter devastation of the Canaanites which Joshua made.

Why did God order such a radical judgment? In answer, here is the comment made by Unger in his *Bible Dictionary*:

The severe treatment of the Canaanites has provoked considerable comment. But that Joshua was right because he acted under the command of Jehovah has been justified by two facts:

1. The excessive wickedness of the Canaanites. Leviticus 18:21–24 describes some of it. It included burning their babies alive as sacrifice to a Satanic god Moleck, homosexuality and other sins, and it adds, 'defile not yourselves with any of these things; these defile the nations which I, the Lord, cast out. The land is defiled and I visit the iniquity upon it. The land itself vomits out its inhabitants.'
2. God warned that if any of it were left in the land, it would contaminate the Israelites.

Archaeology has corroborated the abandoned wickedness and utter debilitating effect of Canaanite cults. Religious literature excavated at Ras Shamra presents the Canaanite gods as utterly immoral. The chief god is a master of wickedness. His son, Baal, is no better. The three famous goddesses, Ashera, Anath and Ashtoreth are patronesses of sex and war and their bloodiness and lustfulness must have reduced Canaanite culture to extremely sordid depths. This archaeological picture of Canaanite religion fully supports Philo's estimate of the utter corruption of Canaanite cults.

Abraham himself had been told by God, 400 years earlier, that when the sins of the Canaanites had ripened in 400 years' time, his descendants would bring judgment upon the land (Genesis 15:13–16).

Yet the example of Rahab showed that if any had believed and repented and changed, God would have spared them, as he did in a number of cases. But the majority refused to change and only resisted. Yet they all had plenty of evidence, as Rahab said, about God's miracles, in Joshua 2:9,10:

> I know that the Lord has given this land to you and that a great fear of you has fallen on us, so that all who live in this country are melting in fear because of you. We have heard how the Lord dried up the water of the Red Sea.

Also the Canaanites knew that God had given the Israelites their land because of their sins. That is also stated, but satanic religion held them as slaves to sin to the end.

Today a greater power can release Satan's slaves. It is salvation and deliverance through Jesus Christ.

SUMMARY

MIRACLE TIME

1. Three main miracle periods:
Exodus, Elijah, Emmanuel (the Messiah).

2. The God of Nature:
- Ten plagues. Years normally separating natural calamities happen together miraculously in months (but 'first-born' fatalities were supernatural).
- Sphinx slab evidence to Pharaoh's first-born fatality.
- Red Sea recession by gale (Ex 14:21).
- Jordan dammed up by soft soil slip (Josh 3:13–16). Happened again in 1927 – Jordan blocked for 22 hrs.

3. The God of righteousness:
- Jericho cursed and mound left desolate.
- 'The spy who loved me' (see next chapter). Rahab ancestress to the Redeemer (Matt 1:5).
- Amarna tablets plea for help, 1400 BC. All four tablets ignored.
- Pharaoh frightened of Jehovah!
- Canaanites' cruelty to children.

5 JOSHUA'S GUINNESS BOOK OF RECORDS
CONQUESTS IN THE PROMISED LAND

H. G. Wells, well known as a novelist, was often voicing his unbelief in God and the Bible. One of his stories was called *The Man Who Stopped the World*. It was aimed to discredit Joshua's report of a day which had nearly 24 hours' sunlight. However, in the end, Wells had to admit that God had won.

You see, astronomical evidence and the records of other ancient nations, show that there was actually a day almost twice the usual length.

A DOUBLE-LENGTH DAY

Q Why did God see the need for this extra special miracle?

The account is in Joshua 10. There you are told of the big amalgam of armies and kings to fight Joshua. Joshua saw that they came out in open battle upon the open field. They did not stay in their strong-walled cities. God gave Joshua a quick victory. But the enemy armies were rushing back to their walled cities. 'This must be stopped,' said Joshua. If they got back to their castles, this could prolong the campaign into siege warfare. One of those cities was Lachish and we know from pictures on tablets that the walls were built on the top of impregnable cliffs (see Fig 5.1).

Joshua saw that half the day was gone already. The sun was at mid-day height over Gibeon. The moon was rising just above the Aijalon Valley. Half the day gone! So, suddenly guided, Joshua shouted to God in the hearing of the armies of Israel, 'Stop the sun! Lord Jehovah! Stop the sun from going down until victory is complete.' Then Joshua turned to the sun and ordered it not to go down. He said, 'Sun, stand thou still over Gibeon and thou moon over the valley of Aijalon.'

They obeyed and the sun stopped in mid-sky for nearly a whole day. How's that for a Guinness Book of Records entry? As a matter of fact, it was recorded in the Guinness Book of Records of that day. It was called the 'Book of Jasher'. In it was recorded all the outstanding events of those times and Joshua chapter 10 mentions it in the second part of verse 13 when referring to the sun and moon standing still.

Figure 5.1. Typical strong-walled city of Joshua's day. View of modern Urbil in Iraq which shows what Lachish and Jericho would have been like. The walls were built high up on a ramp.

Source unknown

But how could it happen? Joshua would not realise the momentous miracle he was demanding. This could have upset the whole solar system! All that Joshua knew was that the Creator was greater than all his creation.

The Long Day Substantiated

Now what evidence is there for such a remarkable miracle as the double-length day? First of all, history records it!

1. **Heroditus**, the great historian of ancient times, tells you that the priests of Egypt showed him in their records the existence of an unusually long day.
2. There are **six independent records** by ancient nations of this long day. The Indian Hindu account says, 'In the life of Chrishnu, the sun delayed setting to hear the pious ejaculations of Akroon; that planet went down to make a difference of about 12 hours'. The date? It corresponds with Joshua's date (about 1400 BC).
3. **Professor Totten** has stated that research shows that a whole day of 24 hours has been inserted into the world's history. Professor Totten has found that the sun and moon have been only in that juxtaposition once. I quote, 'by taking the equinoxes, eclipses and

transits, and working backwards to the winter solstice of Joshua's day, it is found to fall on Wednesday, whereas by calculating forwards to the winter solstice of Joshua's day, it is found to fall on a Tuesday. So a whole day of 24 hours has been inserted into the world's history.' So Professor Totten affirms that 'not before or since has there been a date which will harmonise with the required relative positions of the sun, moon and earth as conditioned in the Holy Scripture'.

4. **E.W. Maunder,** Fellow of the Royal Astronomical Society, late of the Royal Observatory Greenwich, wrote about the subject and traces not only the actual spot on which Joshua must have been standing at the time, but the date and time of the day when this remarkable phenomenon took place. Does the Bible give so much detail? Yes! Joshua 10:12 says, 'Sun, stand thou still at Gibeon, and thou moon, over the valley of Aijalon.' You see, the Bible is so accurate that it tells you the actual position of the sun and moon in the sky at the time.

5. **The Superintendent of Greenwich Observatory** noted, from Joshua 10:12–13, that the sun was at midday and the moon at the horizon – the valley – which is north-west at Aijalon. With this astronomical information, he was able to project back and find that it happened on 21st July, 1400 BC.

6. The **scripture says** that the sun stood still for about a whole day, so that could mean nearly 24 hours.

7. Then **computer programs** used by astronomers found out that a day has been added to the astronomical calendar. The final 40 minutes or so (10 degrees of the sun) could be that added as a sign to Hezekiah in 2 Kings 20:10.

How Did it Happen?

We have abundant evidence to show that Joshua's record day happened. The question is, how? Scientists have given some possible explanations.

Sir Ambrose Fleming, the renowned scientist, says that 'krypton' in the atmosphere would enable the refractive powers to reflect the sun right round the world so that it would be seen for nearly 24 hours.

A clue to the means used by God, however, may come from the record of a hail of huge rocks which killed more of the enemies of Joshua than the actual battle. This is what the Bible says in Joshua 10:11:

As they fled before Israel on the road from Beth Horon to Azekah, the Lord hurled large hailstones down on them from the sky, and more of them died from the hailstones than were killed by the sword of the Israelites.

If this was the tail of a gigantic meteor, the gravitational pull of that body passing near the earth might have slowed the earth's revolution.

The actual word used for the sun 'standing still' is 'silent'. This would therefore refer to its influence rather than its apparent lack of movement due to the earth's revolution.

The Bible does not require us to know what physical or astrophysical means God used before we believe the very detailed record. The lesson for us is that our God is the God of the universe and can do all things by the word of his power. He is not at the mercy of scientific laws of nature. On the contrary, they are at his mercy and use.

God's Watch over Events

In bringing the evidence for that miraculous day which was nearly twice as long as a usual day, Mr Kenneth Anderson says, 'Many unthinking people mockingly say that this miracle is impossible . . . but surely the Creator could alter the normal laws of nature if he wanted to.' He is an expert civil engineer and so suggests: 'If I were to show you my watch and tell you that the watchmaker who made it could have constructed it, had he wished to, so that the hands could go the other way round, or even stop for a minute or two and then go on again without disorganising the mechanism, you would agree that with modern microchip technology, this could be done. In the same way, I would point to the gigantic watch which God has made and which we call the solar system. I believe,' says Anderson, 'that the Creator and upholder of the sun, moon and stars could make a slight alteration in his own arrangements without any accident ensuing, if he wished to.'

The story of Joshua provides us with many instances of God's intervening power – the crossing of the Jordan, the fall of Jericho, the longest day, to mention but the best known.

The flush of victories resulting both from military prowess and from divine intervention was to be balanced later by the failures recorded in the book of Judges concerning the places the Israelites were unable to occupy during the succeeding 400 years. However, alongside these valiant exploits of Joshua's time, we also have some amazing personal stories of honesty and truthfulness, faithfulness and perseverance. Such are the insights the Bible gives us through the personalities of Rahab and Phinehas.

Let us go back to a short time before the destruction of Jericho.

RAHAB'S RESCUE FROM JERICHO

Rahab, the prostitute, must have been full of fear as she watched those thousands of Israelites marching around her doomed city in Joshua chapter 6. Was her faith going to be in vain? Her faith had made her resolve to pledge herself to the Lord, the Lord of heaven and earth, as she called him. She had renounced the idolatry and horrible practices of her people. It had changed her outlook and way of life. But would she perish with the rest after all?

She had brought her mother and father and relatives into her house on the wall, but would they be rescued as the spies had promised? There seemed no escape. They were cut off by those marching hordes as they tramped around the walls of Jericho day after day for a week.

Tramp, tramp, tramp went those feet of 12 marching regiments with their Bronze Age weapons. She watched them followed by the strange sight of priests carrying a gold box. They were draped in white and gold, with Phinehas leading them. They reverently carried the golden box on poles and above the box were the outspread wings of two angel cherubim all in gold.

The priests blew on the curved horns of rams. Rahab's heart trembled as those weird notes echoed and re-echoed around the valley. Their mystic notes wailed and whooped in curving cascades of ominous sound.

Following the priestly band was the main body of the Israelites – absolutely masses of them. Yet, with all this mighty tramping host, there was no sound from their throats – not a word or a shout. This made the tramping sound of their feet all the more obvious.

When were they going to do something? As this was repeated daily, the citizens crowded the walls more and more. They would have thrown missiles and shot arrows, but the marching host kept out of range.

Rahab felt her nerves breaking. Then very early on the seventh day, it started all over again. But this time over and over, not just once but six times. The Jericho citizens jumped about on the walls in fury shaking their fists. For the seventh time, the Israelite host tramped round. The very vibration of their feet could be felt in the city. The rams' horns changed their wavering note into one long sound. Suddenly, the metal war trumpets blew a special signal and the silent host exploded into a shout.

'The Lord Jehovah has given us the city.'

A terrifying rumbling grew into a thunder and dust rose up as the city walls collapsed. The rumbling reached Rahab's house on the wall and stopped. The house was propped up by a stronger citadel next door. Into Rahab's house clambered one of the spies. Both he and God had kept their promise to Rahab's repentance and faith.

The Spy who Loved Me

I hope you will forgive me, but I have made a little romance out of the story of Rahab. This is how I imagine it, reading between the lines. I have called it 'The Spy who Loved Me'.

As the strong arms of the handsome soldier lifted her out of the ruins of the city of Jericho, she felt deep feelings which she had never felt before for any other man. But then other men had only wanted her for her body. Here was something different, but would this soldier-hero ever forgive her for her past way of life?

When this man first visited her house, she thought he had come for the usual. He and his friend said they had just followed the engraved footprints which led to her house. Yes, they did know what those foot-shapes meant. They had been chiselled into the stone slabs with the outline of a woman above them. Yes, they recognised the significance in a society where prostitution was part of the culture. Those foot indentations led them to her house on the city wall. They were spies but, as curious spectators were used to seeing men go to her house, they thought their visit would not arouse suspicion.

But why had they come if it was not for the usual? She soon found that the name of the leader was Salmon. 'I could have thought of a better name than that for you,' she thought. Salmon was immediately captivated by her amazing beauty. 'They certainly chose the best for this job,' he thought.

Salmon and his fellow spy promised to come back and rescue her when the walls of Jericho fell down. They had been impressed by her faith in the true and only God, but she secretly hoped that handsome Salmon would come back for another reason as well – love and marriage.

Although her culture excused her manner of livelihood, she had often felt shame and a deep desire for a faithful life of true love and marriage. And now this young spy Salmon had appeared with high ideals. 'Could he ever become the spy who loved me?' she thought.

She was thrilled now that he had kept his promise and come to rescue her. The walls of Jericho had collapsed and with it her dazzling but unsatisfying world. From her house on the wall, she could see Commander Joshua's strange manoeuvres. When she had watched the invading troops marching around, her heart had leapt to see that one of the important officers was Salmon, the spy, marching at the head of his regiment, and now here he was holding her in his arms.

'I will take you back to my tent,' he said. 'But Salmon', she said, 'please not for the old kind of life. I want a new start, a pure start.'

'You shall have a new start,' replied Salmon, 'for I want to marry you. I will get Phinehas the priest to marry us.'

'But wasn't it Phinehas who was angry with those Moabite prostitutes? What will he think of me?'

'I am sure he will delight to start you on the new life of repentance and faith. He loves the Lord God.'

Well, I don't know whether you agree with my version of 'The Spy who Loved Me', but within five verses of the New Testament, you are told that Salmon did marry her. Rahab the changed character, in God's compassion became the ancestress to King David and the Lord Jesus Christ himself – that's real love – God's love!

PHINEHAS FINISHED IT!

Are you a private secretary? Then do your job well – it's important. Most of the people that God inspired to write the Bible had private secretaries. They preserved the sacred writings and added important notes at the end.

Jeremiah's secretary was Baruch. Paul's secretary, when writing to the Romans, was Tertius. Yes, at the end of the letter to the Romans, you read, 'I, Tertius, who wrote this letter [for Paul] greet you in the Lord'.

We are looking at Joshua's exciting memoirs. Who was his private secretary? Well look at the end of the book of Joshua. Whose name do you see? It is Phinehas. Yes, Phinehas finished it. These are the last words of the memoirs of Joshua. 'Eleazar, the son of Aaron, died, and they buried him in a hill that belongs to Phinehas his son, which was given him in Mount Ephraim.'

Notice that Phinehas is still alive when writing this. He must be the one who added the note in Joshua's memoirs about Rahab. So yes, it is Phinehas, Joshua's private secretary, saying, 'She is still alive and lives in Israel to this day' (Joshua 6:25).

That answers the one who thought the book of Joshua was not written until hundreds of years later. Why didn't he want to believe that the memoirs of Joshua were contemporary? Well, let's have a look and see.

Joshua's Contemporary Memoirs

The book of Joshua can be likened to a field marshal writing up his battle accounts or memoirs, just as Montgomery did when the war was over.

Q How do we know that the book of Joshua was written in the time of Joshua?

I ask the question because a lecturer recently upset the faith of young men he was teaching by saying that Jericho was all myth and the account was not written until hundreds of years later. Well, if that were so, did you ever hear of a woman living until she was 600 years old? Yet we have seen that Rahab was still alive at the time the memoirs were being written!

Well, people did not live more than the 70-odd years then, so that makes the account contemporary with the events, doesn't it?

Q Why did the lecturer express his doubt?

It was because he did not believe in miracles. He did not believe that the walls of Jericho fell down by God's action. He thought it was all folklore. It is never wise to reduce God to the size of your own doubts. If you do, your faith will be in a self-made god – too small to meet your crises. Jericho's walls will still stand as a defiant barrier against your entering the promised land. Your god is too small to make the walls collapse.

Humble Phinehas

Now this Phinehas is rather like Luke who wrote the Acts of the Apostles, Paul's memoirs, and who kept himself in the background. He refers only to himself as 'us' and 'we'. They are called the 'we' passages. When they occur, we know that Luke has joined Paul and his other companions.

Similarly, the name of Phinehas pops up here and there occasionally and unobtrusively. He must be the faithful private secretary. He pops up in Moses' writings as well and must be the one who appends the note about Moses' death – that is at the end of Deuteronomy. It comes after it says that Moses had finished writing the Torah – that is, the five books of Moses, the book of the Law, the Pentateuch.

Yes, Phinehas must also have been Moses' private secretary. That is why his name appears twice in Moses' writings as well as Joshua's. It must have been Phinehas who suggested that the safest place to keep Moses' writings was in the ark of the covenant. Why? Because he was Aaron's grandson who guarded it! The preservation of the Scriptures is one of the wonders of the world!

Clues to Faithful Phinehas

Phinehas, Aaron's grandson, was also a brave and faithful venturer for truth and goodness. Phinehas followed in his father Eleazar's footsteps. He was dedicated to God's truth. His father disassociated himself from the betrayal of truth which two of his brothers showed. These were uncles of Phinehas. Those two uncles betrayed their responsible positions. They showed little regard for God's careful instructions.

The first little note where Phinehas appears in Moses' memoirs is in Exodus 6:25. It is this: 'And Eleazar, Aaron's son, took one of the daughters of Putiel as his wife, and she bare him Phinehas.'

Now what makes this look like a note by Phinehas? He is a grandson with four uncles whom he names, but no names are given of his other nephews or brothers.

The next glimpse we have of Phinehas is when he proves himself a champion against immorality. The story is in Numbers 25. Many of the Israelites had fallen prey to the prostitutes of a neighbouring heathen country, Moab. Like many countries, Moab started with God's revelation of truth, but soon departed from it. They became deceived and captivated by a satanic religion with its many horrors. The king found that he could not defeat Israel in battle, so he infiltrated the Israelite men by alluring them to immorality by his Moabite prostitutes.

To please these prostitutes, the men began to worship their gods and idols. Many were forsaking God's truth. This was serious because it was this truth which would eventually lead to salvation in Jesus Christ when he came. Twenty-four thousand men were involved and they became infected by a plague – perhaps it was a venereal disease. It was then that Phinehas proved his worth. When Phinehas saw what was happening, he grasped a javelin and killed the chieftain's son who was primarily responsible for this immorality and for forsaking God's truth. For this act of zeal and bravery, God commended him. The Lord said in Numbers 25:11:

> Phinehas, the son of Eleazar, the son of Aaron the priest, has turned away my wrath from Israel. He was zealous for my sake. Therefore, behold I give to him my covenant of peace . . . of an everlasting priesthood, because he was zealous for his God, and made an atonement for the children of Israel.

What a wonderful reward for faithfulness to God – an everlasting priesthood, so it proved. It was Phinehas' descendants who were priests for Solomon 500 years later. It was his descendant Hilkiah 900 years later who rediscovered Moses' copy of the Torah. It was 1,400 years later that the Virgin Mary, who inherited Phinehas' priestly lineage (as well as a royal descent), gave birth, by the Holy Spirit, to the One who is now a priest for ever, Jesus Christ the Son of God!

Phinehas' Post-War Crisis

It is sometimes said that a country won the war, but lost the peace.

Post-war conditions often bring a greater challenge than the war itself. It was so after Joshua had conquered the Promised Land in 1400 BC. Two-and-a-half tribes of Israel had settled in Gilead. That was on the east side of Jordan, before Joshua's conquest, but they had promised to help the other nine-and-a-half tribes in Joshua's campaign on the west of Jordan. When the land was conquered, the two-and-a-half tribes marched back and settled in Gilead.

On the way back, on their side of the River Jordan, they built an altar. This sounded highly suspicious. Were they revolting against God? Were they setting up a rival religion? The report and the rumours started a big reaction. Big protest meetings by the nine-and-a-half tribes sprang up. The furore heightened so much that a national gathering was called. At this national assembly, the nine-and-a-half tribes said they must elect someone who was trustworthy; someone to send over to Gilead to see what they were up to. Whom did they elect and send? Why, Phinehas, the son of Eleazar the priest. He had proved his worth from the time of Moses and God had commended his earlier courageous action for truth.

So off to Gilead went Phinehas to settle this post-war crisis. First, he delivered the message from the national gathering:

What trespass is this that you have committed against the God of Israel? Are you turning from the Lord – that you have built this altar? Are you rebelling against the Lord Jehovah? Remember the plague that broke out when 24,000 Israelites went after those Moabite prostitutes. It was only when I, Phinehas, took action against the immorality that God stopped the rampant disease. Will not God punish you for building a rival altar to the one in the Tabernacle? Did not Achan bring God's anger on Israel when he took loot from the fallen city of Jericho, when Jericho was under a curse? Do you want to incur God's anger?

The two-and-a-half tribes stoutly denied the accusation. These tribes were Reuben, Gad and the half-tribe of Manasseh.

'God forbid!' they said. 'The Lord God of all gods knows everything. He knows whether this was an act of rebellion. In fact we built this altar to avoid rebellion. We thought our children might think, one day, that the River Jordan divided us from the God of Israel. So this altar is a witness to the one true God. No sacrifices have been offered on this altar, nor will be. We shall get atonement only from the altar of the Tabernacle. Our altar we have named, "The Witness". It witnesses that Jehovah is God. There is only one true God and Creator, the Lord Jehovah.'

Phinehas returned to the nine-and-a-half tribes with this report. All Israel was greatly relieved that this post-war crisis was over. They blessed God and pledged their own faithfulness.

In modern times, some nations do not realise that their troubles develop because they cease to witness to the revelation of God in Christ. No longer are they 'defenders of the faith'. Phinehas preserved Moses' Torah by placing it in the ark (Deuteronomy 31:26). His faithfulness, and that of his descendants Hilkiah and Jeremiah, established the reading of God's truth down through the centuries.

FROM PHINEHAS TO JEREMIAH

I once heard a man get excited when he found that he could trace his ancestors back to Shakespeare. Famous authors are thrilled if they can trace their talent back to a historical character. Well, did you know that the prophet Jeremiah could trace back to the hero priest of Moses' time, Phinehas? It was to Phinehas that God awarded an 'Oscar' for a brave stand against an invasion of immorality which was corrupting his nation. That is what Oscars should be awarded for – encouragement of purity.

I showed you that Phinehas also had another important task. It seems that he was Moses' private secretary – the one who wrote the postscript to Moses' great work of the Pentateuch, the book of the Law, the five books of Moses, called the Torah, which is the first major section of our Bibles.

Well, God promised that Phinehas' successors would continue the work down the centuries and they did. One important part was the preservation of God's inspired Scriptures. It would be Phinehas who preserved Moses' original copy of Genesis to Deuteronomy by putting it in the side of the ark, safe in the Holy of Holies. It was a descendant of his, 800 years later, who found that original scroll there. At that time, copies in the kingdom had been lost or neglected in a godless age. That descendant's name was Hilkiah. He reported his find to King Josiah in 2 Kings 22.

'I have found the Torah of Moses' *which was actually written by his own hand* (Deuteronomy 31:24; 2 Chronicles 34:14,15).

That find brought about national repentance and revival. It postponed God's judgment on the southern kingdom.

Do you know who Hilkiah's son was? It was Jeremiah! Yes, Jeremiah was also a descendant of Phinehas. Jeremiah was a priest as well as a prophet. He records this momentous find in Jeremiah 15:16: 'Thy words were found, and I did eat them and they became a joy and delight of my heart.'

Now Jeremiah did what Phinehas his ancestor did. His ancestor had collected the memoirs of Joshua and added them to Moses' work. That is why many have remarked that the book of Joshua reads like a continuation from the epilogue that Phinehas had appended to the end of Moses' book. Phinehas did his bit even before Rahab was dead, as he said. God's promise to perpetuate Phinehas' faithfulness down to his descendants was certainly fulfilled. They too preserved the inspired Scriptures.

According to the rabbis and Josephus, it was Jeremiah who collected together all the contemporary records made since Joshua's book, that is from Judges onwards. Yes, they say he collected together the writings of Samuel, Nathan (David's prophet), Gad and other records, then welded them together in a continuous account from Judges to 2 Kings.

God's Word True from the Beginning

The evidence for this is in the list of credits given in 1 Chronicles 29:29 and 2 Chronicles 35:25. Further evidence for this is in the language Jeremiah uses. In his prophecy, typical phrases such as 'Their ears shall tingle' and 'God sent them prophets to warn them continually', appear both in his history of Israel and in his 'Book of the Prophet Jeremiah'.

Yes, Jeremiah was a worthy successor of his ancestor, Phinehas. God used him to preserve for us all those reliable contemporary records. So ignore those sceptics who pretend that they are only folklore.

Do you see the incredible internal correlation between the various parts of the Bible and the individuals God called to compile and preserve them? In that same way, it correlates perfectly with the contemporary history of the nations recorded at that time.

'Thy Word is true from the beginning,' says Psalm 119:160.

Table of Events: Joshua to Solomon

A. 300 Years from the Conquest to Jephta's first year

West of Jordan	No. of years	East of Jordan	No. of years
Joshua and Elders	20		
Mesopotamian oppression	8		
Rest (Othniel) – Judges 3:11	40		
Moabite oppression – Judges 3:14	18		
Ehud and Shamgar – Judges 3:28 to 4:1	80		
Sisera's oppression – Judges 4:3	20		
Deborah and Barak – Judges 5:1,31	40		
Midianite oppression – Judges 6:1	7		
Gideon – Judges 8:28	40		

(Continued)

Abimelech – Judges 9:22	3	Jair's era – Judges 10:3	22
Tola of Ephraim – Judges 10:2	23		
		Ammonite oppression in East Jordan ending with invasion of West Jordan	18
Ammonite invasion of West Jordan – Judges 10:9 – after the 18 years in East Jordan	1		
Jephta's total – Judges 11:26 **Total**	**300**	Since 2½ tribes entered East Jordan 300 years earlier	

The problem now is in accounting for the remaining 180 years between Jephta and Solomon, to bring the total to 480 years (1 Kings 6:1). There are two factors to note, the first is that the Philistine oppression runs concurrently with Samson and Eli judgeship. This is clear from Judges 13:1, 15:11,20 and 16:31. The second is that the duration of Saul's reign is unknown in the Old Testament record. The 180 years work out thus:

B. 180 Years Between Jephta and Solomon

Jephta – Judges 12:7	5	
Ibzan of Bethlehem – Judges 12:9	7	
Elon – Judges 12:11	10	
Abdon – Judges 12:14	8	
Samson – Judges 15:20, 16:31	20	Note 1
Eli – 1 Samuel 4:18	40	
Samuel – 1 Sam 7:2, 14:18	20	Note 2
Saul (by deduction)	27	Note 3
David – 2 Samuel 5:4,5	40	Note 4
Solomon to 4th year – 1 Kings 6:1	3	
TOTAL	180	
Plus 300 to Jephta	300	
GRAND TOTAL (1 Kings 6:1)	**480**	

Note 1. Philistine oppression of 40 years runs concurrently with Sampson and part of Eli's judgeship.

Note 2. Unlikely to be longer as he was a boy in Eli's 40 years and did not die until the end of Saul's reign.

Note 3. At Saul's death, David and Jonathan were about 30 years old (2 Samuel 5:4,5) therefore were teenagers together 15 years earlier when Saul had reigned 12 years. Jonathan would be about 3 years old when Saul was crowned (say at the age of 23 years – married at 19).

Note 4. Saul would be 50 when slain: men usually ceased to go into battle after 50 years of age.

SUMMARY

JOSHUA'S LONG DAY

Reasons for the Long Day
- Enemy rushing to city safety.
- Joshua not equipped for siege warfare.
- Josh 10:13; 2 Sam 1:18.

Records of Long Day
- Heroditus (500 BC) and Egyptian records.
- Jasher, The Guinness Record book of ancient times.
- Indian Chrishnu account.
- Other ancient records – China, Aboriginal, American Indians.
- Prof Totten's equinoxes, eclipses and transits.
- Superintendent of Greenwich Observatory, 21st July, 1400 BC.
- Position moon and sun. Josh 10:12.
- E. W. Maunder, Royal Astronomical Soc.

How?
- Sir Ambrose Fleming and 'Krypton Factor'.
- Comet influence or meteorites.

Other notes
- Rahab was still alive when book of Joshua was written.
- Phinehas was Moses' secretary.

Table of Time
- 1400 BC Bible date for the Long Day.
- 300 years to Jephtha (Jdg 11:26).
- 180 years Jephtha to Solomon 1 Kgs 6:1.

6 SOLOMON'S GREAT EMPIRE
EVIDENCE AGAINST THOSE WHO DISPUTE IT

The wisdom and architecture of Solomon are resplendent in Scripture, yet at Jerusalem practically nothing of his work remains. One critic, however, does not tell his TV audience why. He wrongly infers that therefore it never existed.

It was in fulfilment of our Lord's prophecy that 'not one stone should remain upon another' (Matthew 24:2). The Roman army thoroughly devastated the city in AD 70 and levelled the whole site, thus obliterating all buildings of Solomon, Nehemiah and Herod, except for the Wailing Wall.

GREAT CITIES BUILT BY SOLOMON

According to Scripture, there are three other cities which Solomon built with his special style as at Jerusalem. This style is described in 1 Kings 9:15 and is characterised by double casemate gates at the entrances of the cities. The passage names Jerusalem as one of those places which Solomon had built on this design by forced labour and, although Jerusalem was destroyed, three of these other examples have been excavated. Professor Y. Yadin showed the accuracy of the Bible description on Solomon's six-celled casemate gates at Gezer, Hazor and Megiddo, all of the same period as the Jerusalem temple in the tenth century BC (960 BC).

They had been built by Solomon to the same blueprint and even to the same measurements. Tenth-century pottery has since been identified at all these sites, thus fixing the period correctly. Alan Millard of Liverpool University writes, 'There is little room to doubt that these structures were all erected on a uniform plan at Solomon's command.'

King Solomon's Mines

Tourists are often shown mines at Arava at the Gulf of Aquaba and told that they are Solomon's Mines. The 'Solomon's Mines' fable was started by Dr Glueck, who thought that this site was a roasting valley where Solomon refined his copper for the temple. It is now seen to be Egyptian and of much older date. Had Glueck been guided by Scripture, he would have seen that, according to 2 Chronicles 2, it was King David who provided all the copper, gold and silver for Solomon from the Phoenicians, not from any Hebrew mines. The associated Phoenician craftsmanship amply illustrates this.

Treasures under the Rubble in Jerusalem

The Romans were determined to wipe out any vestige of the Hebrew capital and actually levelled and distributed all the rubble over the whole site to a depth of many feet. They actually 'ploughed Zion with oxen' (thus fulfilling the prophecy of Micah 3:12). So all the features spoken of so graphically in St John's Gospel, as if they existed when he was writing, were obliterated and forgotten to history after AD 70, which is why Dr John Robinson thinks that John's Gospel was written well before AD 70, indeed before the 'Wars of the Jews' started in AD 66.

That devastation has actually preserved evidence for us. In recent years, places mentioned in Scripture have been uncovered from the rubble. Three examples are Hezekiah's conduit, mentioned in 2 Kings 20:20, the Pool of Bethesda, John 5 and the Pavement, John 19. The first instance we will deal with in a later section.

Pilgrims to the Holy Land are always shown 'The Pavement' (*lithostratos*). Upon these calcined flags in the centre courtyard of Pilate's fort, stood our Lord at his trial. No secular historian mentions this pavement. Its existence was doubted until it was unearthed eight feet below the rubble.

A link with the Pavement, John 19, is the discovery of a fragment of that chapter copied from St John's Gospel within a few years of his writing it. This defeats the sceptics who thought the Gospel was written later. This fragment in Ryelands Library also supports the theory that it was the Christians who invented paged books so that they could refer to texts more quickly than by unrolling a scroll.

Some People Don't Like Camels!

Critic 'R', in another series on TV, also attacks Solomon. He says that the Bible reference to Solomon's use of camels is fictional. Why? Because, he asserts, camels were not in use until 601 BC. This shows how some ignore up-to-date information.

Even while I was at Oxford in 1964, Professor Zeuner was telling us that camels were domesticated as long ago as 2000 BC. The ironic thing was that Professor Zeuner was an atheist, but as an anthropologist and a specialist in animal bones, he had first-hand knowledge. While he was imparting this knowledge to anthropologists, the theologians in Oxford were still teaching what critic 'R' has more recently (erroneously) repeated. Some people just don't like camels!

As always, the biblical account of Solomon's use of camels is therefore accurate. The evidence is given by a Phoenician priest of the time called Sanchuniathon. His description is written from Hiram's viewpoint. King Hiram had timber for the temple transported from Lebanon to Jerusalem on 8,000 camels! 1 Kings 5:8–11 (AV) says:

> And Hiram sent to Solomon, saying, 'I have considered the things which thou sentest to me for: and I will do all thy desire concerning timber of cedar, and concerning timber of fir. My servants shall bring them down from Lebanon unto the sea; and I will convey them by sea in floats unto the place that thou shalt appoint me, and will cause them to be discharged there, and thou shalt receive them: and thou shalt accomplish my desire, in giving food for my household.' So Hiram gave Solomon cedar trees and fir trees according to all his desire. And Solomon gave Hiram twenty thousand measures of wheat for food to his household, and twenty measures of pure oil: thus gave Solomon to Hiram year by year.

These details are fully confirmed by the report from the Phoenician priest of Tyre. It also supplies the actual names of the mariners in the ships mentioned in 1 Kings 9:27. To help Solomon build up his ships' crews with experienced men, Hiram sent his well-seasoned mariners.

Riches from India

With this fleet, Solomon brought riches from Ophir. They were cargoes of 'gold, silver, ivory, apes and peacocks' and the journey took three years.

Where was Ophir? Some have suggested Yemen in the south of the Red Sea, but better evidence is for India, at a place 60 miles north of Bombay. To support this is the three-year journey. It would not take that long to Yemen. Also, the commodities mentioned were more typical of India, especially apes, of which there were none in Yemen. We know, too, that there was a lively sea trade between the Near East and India from the second millennium BC. Jerome of the fifth century and the Greek Septuagint of 288 BC also interpret Ophir as India.

SOLOMON'S DEBT TO THE CAMEL

The visit of the Queen of Sheba is a well-known story and Handel's majestic music played on royal occasions still stirs the imagination.

Although camels were in use among the elite from Abraham's time, large camel caravans came into greater use during the reign of Solomon. The information from Tyre spoke of 8,000 camels on one enterprise. These 'ships of the desert' opened up trade routes that plodding donkeys could never attempt, says Dr Dent. The road from Sheba to Solomon's port at Ezion-Geber where Solomon kept his navy on the Gulf of Aquaba, stretched for more than 1,000 miles of open desert.

Sheba was able to export large quantities of spices to markets throughout the fertile crescent. It is obvious from the Bible details that the Queen of Sheba also had commercial arrangements in mind when she visited Solomon.

A Load of Great Riches

Professor K. A. Kitchen, the great expert, describes from archaeological tablets the great loads of gold which were transported in ancient times. He writes, 'Over a thousand years before Solomon's day, a defeated king of Mari paid tribute to Ebla of ten tons of silver and over a third of a ton of gold' (Ebla tablets). 'Five centuries after Solomon, one province of India (just the Indus basin) yielded an annual 360 talents (sacks) of gold to the Persian emperors.' Solomon's 666 talents would be about 20 tons of gold.

Professor Kitchen gives detailed information about the history of the camel in the *New Bible Dictionary*. 'The evidence clearly indicates that the domesticated camel was known by 3000 BC, but continued in limited use as a slow-moving burden carrier' until later. From the period of the Patriarchs until Moses (2000–1400 BC), he lists the evidence from pottery figures, including a camel with two water jars from Memphis in Egypt, as well as bone remains.

Made to Measure

The camel seems to be specially designed by God for desert use. Unger's *Bible Dictionary* describes it as:

> One of the most useful of the domestic animals of the East. With the exception of the elephant, it is the largest animal used by man. It is often eight feet or more in height, and possessed of great strength and endurance. It has a broad foot, which enables it to walk over sandy wastes without sinking deeply beneath the surface. It has a provision in its stomach for storing water enough to enable it to travel for days together without drinking. It is capable of subsisting on the coarsest and bitterest of herbage, and can take into its horny mouth the most obdurate thorns, which it grinds up with its powerful teeth and digests with its ostrich-like stomach. To offset its great height, it is formed to kneel, so that it can be loaded as easily as an ass, and then rise with its burden of five hundred pounds and plod on through the hottest day, and the most inhospitable waste of the deserts, in which it finds its congenial home. The hump on its back is not only a help to retaining its pack saddle, but a storehouse of fat, in reserve against its long fasts.

Anthropologists learn that in an emergency, if a camel driver runs out of water, he pushes a reed down the camel's throat and drinks from the camel's reserve. The pad-like feet of the camel spread out for support from the sand and the double eyelid flap closes down to protect the eye from flying sand.

ANSWERING THE DOUBTERS

Now look at some answers for anyone influenced by the critic's doubts.

> *Q Victor, the critic in his television programme, comes up with the astonishing statement that there's no evidence whatsoever that King Solomon ever existed. What do you make of that?*

Well, he is not saying that archaeology shows that Solomon did not exist. He actually agrees that archaeology harmonises with the Bible about the culture and background described in the Bible, but he thinks that that doesn't prove that King Solomon existed. So he says that the story of Solomon and all his glory was just made up by the writer in the Bible. But I have evidence that he doesn't seem to know about. One, the Bible presents Solomon as an historic character and refers to two history books in existence at the time. They were the official court records and we know that it was the custom of the nations to keep them. Second, the fact that the Bible gives correct details of the culture and of other personalities who lived in 960 BC does argue that what it says about Solomon must also be reliable. Lastly, he does not seem to know that tablets have been found that refer to Solomon and his temple.

> *Q But the same critic says that there are no signs in Jerusalem of the remains of a temple or of any of Solomon's other magnificent buildings.*

Of course there aren't. The Bible says they were all destroyed in 587 BC by Nebuchadnezzar (and again the second temple was destroyed by the Romans). They destroyed Jerusalem so thoroughly that historians of the time say you would not have known that a city ever existed there. In fact, the Romans ploughed it like a field to obliterate everything, but there are buildings by Solomon which testify to him in other parts of the country as mentioned in the Bible.

Now, tablets found actually describe the transport of timbers from King Hiram to the temple of Solomon. Hiram was a Phoenician and these records were written by a man named Sanchuniathon. He is the one who says that King Hiram transported timbers and planks on 8,000 camels.

Q But hang on a minute, Victor. Critic 'R' said that camels weren't in use until 360 years later than this.

He did. But this tablet proves him wrong, doesn't it? Think of it! Eight thousand camels to transport cedars to the temple building project. Now listen to the equivalent account in the Bible. It's in 1 Kings 5:6: 'Solomon said, instruct the cedars of Lebanon be cut for me for no one among us knows how to cut timber like you people of Tyre.' Hiram replied 'I'm ready to do all that you desire in the matter of cedar and cyprus timber.'

This tablet by Sanchuniathon sheds light on why Solomon needed to get all this timber from Lebanon. It says that there were plenty of palm trees in Judah, but no wood suitable for building material. These archaeological tablets add other interesting details to 1 Kings 9:26. We read, 'King Solomon built a fleet of ships and Hiram sent with the fleet his servants, seamen who were experienced mariners.'

Q But what do the tablets add to the information in the Bible?

It gives the actual names of those mariners. There were Kedorus, Jaminus and Kotilus. It also says that Hiram sent highly skilled bronze workers to Solomon's temple. One such worker is mentioned here in 1 Kings 7:13, I quote, 'He was the son of a widow of the tribe of Naphtali and his father was a man of Tyre, a worker in bronze, very skilful for bronze work. He came to King Solomon and did all his work.'

Q So this man was mentioned in despatches in both the Bible and on these tablets that have been found?

Actually, that workman's name was also Hiram (or Huram), like his king. That's also mentioned both in the Bible and on that tablet of Sanchuniathon. Critic 'R' may not have known about these tablets, but it should warn anybody not to doubt a Bible story just because we've not found the evidence. You might find the evidence any time, as apparently we found evidence he did not know about. Do you know that so many tablets have now been unearthed from the ancient world that only five per cent of them have been deciphered and translated so far?

Some critics also say that King David didn't write the psalms that were attributed to him. They say that, instead, they were written in the times of the Maccabees which was about 800 years later. They say actually that poetry in that style wasn't written as early as the time of King David.

Wrong again! The Ras Shamra tablets from the coast of Syria are poems and psalms about David's time and of course Solomon was famous for his wisdom, his proverbs and natural history. Solomon was a great expert on horses. He imported horses from a place which the Bible calls 'Que'. We've only learnt recently that this was a place away in Asia Minor (Turkey). This was where the famous horse culture of the Hittites arose. They took to breeding white horses. One white horse was worth four times as much as an Egyptian horse. You can imagine Solomon riding a great white horse.

Q Doesn't the Bible say that Solomon had thousands of horses and mounted soldiers and that in fact he built garrisons complete with stables for the horses? Have we found any of those?

Yes, the remains of them are at Gezer, Hazor and Megiddo.

Now, critic 'R' said something about Megiddo. He said there was no sign of Israelite occupation there when Israel entered the land under Joshua's conquests a bit earlier on.

That confirms the Bible. If he had read Joshua 17:11 and Judges 1:27, he would see the statements that Israel failed to capture Megiddo. It says that the Canaanites continued to live there; but now go back to Solomon's temple. Although that was thoroughly destroyed, we have the same pattern of his building at Gezer, Hazor and Megiddo.

Q What pattern was that and how do we know about it if Solomon's temple has vanished?

Because the building instructions in the Bible for the temple describe a double casemate style (dummy entrance) and that is the same style which has been found in Gezer, Hazor and Megiddo, which Solomon also built.

Q But look, critic 'R' in his television programme, showed a Canaanite temple down in the south and said that's where Israel had got the idea of the temple from.

Ah, that temple was nothing like Solomon's, but what the Bible does say in Judges 3:6 is that the Israelites went and served the Canaanite gods. They could not drive out the Canaanites in many places and eventually, sadly, the Israelites inter-married and served the Canaanite gods. That's why Israelites were in a Canaanite temple.

200-YEAR CRITICISM OF LITERATURE

Here is a typical conversation arising out of an actual TV programme. It may suggest replies for you to give when friends report such a programme to you.

In the Bible you are often told who wrote parts of it. A television series showed that there are people who question this and it suggested that many parts were not written by the author who was named.

Well Victor, when did people actually start questioning who wrote these various parts of the Bible? Was this something that only happened recently?

No, it was nearly 200 years ago. It started with the French Revolution. Rationalists like Wolf. They doubted and mistrusted lots of other books as well as the Bible. They said that all literature was open to examination.

Well, that sounds reasonable, doesn't it Victor?

Ah, maybe, if it's done fairly and without prejudice.

Now, you said there are other old books they examined to see if their authorship was correct. Can you tell me what they were?

Well, there were Shakespeare's plays.

Oh yes, now I've heard something about that. Some people say that Shakespeare didn't actually write the plays at all, but some fellow called Bacon.

That's right. But a more recent writing than that was under attack. It was that lovely poem by Coleridge called the 'Ancient Mariner'.

Ah, now that's the one about the curse on a seaman because he killed an albatross, isn't it? That brought a curse on the whole crew and the ship so that the ship was stranded in a dead calm in the middle of the Pacific Ocean. But why did the critics think that Coleridge didn't write that at all?

Because the style altered so much in the various verses. However, a friend of Coleridge, named Lowas, produced Coleridge's notebook. These were the notes Coleridge made in preparing to write that famous poem. So that proved the authorship was genuine.

Yes, OK, but what other classics did these rationalists test?

A very old one – the ancient books of Homer, probably written eight centuries BC.

Oh, about Helen of Troy and the Wooden Horse and all that. Now, there were two books there, weren't there? Illiad and The Odyssey?

Yes; well the rationalists said Homer could not have written both. Then another man named Wellhausen criticised the Bible in the same way, doubting the authors of the Bible.

Well, you know, they must have had good reason for saying that. Why did they say it about Homer's books?

The reason was that there were a lot of words in one book which were not used in the other. They actually counted the words. There were factors they did not think of though. One book was all about a town and house furniture, but the other book was set in the countryside – an entirely different environment. When scholars looked at the word differences, they found it was due to a different environment being described.

(Continued)

So, did the scholars then reject Wolf's theories?

Yes, they did, but not the critical views about the Bible, even though their theories were based upon the same wrong assumptions.

Yes, but perhaps there's more reason to doubt the Bible's authorship. After all, the Bible claimed to be much older than any other book in the world.

True, and that highlights another assumption they made. They thought that writing was not invented when Homer wrote, so it must have been folklore – stories told over and over again and written down much later.

Well, that's what they said about the Bible too and, since the Bible talks about even more ancient times, that seems very reasonable.

Ah, not now, because archaeology has shown that writing was invented long before Homer and long before the Bible. In fact, writing started around 3400 BC. The television critic referred to the Oxford Museums. Now I worked in them, of course. If he had looked in the Ashmolean Museum, he would have seen the first tablets when writing began, 2,000 years before Moses.

But many critics today admit that writing was known long before Moses.

Yes, but it did not change critical theories as it had done with those secular works. In that museum are the works of Mindenhall as well, who discovered that new words and different styles were due to a different subject. All the writings of Moses were composed in the legal style of his day, based upon the Hittite code.

You told us about that previously, but perhaps Mindenhall was alone in his views and not supported by others.

He has been supported by many others. Dr J. Martin of Liverpool University, Kitchen of the same university, Finn, Orr, Baker, Mitchell, Wiseman, Bruce.

OK, OK, that's enough names for now, but why hasn't their evidence been accepted? If similar evidence was accepted for Homer and others, why don't they accept it for the Bible? Didn't you say that scholars now accept these secular books as genuine?

It's because of the climate of unbelief in the world today. Unbelief in the Creator, unbelief in spiritual beings, miracles and unbelief that God has spoken through the prophets and through his Son, Jesus Christ. Jesus prophesied that this scepticism would come in the latter days. He said that many would fall away from the faith and that lawlessness and wickedness would result.

Now you're beginning to preach, Victor. I'm sure we don't want that.

That's right, many don't want it. They want an excuse to hide from God and false theories help them to do it. What is more, their theories were based on wrong assumptions when little was known about archaeology and the literary methods of the ancient Middle East.

But we know about them now, don't we?

Yes, but they ignore them and often refuse to let Bible-believing scholars have their say. It was with great difficulty that we managed to get one minute on television to reply to their critic – one minute to reply to seven hours of unbelief in a series of programmes.

(Continued)

Whatever did you say in that minute then Victor?

Here it is. This series doubted Bible accuracy. I am an anthropologist and archaeologist of Oxford and wish to correct this. He said there was no Exodus because Jericho had fallen by 1250 BC, but the Bible date in 1 Kings 6:1 is 200 years earlier. This date fits Egyptian history and Palestine archaeology perfectly. The Amarna tablets report Israel's invasion. He says stories of Abraham were not written until 600 BC because camels are mentioned, but evidence shows camels were used 2000 BC, in Abraham's day. He questions Solomon's existence. Sanchuniathon's tablet says 8,000 camels carried materials for Solomon's temple. He said the author of Genesis never knew Egypt but 21 Egyptian words and customs occur in Genesis which only a contemporary dweller would know. So it's the Bible which is accurate; certainly not that critic.

But Victor, many church leaders agree with the critics.

Yes, these are the days spoken of in Acts 20:29: 'I know this that grievous wolves will enter in among you not sparing the flock and also of your own selves. Men will arise speaking perverse things.' Also in 2 Timothy 3 this warning is given: 'Know this that in the last days, perilous times will come. Men will have a form of religion, but deny God's power. They will be forever educating, but never able to come to the knowledge of the truth.' Peter wrote in 2 Peter 3:3: 'In the last days sceptics will come, living according to their lusts, asking where is Christ's promise to return and willingly ignorant that God created by words.' Jesus warned about the Sadducean spirit which refused to believe in miracles or spiritual beings or the resurrection and which rejects a large part of God's inspired Scriptures.

But the critics were only putting the Bible to the same tests as other books.

Actually, they were not. They refused the evidence which showed the Bible to be genuine. Also they ignored the many warnings not to tamper with God's Word.

Warnings! What warnings? Where are they?

Jesus said 'He who rejects my words has one who will judge him at the last day. The words that I have spoken will judge him . . .' And also I'll quote the Bible's closing words on the last page. 'I testify unto every person who hears the words of the prophecy of this Book that if anyone shall add to these things, God will add the plagues which are written in this Book and if anyone takes away from the words of this prophecy, God will take away his part out of the Book of Life.'

That sounds a bit harsh.

They sound harsh words because the consequences in the world are harsh. Scepticism of God's Word reaps a bitter harvest in society as well as in a person. Warnings of danger are a kindness. Also the Bible ends with a gracious invitation to believe and have life. Here it is: 'I, Jesus, sent my messenger to testify to you. The Spirit and the bride [that's the saved ones] say come and let him who hears these words come and let him who is thirsty for truth come, and whoever is willing let him come and take of the water of life freely.' There's a very generous invitation.

S U M M A R Y

SOLOMON'S EMPIRE

1. Two TV critics said there is no evidence of Solomon's buildings.
The reason: 'Not one stone left' at Jerusalem's prophesied fall in
AD 70 but Solomon's casemate style visible. Gezer, Hazor,
Megiddo Forts (A. Millard, Liverpool Univ.). Phoenician
materials (2 Chron 2) confirmed.

2. Camel blunder by critic 'R', said not used until 601 BC.
Corrected by experts:
  Prof Zeuner – camels domesticated in Abraham's time 2000 BC.
  Sanchuniathon says Solomon's transport had 8,000 camels! He
  confirms all the details of 1 Kings 5:8–11.
  Prof K. Kitchen lists evidence 2000–1400 BC.

3. Ingots from India.
Confirmed by Jerome and Greek Septuagint.

4. Critic 'R' lacks tablets to correct scepticism:
  • Hiram of Tyre confirms temple materials.
  • Hiram sent experienced sailors.
  • David's psalms style on Ras Shamra tablets.
  • Solomon's horses from 'Que' Turkey (Ras Shamra tablets).
  • Solomon's stables unearthed at Gezer, Hazor, Megiddo.
  • Bible lists cities Israel failed to capture.

7 CAN YOU SWALLOW JONAH?
EVIDENCE ON WHALES, SEA CRUISES AND NINEVEH

If ever there was a book in the Bible which was unlikely to be true, it is the book of the prophet Jonah. Yet all its impossibilities have now been proved factual. Here is a partial list:

1. That Jonah paid a passenger fare for a sea trip as far as Gibraltar.
2. That God had created a sea mammal able to swallow a man for three days and keep him alive.
3. That Jonah was swallowed by the whale and was coughed up alive.
4. That Jonah saved Israel as well as Nineveh.
5. That Nineveh was an exceeding huge city of 60 miles across ('three days' journey').
6. That the ruling despot noted for cruelty would take any notice of Jonah's threat of God's judgment.
7. That God had a plant which could grow up in one night and wither away the next morning.
8. That Jehovah God is a God of love who wants to spare the children and cattle of cruel foreigners.

Some have even questioned whether Jonah existed. 2 Kings 14:25 states clearly that he did. 'God spoke by the hand of his servant Jonah, in the reign of the northern Israel king, Jeroboam II. He was contemporary with Hosea about 765 BC.

JONAH AND THE WHALE

Sceptics as far back as the French Revolution said that a whale could not swallow a man. Why? Because it had a grill in front of its mouth which filtered out small fish. Sceptics still propagate this objection. The British Museum exhibited one to cast doubt on the story of Jonah. Then it was discovered that there were 14 types of whale. Most of them could swallow large-sized articles, especially the cachalot species which frequents the Mediterranean where Jonah was swallowed.

Four Documented Stories

There are four well-reported cases since Jonah in the Bible 800BC. Their dates span nearly three centuries.

The first case is that of Marshall Jenkins who belonged to an eighteenth century US whaler. The ship's boat went out and harpooned a huge whale. In its fury, it turned the boat upside down and threw the crew into the sea. They saw Jenkins swallowed by the whale and chased the whale and succeeded in harpooning it. In its death struggles, it vomited up, as was common, its last meal, which was Jenkins who to their surprise was still alive after many hours.

In the second case, the whaling ship Star of the East was in the vicinity of the Falkland Islands in 1891. One morning the lookout sighted a whale which was eventually harpooned but swam away at terrific speed, dragging the small whaling boat after it. The whale struck the boat throwing all the men into the sea. James Bartley was not recovered. In due course, the dead whale was tied to the side of the ship, the stomach was hoisted onto the deck to be cut open and out fell Bartley, alive but unconscious. A bucket of seawater revived him, but he was 'a raving lunatic'. He was carefully treated by the captain and officers, recovered from the shock and 'resumed his duties'. Bartley had been alive, breathing inside the whale for a whole day.

The third case was in the English Channel in 1927, reported in the Literary Digest by Rimmer. In an attempt to harpoon a 'whale shark', a sailor fell overboard and was swallowed. The entire trawler fleet put out to hunt the fish down and 48 hours later the fish was sighted and slain. They towed the carcass to shore and opened it, and were amazed to find the man alive! He was rushed to hospital and a few hours later was discharged physically fit.

The fourth case was an Arab from Kuwait. This man cut his way out of the whale's stomach with a knife which he carried in his belt.

God 'Prepared a Great Fish'

How did God prepare this great fish? We saw in Volume 1: Science, that it appears suddenly in the fossil record, and comparatively recently, yet too early to have been evolved from a mammal. Why do I say that? It is because evolutionists say that the whale was at one time a land animal breathing air and giving birth to offspring which were breast fed - in other words, it was a mammal which lived on the land. Therefore, the evolutionist says that the whale must have a lot of ancestors who lived on land like the mammals we know, and after that grew into a big whale and took to the sea.

What an extraordinary series of developments there must have been if this were true. There should be thousands of fossils leading up to this. But there aren't! The whale appeared suddenly in the fossil record, at the same time as the first earth mammals, so there is no time for evolution to explain its appearance and, in any case, there is no long fossil record of such an extraordinary development of a mammal gradually turning into a sea mammal.

What it does explain is the statement in Jonah chapter 1 verse14, 'Now the Lord had prepared a great fish to swallow Jonah'. God prepared it on the fifth day, before man was created at the end of the sixth day. That fish was well-prepared, too, because all the sailors who have been swallowed alive and come out alive have said that they could breathe inside the whale.

Luxury Cruises in the Sun

Was there really a regular passenger sea trip to Gibraltar as long ago as Jonah's day, 800 BC?

Fortunately, my training as an anthropologist says yes, and long before that. Modern thinking had underestimated the advanced state of civilisation millenniums before Christ. Britain was called The Pretanic Islands in Jonah's time, but by the Irish, Britain was called Albion (white) because of the white cliffs of Dover and the south-east coastline. The Irish called their island Ierne.

Trade routes in Jonah's day called at Marseilles (Massilia), then ships would sail through the pillars of Hercules (Gibraltar) to Tartessos nearby (Tarshish). Note the map of sea lanes in Joshua's day (Fig 7.1).

So we cannot underestimate the civilisation of Jonah's time, nor their ability in the fields of science, education, music and travel.

Jonah Saved Israel

Did you know that Jonah saved Israel from being invaded by preaching repentance to Nineveh? Nineveh was in northern Mesopotamia now called Iraq.

We saw how James Bartley, like Jonah, was swallowed by a whale and came out alive. Well, when Jonah came out alive, he was told by God to be obedient and preach repentance to Nineveh. Jonah did not want to because this capital of Assyria was a threat to Israel.

If God threatened to destroy it for its wickedness, that was OK for Jonah, but God had a more compassionate way: it was the way of repentance and change of heart. This would involve Jonah in risking his life to preach at Nineveh. Instead, he would rather let God punish and destroy Nineveh.

We now know from archaeological history that Nineveh's repentance saved Israel from invasion for 40 years until Israel itself needed to repent. Reluctant Jonah saved Israel as well as Nineveh. It shows that more things are influenced by spiritual matters than by armaments.

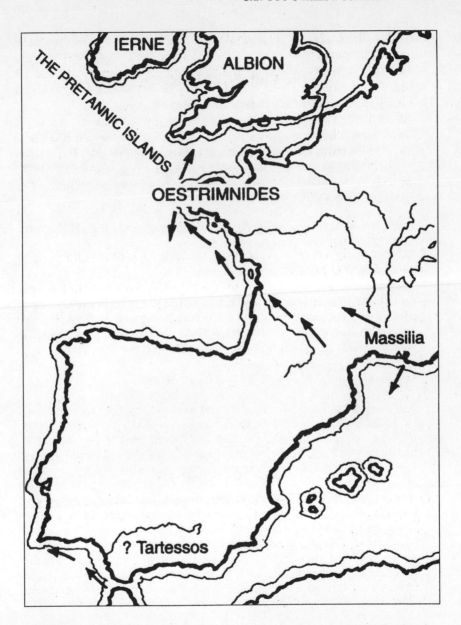

Figure 7.1. Ancient Tarshish: Jonah's escape route in the ancient world Tartessos or Tarshish was near Gibraltar, which was a port of call on the way to Brittany (Oestrimnides) and the Western Isles. A stop would also be made at Marseilles (Massilia).

ANCIENT NINEVEH AT THE TIME OF JONAH

The Culture of Nineveh

Dr Leslie Dent states in his broadcast notes:

> Two rooms were found in which was stored a library which had been added to the palace of Senancherib's grandson, Ashurbanipal. The tablets were arranged according to a definite system and included works on such subjects as exorcism, philosophy, astronomy, mathematics, philology, history, education, poetry, and devotional music.

In his book, *Nineveh and its Remains* (Murray, 1851), A. H. Layard reports on his expedition to Assyria. He says:

> On the walls of Nineveh in Jonah's time there are depicted boats of all sizes and shapes and sails and rowed by slaves. A double tier of oarsmen are depicted, half on the upper deck, and half on the lower deck. The lower deck rowers are partly concealed, their oars being worked through portholes. On the top deck passengers are seated. The women are smartly dressed with high turbans from which veils hung down their backs.

Concerning another low relief mural, he wrote:

> Ships or galleys, filled with warriors and women, were seen leaving a castle, built on the sea-shore at the foot of a mountain. At a gate opening upon the water stood a man placing a child in the open arms of a woman, who had already embarked in one of the ships. The sea was indicated by wavy lines, covering the slab from top to bottom, amongst which were fish, crabs, and turtles. The vessels were of two kinds. The larger had one mast, to the top of which was attached a long yard held in its place by ropes. The sail was furled. The fore part of the vessel rose perpendicularly from a low sharp prow, resembling a ploughshare, which may have been a metal ram, like that of the Roman galleys, to disable and sink the enemy's ships. The stem was curved from the keel, and ended in a high point rising above the upper deck. The ship appears to have been steered by two long oars. Eight rowers were seen on a side, but the number was only representative of a larger crew.

A Repentant Despot?

The experience of James Bartley gives us a clue as to why the despot king of Nineveh would repent at the preaching of a foreign prophet.

The Ninevites were known as 'a hard and bitter nation', to use the words of God to another prophet, Habakkuk. The semi-relief panel pictures which Layard unearthed at Nineveh showed the Assyrians cutting off the hands of conquered people and skinning them alive.

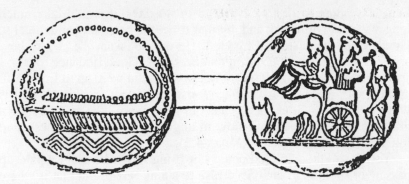

Figure 7.2. Coin probably of a city on the Syrian coast during the Persian occupation. Note the very large numbers of oarsmen.

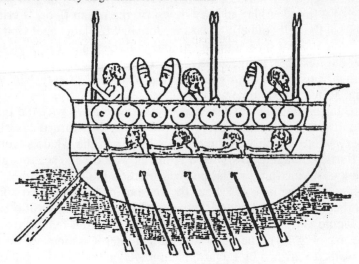

Figure 7.3. A galley (kouyunjik) at the time of Jonah. As found by Dr Layard, carved on the walls of Nineveh. His first book written in 1851 and in my possession is of special value, because many of the finds have since been carried away by the local people.

Soldiers would then cut off their heads and bring them for payment by their quartermasters at so much a head. Captured leaders would have hooks put through their lips and tied to horses to walk all the way to Nineveh. There around the walls they would see their next fate, already suffered by those before them, people impaled upon stakes down which they would slide, to be eaten at the bottom by wild animals.

Jonah did not run away to the west because he was afraid. No, he believed in a God who was greater than all these things. He went on a long sea voyage, 3,000 miles west to Gibraltar (Tarshish), because if

God was going to destroy Nineveh in 40 days, it would take much longer to bring him back and, by that time, the hated city and threat to Israel would be destroyed by God. He did not want the city to hear about coming judgment, repent and be saved. Good riddance to it!

Later he confessed to God, 'I knew what you were up to Lord. You are too soft, that is your trouble.' Jonah was blunt speaking. 'That is why I set out for Gibraltar, because in your Word, you said you are a gracious God and merciful, slow to anger and of great kindness, and reluctant to send judgment' (Jonah 4:2).

Yes, Jonah thought God could not bring him back from a paid-up passenger spot in the sun on a cruise to sunny Spain. But that is where he underestimated God's natural resources. God had already created an air-conditioned submarine sea mammal. Jonah was going to have a whale of a time learning to pray down on the ocean floor, 'I cried to you out of the belly of hell!' Dear me, Jonah, what language! God used his remote control speech intercom and told the whale to cough up on shore that irascible, indigestible meal, as they sometimes did.

Jonah was disgusted to get the same command, 'Go to Nineveh – judgment in 40 days' time!'

So, James Bartley's experience gives a clue as to why the tyrants would listen. The gastric juices of the whale had turned his skin a leathery white. Jonah was three times longer in the whale's stomach than Bartley. Imagine how scared Nineveh would be to see this ghastly hunk of divine fury proclaiming destruction in 40 days' time!

Then when he had told them the reason for his parboiled appearance, that he had come out of the belly of a fish, the superstitious citizens would shriek with terror. They worshipped the female fish god 'Nina' (see Fig 7.4). Their city was named after it – Nineveh. On their very walls, excavated by Layard, is engraved a man coming out of the mouth of a large fish.

A Vast City of Old

But the usual doubters doubted the story of Jonah, not only about the whale, but also about what the Bible said of the size of this immense city. It was 'three days journey in breadth'. This was nearly 800 BC and was about 100 miles NNW of Baghdad. Dr Layard was a Higher Critic at first. He accepted without question all that criticism asserted. He believed that the story of Jonah was only a myth with a moral. Archaeology had hardly started to correct corrupting concepts. Then Dr Layard made an expedition to ancient Nineveh and excavated its ruins. The public were astonished when he wrote his famous book *Nineveh and its Remains*. He found that Nineveh was all that the Bible said it was. I quote Jonah 3:3:

Nineveh was an exceedingly great city, three days' journey in breadth and Jonah began to go into the city, going a day's journey, and he shouted, 'In 40 days' time Nineveh will be destroyed by God.'

On page 336 of his book, Layard says, concerning the extent of the city:

The dimensions of the city were 150 stadia for the two longest sides of the quadrangle, and 90 for the shortest, the square being 480 stadia or almost 60 miles . . . The three days' journey of Jonah should correspond exactly with 60 miles of the square formed by the great ruins . . . 20 miles is a day's journey in the East, and we have therefore exactly three days' journey.

Layard found that Nineveh was indeed a 'mighty city'. Its walls were even bigger than Babylon's. The inner wall was 76 feet high and 32 feet thick. That is wide enough for four traf-

Figure 7.4. Fish god Nina. Found on a wall in Nineveh. The city was named after the god Nina. Jonah, who came out of the belly of a 'big fish', would have frightening portent for Ninevites.

fic lanes – the motorway of ancient times, like an M25 around the outskirts. It provided the possibility for chariot races upon the walls. Fifteen-hundred towers 200 feet high dominated the whole complex at regular intervals.

Bas relief sculptures on the walls show what a powerful culture it was – soldiers and chariots, shields and projectiles. And yes, there is that low relief on the wall – a man looking out of the mouth of a fish – could it be Jonah? Who knows. Too much for some to believe of course, but the preaching of repentance certainly saved Nineveh, for Jonah 3:5 says, 'And the people of Nineveh believed God. They proclaimed a fast and put on sackcloth from the greatest to the least' and the king ordered, 'Cry mightily to God, yes, let everyone turn from his evil ways and from violence . . . that God may turn from his fierce anger, that we perish not'. And God saw their change of heart and behaviour and said he would not destroy the city.

Jesus said that in the judgment day, the people of Nineveh who repented will rise and condemn a generation who did not repent at the preaching of Jesus, who was greater than Jonah.

JONAH'S FAST-GROWING PLANT

Another source of doubt was whether a plant could grow up in one night so quick as to shade complaining Jonah's head from the scorching sun (Jonah 4:5–10).

Reports have been brought back from the Middle East of the palm-crist which can do this. It has a fleshy, succulent leaf, able to hold moisture in the parched desert. There is a particular grub which attacks it, so that it shrivels up and collapses very quickly.

GOD'S LOVE FOR SINNERS

The teaching that the Lord was a God of love who wanted to spare the children and cattle, even of cruel foreigners, was contrary to those who wanted to believe in the evolution of religion. According to their theory, this view of God could not have 'evolved' until later as an invention of man.

But Jonah quotes God's own description of himself given in the Torah, that is the covenant given through Moses to Israel. We have already seen that factual evidence now establishes that Moses did write the Torah. It was set out on the Gattung legal system of his day.

You may have heard some say that the Old Testament does not teach that God is a God of love, but I have broadcast a series on passages throughout the Old Testament which speak of his love, but of how it is balanced by his justice. Examples are God's forgiveness to the wicked King Ahab on his repentance and that beautiful assurance to those who thought they were forsaken in Isaiah 49:15, 'Can a woman forget the child sucking at her breast that she should not have compassion on the son of her womb. Yes, they may forget, yet I will not forget you.'

God's Power over Nature

The story of Jonah and the great fish also raises the question of God's power over nature.

The reductionists are always ready to reduce God's power. One of them said to me that it was not necessary to take the story of Jonah literally. He thought it was only a parable to teach a wider concept of mission to other nations, so it does not matter whether such remarkable events happened or not.

Can you think why it does matter? A person who rejects the possibility of God's control of nature has a limited view of God, certainly not the God of the Bible. A limited God breeds a limited faith, unable to meet life's challenges.

I have heard the same attitude question whether the stories of Christ's control over nature could be true; the stilling of the storm; the miraculous catch of fishes; also that knowledge that a fish Peter caught would have a silver coin in its mouth with which to pay a tax demand.

The reductionist approach goes on to doubt even more fundamental issues regarding the divine nature of Christ. Jesus said that Jonah was a sign of his resurrection. 'As Jonah was in the stomach of the whale three days and three nights, so must the Son of Man be three days and three nights in the heart of the earth.' 'The men of Nineveh will rise in the judgment with this generation and shall condemn it, because they repented at the preaching of Jonah; and behold, a greater than Jonah is here.'

Abraham Lincoln's Revival

Did you know that a gospel revival caused Abraham Lincoln, President of the USA, to call for national repentance in 1863? Here is part of the script. It called the nation and people, I quote:

> to confess their sins and transgressions in humble sorrow yet with assumed hope that genuine repentance will lead to mercy and pardon, and to recognise the sublime truth in the Holy Scriptures and proven by all history, that those nations only are blessed whose God is the Lord.

We have forgotten God. We have become too self-sufficient, too proud to pray. We must humble ourselves, confess our national sins and pray for forgiveness.

The USA's revival not only cleaned up the nation, it also led to a rapid economic recovery.

The story of Jonah is probably one of the first we learn as children. It is also one that the sceptics rapidly discard. Yet the evidence of science, archaeology and anthropology shows that this is a faithful portrayal and, in doing so, helps to assure us that all God's Word is faithful and true.

Can you swallow Jonah? I thank God for my scientific training, for it is precisely because of it that I can re-affirm the truth of Jonah and the Bible.

S U M M A R Y

JONAH – USEFUL POINTS

1. Cachelot whales can and have swallowed men, e.g. James Bartley.
- Mystery of when and why whale was created.
- Habit of coughing up meals onto beaches.
- Jonah's parched appearance would frighten superstitious tyrant.

2. Passenger sea trips featured in ancient times.
- Frequent trips to Gibraltar (Tarshish) and beyond.
- Pictures on Nineveh's walls.

3. Sceptics doubted Nineveh's size until Layard excavated it (60 miles diameter).
- Walls 76 ft high, 32 ft thick.
- Powerful nation threatened Israel at time of Jonah.

4. Palmcrist plant does grow and wither rapidly as in the biblical record.

5. God revealed his love to Jews and Gentiles alike.
- Ex 20:6 (cf. Jonah 4:2); 1 Kgs 21:25–29; Ps 18:6,18; Jer 9:23,24; Lam 3:23; Hos 2:20.

8 GREAT TIMES OF CRISIS

EVIDENCE CONCERNING ELIJAH, DANIEL AND BABYLON

There comes a time in the history of nations when organised attempts are made to turn its peoples from God's truth. It was so in Elijah's time, 870 BC. He almost stood alone in turning back the tide of satanic Baal worship which was eclipsing Jehovah's revelation. It was a satanic attempt because God had chosen Israel to produce the Messiah to be the Saviour of the world. It was a major crisis for truth and goodness.

ELIJAH AGAINST BAAL WORSHIP

King Ahab had taken for his wife, Jezebel, a Canaanite daughter of Eth-baal of Sidon. Jezebel was a high priestess of Baal and she pledged herself to pervert all Israel to this cruel heathen god, to whom children were sacrificed and who demanded prostitution. Jezebel had almost accomplished her campaign. The Levitical priests of Jehovah had withdrawn to Judah; most of the prophets of Jehovah had been slain and the last mopping-up operation, in which caves were searched for hidden prophets, was under way.

Meanwhile, Jezebel had established Baal worship on a grand scale and appointed Baal priests and prophets in crowds.

It is in this context that God began to do great miracles in support of his champions Elijah and Elisha. There are three great miracle eras in the Bible, required because of crises or for the Messiah. They are the Exodus; the time of Elijah; and the life and miracles of Christ. Between these times, there are very few special miracles. This answers the objection that Bible history is all miracles and that this is not typical of life. Between these miracle eras there are the times when such as Gideon could complain, 'Why has all this befallen us? Where are all the miracles that our fathers told us about? Did not Jehovah bring us up out of the land of Egypt?'

One Man with God against 450

Elijah's faith was in the greatness of God who was greater than any satanic challenge. Baal claimed to be the source of rain, sun and crops, so in the name of Jehovah, Elijah said, 'Let there be no rain for three-and-a-half years'. He believed that one man with God could confront 450 prophets of Baal, 400 prophets of Ashera, all who were personal guests at 'Jezebel's table' and the king himself. Moreover, he could confront them at their very stronghold at Carmel in north-west Israel. Interesting information has come in about this from Dr Dent:

> The significance of this move is seen in the poetry of the Ugarit Tablets, found in Syria. In them, we are informed, it was Baal who carved his castle from the rock with fire. The fire ate out the windows, doors, carved the corridors and the rooms. So fire was used by Baal and its castle was in Carmel. They believed their god was a god of fire. When the people heard that Elijah wanted the contest to be determined by fire at Carmel, the priests of Baal considered it a good idea. During the morning the priests of Baal performed all the rites attributed to this god and by noon the prophets of Baal were jumping on the altar and performing the rituals necessary to call Baal's attention to their contest, and Elijah mocks them. The prophets cut themselves and the blood flowed out.

The God of Israel Is the True God!

This concept of self-flagellation has been used by many cults down through the centuries. Prior to the Reformation, men like Martin Luther would crawl up the so-called Pilate's staircase in Rome until their knees and hands were bloody, in an attempt to appease God. The Ugarit tablets and extant literature of the time show that men would cut off their fingers and throw their amputated fingers onto the altar of Baal and Ashera to pacify them – all to no avail.

About the time of the evening sacrifice, Elijah said, 'Draw near'. Twelve stones from the broken-down altar of God were built up again. A trench was dug and wood placed on the altar and the cut-up bullock placed on the wood. Everything was drenched with water so that no one could say it was an accident or spontaneous combustion. Elijah had complicated the whole system. We are told that this man of God prayed and as he prayed so fire fell from heaven from Jehovah, not from Baal.

The evidence was undeniable – the God of Israel is the true God. Everything else is fake. Conditions attributed to Baal, strong mind, earthquake and fire were also to be experienced by Elijah, but God communicated in a way Baal never could, 'By a still small voice'.

Q Where did Elijah get his water from, after three-and-a-half years' drought?

This is a shrewd question. Elijah had poured 12 whole barrels of water over the sacrifice. It was to demonstrate that God could send down fire intense enough to lap up the water as well as burn the sacrifice. Yet the land was so scorched that even the king could not find grass for the horses. Then in the story comes this clanger!

'I don't know where Elijah found water after three-and-a-half years' drought, but as God sent the fire I'll ask him to send me the answer,' I decided. 'Perhaps he got it from the sea – that's at the foot of Mount Carmel,' you might suggest.

Good suggestion! Let's read the story in 1 Kings 18:34 to see if it could be the solution: Elijah dug a metre-wide trench around the altar.

'Fill four barrels with water,' he said, 'and pour water over the sacrifice and all the firewood.'

They did this and then Elijah said 'Do it again.' And they did.

'Now do it once more!' he ordered. They did, and the water ran all over everything. It flooded the altar and filled the wide trenches.

The usual time for the evening sacrifice had come, as commanded by Moses over 600 years earlier. So Elijah walked up to the altar in full view of 850 false prophets and priests of Baal, and watched by thousands of Israelites who had been summoned to the demonstration.

Everything went quiet. The Baal priests had stopped dancing and jumping around and cutting themselves and shouting 'O Baal hear us!'

A tense hush fell upon those Carmel slopes. The test had come. Elijah prayed.

'O Jehovah God of Abraham, Isaac and Israel prove this day that you are the God of Israel and that I am your servant. Prove that I have done all this at your command. O Jehovah answer me! Answer me so that this multitude will know that you are God and that you have brought them back to yourself.'

Suddenly, fire flashed down from heaven. It scorched up the sacrifice, the timber, the stones, the dust. The floods of water went up in hot steam and evaporated the ditches dry.

The vivid light flashed on thousands of scared faces as they fell to the ground and a thunderous roar of voices echoed around the bare mountains.

'Jehovah *is* God! Jehovah is God!'

I paused. 'Well what do you make of the story?'

'There's still no mention of twelve barrels of water being dragged up the hill!' you say.

So when I asked the God who sent down the fire to please send down the answer, the answer came from the Government survey office! It was a report on the hydraulic resources of Palestine described in Chapter 20. It had discovered a most astonishing fact. Underlying the whole of Palestine, from Mt Carmel in the north to Beersheba in the extreme south, was a huge curving artesian basin of limestone. It held gallons and gallons of fresh water. It held so much that it would supply enough water for three-and-a-half years, for the whole population – yes, it actually said three-and-a-half years, without a single drop of rain falling. If only Israel had known how to tap it, they could have had their thirst quenched for three-and-a-half years.

Beersheba! What did I remember about Beersheba? Why, yes, Abraham had been guided by God to dig a well. I had seen it.

So Elijah must have been guided to tap the voluminous supply at Carmel, the top end of this great basin, where now there was a well. The survey drawing showed the artesian underground reservoir curving downwards from Beersheba and coming up again 60 miles north at Carmel!

That should teach anyone not to let their feeble faith be extinguished by 12 barrels of water!

DANIEL AGAINST NEBUCHADNEZZAR

One could add an extra time of crisis and miracle, namely Daniel's witness during the exile.

Four Youths Face a Future

Four youths faced a future, a future for themselves and a future for the world. Both were fraught with bright prospects and big perils. Big perils because right living by them could bring collision with the world power and bright prospects because the emperor was looking for the very best youths with brains, brawn, skill, intelligence and good looks.

Daniel and his three friends had qualified in all these and they were presented to the emperor. But the emperor was a despot, a heathen. He had no time for God the Creator, only for magic, the occult and idolatry. Moreover, he laid down rules for eating and living which were contrary to Daniel's God-given principles.

Daniel would refuse to drink alcoholic drinks but this despot insisted on wine. Daniel would eat only health foods sanctioned by God but the emperor insisted on a rich, unhealthy menu. There was going to be a head-on collision and usually in such cases it was a head-off outcome for the underdog! His head was as good as off. In fact, this was what Daniel's trainer said, 'I put my head at risk if I let you eat your own stuff and live your own way' (Daniel 1:10).

But Daniel and his three friends had a firm faith in God. God was bigger than the biggest world power. He would see them through. Daniel didn't know it, but God was to deal with more than this world power. He was going to tell him all about world powers down to the end of time.

What mattered now was that God was greater than this present despot, but how were they going to convince his trainer of that? 'Give us a ten-day test,' they said, 'and if we are fitter and brighter than the other youths who are ready to compromise, then you can't lose.'

'OK,' said their trainer, 'ten-days test it is.' Ten days passed and the test was over. Look at them! They were glowing with health and intelligence! They were leaping with liveliness and handsome looks. Their faith in the Creator of their bodies and minds had paid off. But would their trainer agree to three years of this?

The Right Test

The challenge of the future was met with faith and purity by Daniel and his three young friends. The authorities wanted to give them the wrong kind of test – perverted education, soiled morals, idolatrous religion and strong drink and food. Daniel and friends held resolutely to the principles laid down by God. The proof of the pudding was in eating and drinking God's health foods. By doing this they were fitter and fairer than any and their minds were healthier too, from God's truth.

A bigger test was now to come at the end of their round of education. They were brought to the emperor himself for an oral test. He was a big, blustering, bouncing bully who just loved to catch out people; but did he catch out Daniel and his friends? Not on your life! In fact, he was amazed. Their God-given truth was better than all his magicians' occult stuff. He did not wait until their three-year course was up. He enrolled them among his magicians immediately.

But yet a bigger test was to come. God had a sense of humour. He set this one (though the emperor didn't know it). God gave him a terrible nightmare. It was a nightmare which affected his future. It was a nightmare which affected the world's future. Some instinct told the emperor that the nightmare was a solemn portent. He woke up in a cold sweat. The perspiration was pouring off him. His servants rushed in at his angry shouts.

'Get this soaking nightshirt off me and send in the magicians. What is my nightmare all about?'

'Tell us the dream,' they said, 'and we will tell you what it means.'

'If you tell me what it *was*, it'll prove you can tell me what it *means*. It was horrible – that's all I know!'

The magicians couldn't tell him.

'You're a lot of frauds!' shouted the emperor. 'Send for the Lord High Executioner. Summon all the magicians and wise men and behead them. Off with their heads!'

Daniel was on the list so they summoned him.

'Tell the emperor that I represent the God of Creation who knows all about the future. If he lets me ask God, he will tell me right away.' Little did Daniel suspect the momentous events that dream of the emperor was to unfold. He was to see that God rules and overrules in the affairs of men. Even the schemes of evil despots are turned into events to glorify God. When Daniel learned this, he burst into praise:

Blessed be the name of God for ever . . .
He changes times and seasons;
He removes kings and sets them up.

Secrets Revealed

The Lord High Executioner was ready for Daniel's head and those of
his three friends. The captain of the royal guards came to march them
off with all the magicians for execution.

Emperor Nebuchadnezzar was red with rage and seething with fear.
His nightmare had been so vivid.

'Your most royal highness,' said Daniel. 'My God is the Creator
himself. He will tell me what your dream means!' The emperor nod-
ded and Daniel hurried to his friends and held a prayer meeting.

That night God revealed the meaning in a vision, so Daniel rushed
back into the emperor.

'There is the Lord God in heaven who reveals mysteries. The dream
that worried you was this. It was of a huge metal figure of a man. It
was made of four metals and clay. It was top heavy. Its heavy gold
head was supported by feet of clay. The four minerals were gold, silver, bronze and iron with clay. Then a . . .'

'That's right!' shouted the blustering monarch. 'It has all come
back to me now! Then a stone fell from heaven and shattered the statue. Why Daniel you're marvellous!'

'Not me; it's God who is marvellous. He showed me.'

'What does it all mean?'

'Well, it's the future history of empires from your time down to
God's kingdom on earth. All man-made empires will rise and fall, but
God's kingdom – never.'

'What! What! Are you saying my empire will crash?'

'Oh, not in your time, O mighty one. You are this head of gold.
After your empire will rise the silver empire (only later was it revealed
to Daniel that this would be the Persian empire). After the silver
empire will come the bronze empire (later it was revealed that this
would be the Greek empire). After the bronze empire will come the
iron empire' (only later was it revealed to Daniel that this would be the
Roman empire).

Then Daniel started to go into all the details about the iron empire
(the Roman empire). Even that will divide into two (which it did, like
the two iron legs of the statue; it divided into east and west in the third
century AD).

Then Daniel described how the Roman empire would decline further into more kingdoms – some strong like the iron, some weak like
the clay. The European kings would try to cohere by royal marriages.

That also came true. The kingdoms of Britain, France, Spain, Italy,

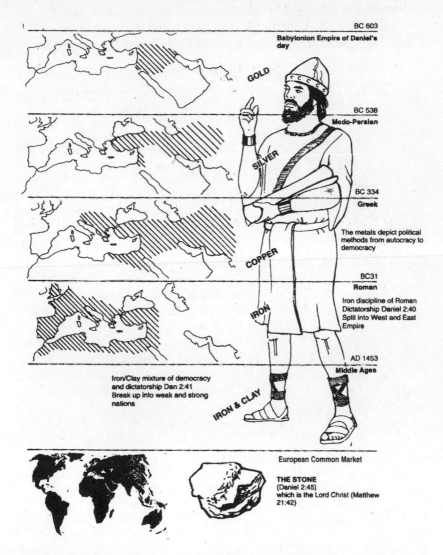

Figure 8.1. Daniel's image. This foretold the great empires from 603 BC to the present time, in which the toes popularly represent European authorities. The stone strikes the toes 'in the days of those sovereignties' at Christ's return to rule the world.

Greece and so on (which arose out of the Roman empire) all intermarried their royal families.

The ten toes at the bottom of the statue popularly represent the states of Europe in the European Common Market and the European Economic Community.

It is in those days that the Messiah would descend from heaven and set up his kingdom which will never be destroyed.

With your knowledge of history, you can see how accurately this has been fulfilled – all except the last part. Volume 3 of this series, which is on prophecy, will show you that there is a God in heaven who reveals secrets.

Smelting the Gold and the Godly

Daniel in the lions' den and his incombustible friends in the furnace are stories well-known by children. Let's look at that story again, to see if the archaeologists have discovered evidence even for this.

Archaeological studies by L. Woolley (*Ur of the Chaldees*, Pelican, 1952) revealed what it was that made Nebuchadnezzar clear a wide area for a huge assembly.

Sometimes people get swell-headed when people praise them. The tyrant Emperor Nebuchadnezzar got swell-headed. That head of gold mentioned in Daniel chapter 2 must have put ideas into Nebuchadnezzar's head. Didn't the head of gold represent himself? Daniel had said so, but why only the head of the statue? He would claim all the statue. He would dominate all Gentile history which it represented.

So a furnace for smelting was built and gold was melted and made to flow into huge moulds. These large gold components were assembled into the biggest image known. It was 90 feet high and 9 feet wide. Was Nebuchadnezzar only the head of gold? Now he was the whole image of gold. Probably it was an image of himself. All his empire must fall down and worship him. He wanted to exalt himself above God – just like Satan wanted to. Satan tried to lift himself above God, but pride was his downfall.

The huge image of Nebuchadnezzar was set up in the largest plain in his province. Millions would be able to assemble around it. Every official in his high-structured organisation would be there. The crowds stretched back a mile or more, but all would see this shining gold likeness of Nebuchadnezzar, because it rose up high in the middle of the Plain of Dura. When the massed orchestra of every type of known musical instrument struck up, that was the signal that everybody must worship the image.

All did, except the Jews. The emperor was furious. He would make an example of Daniel's three friends, Shadrach, Meshach and Abednego.

'You've one more chance!' he shouted at them.

'No go!' they replied calmly. 'The God of Creation will rescue us. Even if he doesn't, we will willingly die for the truth.'

Now the tyrant emperor was not used to refusal. He exploded in fury. His face went from red to scarlet, and from scarlet to purple.

THE HUMBLING OF NEBUCHADNEZZAR

'Heat the furnace seven times as much!' he roared. This was a draught-controlled smelting furnace. The heat became so terrific that the foundry workers shrivelled up and died. Into this intense smelting heat the three believers were thrown. But the only thing the flames burnt were the ropes that bound them. The fires of persecution can do the same for you! They walked at liberty and a fourth person joined them in the fire – the Son of God.

The whole episode was a portent of the fire of persecution which believers would suffer down those 25 centuries of the Times of the Gentiles, as Jesus called them. Believers refuse to worship idols, but in the fires the Son of God walks with them.

The idolatrous emperor was humbled, 'Servants of the Most High God, come out of the furnace!' he ordered. Out they walked. There was not a hair singed, not a garment burnt. Their bodies were unscathed and there was not even the smell of fire upon them.

'I make a decree!' shouted the emperor. 'No one is to say one word against the God of these believers.'

So down those 25 centuries of the Times of the Gentiles, the fires of martyrdom were to rise at various times. The brave witness of believers was to convert more to God then than in times of ease. As Tertullian (AD 160–225) said, 'The blood of the martyrs is the seed of the church.'

'This Is the Place of Burning'

What archaeological evidence do we have for this account in chapter 3 of Daniel, when three friends of Daniel refused to worship the huge golden idol? The evidence for the use of high temperature draught furnaces has been discovered.

Dr Dent comments that it may have been in the plain between the Tower of Babylon and the Palace of Nebuchadnezzar that the 'image of gold' was set up. This statue was 100 feet high and 10 feet wide and was a representation of Nebuchadnezzar himself that was to be worshipped. Records tell us that he made public use of worshipping statues not only in Babylon, but also in Ur.

When the three Hebrew youths refused to bow down to this image, they were punished by being thrown into a fiery furnace. Excavators at Babylon have found a furnace with the inscription, 'This is the place of burning where men who blasphemed the gods of Chaldea die by fire'. Also, a ruined college library was discovered revealing curricula for native princes. They were instructed and trained especially for 'Interpretations of dreams and visions'. Records made reference to 'Impiety to any gods – cast alive into a fiery furnace' and 'Untoward acts relative to a king – cast alive into the den of lions'.

BIG AREA CLEARANCE FOR NEBUCHADNEZZAR
Sir Leonard Woolley Discovers Large Areas for Mass Audiences

Nebuchadnezzar did not confine himself to restoration; he was far more original than most of his predecessors, and even when dealing with an old building was ready to disregard old traditions. One thing he did was entirely new. The old Sacred Area had consisted of religious foundations of all sorts grouped together and in theory forming a unity, but the unity was ill-defined; sometimes the outer walls of adjacent temples were continuous, sometimes the buildings were more loosely disposed, and it would seem that in fact the Sacred Area in many places merged imperceptibly into the lay quarters of the town.

Nebuchadnezzar reformed all this. A space 400 yards long and 200 yards wide was marked out, a rough rectangle which enclosed all the important buildings of Nannar's enclave, and round this was built a wall of mud brick. It was a double wall with chambers in the middle of it, the flat roofs of which would make a broad passage along the wall top available for the manoeuvring of troops in its defence; it was 33 feet wide and probably about 30 feet high; the face of it was decorated with the double vertical grooves which were traditional for temple walls, and it was pierced by gateways of which six have been discovered; the main gate, with a high gate-tower set back in a deep recess, led immediately to the entrance of Nannar's chief temple.

The Temenos Wall was an imposing structure, and with its completion the Sacred Area took on a new character; it was much more a place set apart than it had been in the past. And inside the wall nearly everything bore the stamp of Nebuchadnezzar's creation.

In the old temple, everything had been secret; now a numerous public could watch the priest making his offerings on the open air altar and behind him could see through the dim sanctuary's open door the image of the god.

There is no doubt that the remodelling of the building implies such a change of ritual, but how can this itself be explained? The answer is given by the Old Testament story of the Three Youths in the book of Daniel. Now the gist of the story is this, that Nebuchadnezzar made a great image and set it up in a public place and ordered that at a given signal everybody was to fall down and worship it; the Jews, who seemed to have lived hitherto undisturbed in the land of their captivity, were by this order given the choice between idolatry and disobedience involving death. What was there new in the king's act? Not the setting up of a statue, because each king in turn had done the same; the novelty was the command for general worship which all his subjects are obliged to attend. So striking is the correspondence between the written story and the facts of the ruins and so completely do they explain each other that we must needs accept the background of the legend as historical. The alteration in E-Nunmakh were designed deliberately with a view to the religious reform attributed to its builder by the Old Testament.

L. Woolley, *Ur of the Chaldees*, Pelican (1952).

No Match for the Almighty

The greatest nation on earth at that time was allowed to demonstrate its power and human authority, but it was no match for the Almighty, for God was able to deliver his faithful servants from the tyrant:

a) The keepers of the furnace died because of the intense heat . . . yet the three young men were preserved.
b) The lions were ravenous . . . yet the Lord closed their mouths when Daniel was thrown into their den.

Once again archaeology had proved the Bible records of Daniel 3 to be true and for all to declare, 'There is a God in heaven'.

The Writing on the Wall

Nebuchadnezzar's son, Belshazzar, did not learn his father's lesson. He held a huge feast of debauchery using God's sacred vessels in mockery, at which the finger of God wrote his doom upon the banqueting hall wall. The inscription was, *Mene, Mene, Tekel, Parsin* and this is what these words mean (Daniel 5:26–28):

Mene: God has numbered the days of your reign and brought it to an end.
Tekel: You have been weighed on the scales and been found wanting.
Parsin: Your kingdom is divided and given to the Medes and Persians.

The invading army broke into the city that same night. History tells how Medo-Persian troops avoided the high walls by diverting the river which flowed through the middle of Babylon. They then marched in along the bricked river bed and the Babylonian empire fell on the 16th October, 539 BC.

The old Medo-Persia is now called Iran. In 1988, another sign appeared on a wall in Iran.

The Ayatollah's Writing on the Wall?

A strange report appeared in a Grimsby newspaper. It had been reported in an Iran newspaper that a mysterious sign appeared on the wall of the Ayatollah's residence. It was a glowing cross. All attempts to remove it failed. Eventually, they even broke down and removed the wall, but this was unavailing because the glowing cross appeared on the wall behind the one which had been removed.

The Ayatollah was reported as being extremely upset, he being the religious head of Islam. The report was as follows:

A recent newspaper report has said that the Ayatollah Khomeini of Iran is suffering from liver cancer, and has only three months to live *(Daily Mail,* June 10th, 1988). Now Iranian sources are saying that the Ayatollah had been enraged by a glowing cross which appears on the wall of his room! Khomeini aides at first refused to believe the story, but have now admitted that it is true. The Ayatollah has tried everything in an effort to remove the cross, including knocking down the offending wall – but the cross simply appeared on another wall the next morning. Some international experts claim that the cross, which first appeared some months ago, is responsible for the Ayatollah's decline – they say that after living in a constant state of rage, he fell into a coma.

The night Belshazzar was slain, his kingdom was taken from him – a God-inspired event of history which led to the eventual return of the Jewish exiles. It is tempting to see a similar prophetic meaning in this strange account of the Ayatollah's glowing cross.

Is Babylon Haunted?

In *Volume 3: Prophecy*, you will be given an amazing list of prophecies which have been fulfilled down to our times.

The Lord once told Isaiah, 'The Arab shall not pitch his tent there' (Isaiah 13:20) referring to Babylon. This is true even today. A surprising experience proved this when an Arab was invited to pitch his tent near the ruins. He refused, saying that the place was haunted and that nobody ever camped there. This insight came to Dr Hamlin when he had a shooting expedition around the desolate area which once was Babylon. It was an Arab sheikh who would not leave his tent there. Only howling hyenas haunted the ruins and jackals ran around the once glorious palaces (Hart-Davies in *The Service of God*, p 107). The prophecy in Isaiah 13:20–22 was literally fulfilled which said:

> It will never be inhabited or dwelt in for all generations. No Arab will pitch his tent there, but wild animals will lie down there and its house remains will be full of howling creatures . . . and there satyrs will dance. Hyenas will howl in its towers and jackals in the once pleasant palaces.

Like many despots, Nebuchadnezzar soon forgot the lesson learnt from the 'fiery furnace episode'. He also forgot the dream which Daniel had told him was a warning against his pride and boasting, in Daniel chapter 4. He would be like a tree cut down seven times. That again symbolised the seven Times of the Gentiles (this will be dealt with in *Volume 3: Prophecy*). After twelve months, he had forgotten the warning.

On one occasion, he was walking on the roof of his palace overlooking the mighty Babylon he had built and he swelled with pride. 'Is not this great Babylon that I have built for the house of the kingdom, by the might of my power, and for the glory of my majesty?'

While the king was still speaking, there fell a voice from heaven, 'O King Nebuchadnezzar, to you it is spoken, the kingdom is departed from you.'

For centuries the site of Babylon has lain waste. Critics thought that the Bible's description was myth until archaeology revealed an amazing metropolis. Dr Dent sums up the archaeologist's discoveries:

In the days of Nebuchadnezzar, the city of Babylon was large and grand. The walls were 60 miles in circumference, 80 feet thick and 300 feet high and its foundations went down 35 feet. Around its walls were 250 towers used as guard rooms. Surrounding the city was a moat and in the wall were 100 gates of brass. The city was divided almost in half by the river Euphrates and 25 gates connecting streets with ferry boats. Over the river was a bridge with stone piers half a mile long and 30 feet wide. At night drawbridges were removed. A feat of ancient engineering was the tunnel which went under the river and was 15 feet wide and 12 feet high. The walls were so wide that chariot races were a common occurrence and it is claimed that four chariots in line would race around the city on the wall. Approaching the city of Babylon, the sight must have been impressive, but within the city greater features are still to be revealed. Within the city was the great temple of Marduk or Bel. This was adjacent to the Tower of Babylon or Babel, the most renowned sanctuary in all of the Euphrates valley. It contained a golden image of Bel and a golden table which together weighed not less than 50,000 pounds, or nearly 22.5 tons. Many other deities stood in the temple together with golden lions and human figures.

Truly, Babylon was a city of gold, as Isaiah tells us in Isaiah 14:4.

The Language of Babylon

God loves to tell secrets to those who live close to him, to those who are not self-opinionated but willing to listen. We find that, for this reason, the revelations of Daniel chapter 8 onwards are in the old Hebrew which the general public of Babylon would not understand. The earlier chapters – those from chapter 2 verse 4 to chapter 8 are in Aramaic – the language of Babylon.

At one time, critics said that Daniel could not have written those chapters because the Aramaic speech was not known until later. But here again they are wrong. Archaeology has shown that Aramaic was spoken before Daniel's time. In any case, chapter 1 of Daniel tells you that Daniel and his friends were to be taught Aramaic as part of their re-education.

Another passage in the Bible also shows that Aramaic was spoken long before Daniel – 200 years in fact. This is in 2 Kings 18:26. It was

when good King Hezekiah was besieged in Jerusalem by the triumphant Assyrian armies. The enemy general started shouting threats
to the defenders on the walls of Jerusalem in their Hebrew language.
He told them that Jehovah could not defend them. He was trying to
create a mutiny. The king's messenger said, don't speak in Hebrew but
speak in Aramaic (that was the Syrian language) for we understand it.

Now if the Bible says Aramaic was spoken as early as that, I
believe the Bible, but archaeology also confirms it. Arthur Gibson of
Manchester University shows from the Dere Ala tablets that Aramaic
was known well before Daniel's time.

I won't tire you with further evidence, but it shows how the critics
were wrong again. This Aramaic continued right down to the time of
Christ. The Lord Jesus spoke and preached in this Aramaic. Can you
remember something Jesus said in Aramaic? For a special reason,
St Mark tells us what these words meant. Jesus spoke to a little girl
aged 12 in her native language. She was dead, but he said to her,
'*Talitha cumi*!' Mark 5:41 tells you it meant, 'Little girl, I say to you,
arise!' The term Jesus used was a very loving one. Immediately she got
up and walked around. Everybody was amazed! Then Jesus showed
one of his many acts of thoughtfulness. He knew she was hungry so he
said, 'Give her something to eat'.

There is a spiritual lesson to this. When you are brought to spiritual new life through Christ's words, you become hungry for his Word,
the Bible. I remember a young man saying he found a New Testament.
He took it and read a paragraph, but he had no appetite for it and he
threw it down. Later he was in trouble. He cried to God to save him
and found new life in Christ. Immediately, he was hungry for spiritual
food – the Word of God – the Bible and he read it eagerly.

Were Daniel's Predictions a Fraud?

A greater knowledge of archaeology and of Eastern literary methods
show that the book of Daniel is not of later date, but written as indicated in chapter 8 verse 1, etc. by Daniel himself from 588 BC
onwards. In *Volume 1: Science,* Chapter 18, the reason that critics
thought Daniel was written 400 years later is given. They date the book
as late as 165 BC and claim it was written by an unknown Jew, because
it was assumed that, in spite of the book's claims, the future could not
be foretold and therefore the 400 years of history down to Antiochus
Epiphanes, in 165 BC, so accurately given, must have been written
after the event and then fraudulently presented as a prophecy. But
Daniel claimed, 'There is a God in heaven who reveals secrets'.

In *Volume 3: Prophecy*, we shall bring amazing evidence of the
fulfilment of Daniel's prophecies. They are events which many com-
mentators have overlooked or been afraid to reveal, but they are of

great significance for our times.

> Blind unbelief is sure to err, and scans God's works in vain.
> He only is interpreter, and he will make it plain.
>   (William Cowper).

Truly it has been said: 'The Christian on his knees can see farther than the sceptic on tiptoes.' In the last days, 'None of the wicked shall understand' (Daniel 12:10).

S U M M A R Y

GREAT CRISES, WITH EVIDENCE OF GOD'S INTERVENTION

1. The Elijah Crisis (answered by special miracles)
- Jezebel replacing Jehovah by Baal horrors.
- Baal's castle at Mt Carmel 'carved by fire' (Dr Dent).
- Elijah challenges 850 there. Shows fire comes from Jehovah.
- Water in drought: 12 barrels poured over sacrifice!
- Palestine Government survey reveals artesian outlet at Carmel.

2. The Daniel Crisis
- 10-days test passed with credit.
- Feet of clay image prophesied 2,500 years of history.
- Evidence for furnace furore.
- Inscription 'This is the place of burning'.
- Penalty for impiety – cast alive in furnace fire.
- Training curricula for native princes – included interpretation of dreams (Dr L. Dent).
- Area cleared for mass worship (Leo Woolley).

3. Babylon
- Historical record and writing on the wall.
- City fell 16th Oct, 539 BC.
- Repeated in 1988 to Ayatollah Ð glowing cross.
- Daniel third in kingdom. Discovered that Belshazzar was vice-regent.
- Critics thought Babylon a myth.
- Digs confirm existance. Walls 80 feet wide, 300 feet high.
- 250 towers, 100 gates of brass.
- Impressive main entrance.

4. The Book of Daniel
- Critics wrong on Aramaic, but still ignore discoveries.
- Aramaic spoken 200 years before Daniel. (Dan 8–12 in Hebrew).
- Daniel wrote 588 BC, but critics date it 165 BC because of unbelief in prophecy.
- Greek translation made 100 years before that date!

9 THE VIRGIN CONCEPTION, ENGAGEMENT AND MARRIAGE
EVIDENCE OF GOD'S INTERVENTION IN NEAR-EAST CUSTOMS

Let me read you a letter I received from a listener to one of my radio broadcasts:

> After one of your programmes, I opened my Bible and re-read Matthew 1:18–21. 'Now the birth of Jesus Christ was on this wise; when as his mother Mary was *espoused (married)* to Joseph, before they came together, she was found with child of the Holy Ghost. Then Joseph *her husband* being a just man, and not willing to make her a public example, was minded to put her away quietly. But while he thought on these things, behold, the angel of the Lord appeared unto him in a dream, saying, Joseph thou son of David, fear not to take unto thee *Mary thy wife*, for that which is conceived (marg. begotten) in her is of the Holy Ghost.' So how can you say that Mary was not married and suggest that our Saviour was born out of wedlock?

This shows how one can be misunderstood through not using clear language. We are sometimes obscure through using tactful words on a delicate subject. When Jesus was born, Mary and Joseph were married but had not come together.

Another asks, if Joseph was only engaged to the virgin Mary, why was it that he would have to divorce her when he found she was going to have a baby which he knew was not his?

DIFFERENT MARRIAGE CUSTOMS

The marriage custom was different from our Western one. When a young couple were engaged, that was regarded as binding upon them and it could be broken only if they were divorced, but they did not live together until they had taken the next step which was marriage itself.

Actually, if Joseph had carried out the full law of Moses, he would have done more than divorce her, he would have had her put to death for adultery. But because he loved her and was a just man, meaning that he was merciful, he decided only to divorce her and, to save her as much pain as possible, to do it privately. It is obvious that he did not believe her story. He could not accept that it was the Holy Spirit who had brought about the conception.

Then the angel told Joseph that Mary was truthful, that the conception was a miracle and that he should go ahead with the marriage, but not have sexual intercourse with her until after Jesus was born.

It is obvious that some modern listeners do not grasp the meaning if we wrap up the words in obscure language, so to make it clear, I am using a modern translation for verse 25:

> He did not have sexual intercourse with her until after she had given birth to her first-born son, and Joseph called his name Jesus, as he was told to do by the angel.

This means that when the Lord Jesus was born, he was not born out of wedlock (even though Joseph was not the father). God was the father by the Holy Spirit. All the accounts make this quite clear. Think how providential the rules of engagement and marriage of that time were. They made it possible for Mary to be pledged to Joseph when Jesus was conceived by the Holy Spirit, while she was still a virgin, but made it possible for Mary and Joseph to be legally married before Jesus was actually born. Thus Jesus was not born out of wedlock and Joseph and Mary had not yet come together.

Some of you may wonder why I have gone to such pains to clarify this. It is obvious from that letter I received that such things are not understood these days.

The Betrothal of Joseph and Mary

Further particulars are given by Edersheim in *Life and Times of Jesus the Messiah* (Longman, 1920) about the betrothal customs.

We may take it, that the people of Nazareth were like those of other little towns similarly circumstanced: with all the peculiarities of the impulsive, straight-spoken, hot-blooded, brave, intensely national Galileans: with the deeper feelings and almost instinctive habits of thought and life, which were the outcome of long centuries of Old Testament training; but also with the petty interests and jealousies of such places. The purity of betrothal in Galilee was less likely to be sullied, and weddings were more simple than in Judea – without the dubious institution of groomsmen, or 'friends of the bridegroom', whose office must not infrequently have degenerated into utter coarseness. The bride was chosen, not as in Judea, where money was too often the motive, but as in Jerusalem, with chief regard to 'a fair degree'.

(Continued)

Such a caring home was that to which Joseph was about to bring the maiden to whom he had been betrothed. **Both Joseph and Mary were of the royal lineage of David.** Most probably the two were nearly related, while **Mary could also claim kinship with the Priesthood, being, no doubt on her mother's side, a blood-relative of Elizabeth, the priest-wife of Zechariah.** Even this seems to imply that Mary's family must shortly before have held higher rank, for only with such did custom sanction any alliance on the part of Priests. But at the time of their betrothal, Joseph and Mary alike were extremely poor, as appears – not indeed from his being a carpenter, since a trade was regarded as almost a religious duty – but from the [value of the] offering at the presentation of Jesus in the Temple. Accordingly their betrothal must have been of the simplest, and the dowry settled the smallest possible.

Whichever of the two modes of betrothal may have been adopted – in the presence of witnesses either by solemn word of mouth, in due prescribed formality, with the added pledge of a piece of money, however small, or of money's worth for use; or else by writing (the so-called Shitre Erusin) – there would be no sumptuous feast to follow. The ceremony would conclude with some such benediction as that afterwards in use: 'Blessed art thou, O Lord our God, King of the World, Who hath sanctified us by His Commandments, and enjoined us about incest, and forbidden the betrothed, but allowed us those wedded by Chuppah (the marriage baldachino) and betrothal. Blessed art Thou, Who sanctifiest Israel by Chuppah and betrothal' – the whole [ceremony] being perhaps concluded by a benediction over the statutory cup of wine, which was tasted in turn by the betrothed.

From that moment Mary was the betrothed wife of Joseph, their relationship was sacred, as if they had already wedded. Any breach of it would be treated as adultery; nor could the bond be dissolved except, as after marriage by regular divorce. Yet months might intervene between the betrothal and marriage.

THE VIRGIN BIRTH

There is something else that is not understood. The prophecy which Matthew quotes from Isaiah chapter 7 says that a virgin shall conceive and bear a son. Some think that the word 'virgin' only means a 'young woman'. We now know that it did mean a virgin and those who think that they are cleverer than Matthew had better read Mary's words in Luke's Gospel, where she says to the angel, 'How can I have a baby when I have not had sexual intercourse with a man?' In other words, she knew the conception had taken place while she was still a virgin and that it had happened by the Holy Spirit.

That is why Joseph was told it would fulfil a literal meaning of the prophecy. Jesus would be 'God with us' – the meaning of 'Emmanuel'. That was because there was no human father. God was the father.

However, cynical minds will always remain unconvinced. Another prophecy in Isaiah chapter 9 says that the son given by God would be 'The mighty God, the everlasting Father, the Prince of Peace'.

Now John speaks out very boldly and plainly in his first Epistle, 1 John 4:3. He says that anyone who does not believe that Jesus Christ is God who has become man is not of God, but is of the antichrist, and then he is prompted by evil, deceiving spirits. The Bible speaks of this and sometimes bluntly, in order to be fully understood. Thus in 1 John 5:10 it says that such a person makes God a liar, because he does not believe the gospel record that God gave of his Son. That record is quite clear.

When Mary asked how this could happen because she was a virgin, the angel replied in Luke 1:35, 'The Holy Spirit will come upon you, and the power of the Most High will overshadow you, so the holy one to be born will be called the Son of God.' He who does not believe that record makes God a liar. These are plain and blunt words in Scripture because God's whole plan of salvation is affected if the virgin birth was not a fact.

Why Question the Virgin Birth?

Why is Scripture so outspoken about the necessity of the virgin birth? Only the God-man could be a sufficient payment for sin or substitute for sinners like you and me – we who have done wrong in God's sight. It was essential for your salvation and mine. That is why the angel told Joseph to name him Jesus which means Saviour, because he will save his people from their sins (Matthew 1:21).

The cross and the virgin birth are immediately tied together here. One cannot be effective without the other.

But what is the real reason that some question the virgin birth? It is because they do not believe in miracles. The Lord said beware of the yeast of deception of the Sadducees. He warned us that such unbelief would come into the Church later.

Now, we are clearly told in Acts 23:8 what kind of unbelief this is. The Sadduccean religion did not believe in miracles they did not believe in resurrection, they did not believe in angels and we know also that they did not believe in all of the Old Testament.

That is certainly with us today and the Scriptures say that it is one of the signs of Christ's near return.

How Did God Create a Virgin Birth?

Have you ever asked how God might create a virgin birth? It is amazing how some cannot believe that God did something remarkable unless they know how God did it. Will it help you if I tell you how I think God chose to do it? I will try to take some clues from Scripture.

We have seen from the Bible that God created by words. We have seen from science that the secret of creation is in a language God used. 'God spoke and it was done.' Science has discovered that every living thing on earth is created and recreated by a language. All life is determined by a language say the scientists, called the DNA code. The Bible agrees and says that life resulted from language. 'God said, let the waters bring forth swarms of living creatures'; 'God said, let us make man in our image'; 'God upholds all things by his powerful words'.

If I speak into a microphone, it can be recorded on oxidised tape. Have you ever recorded your thoughts and instructions on a tape recorder? Have you played it back to yourself to make sure that it has been recorded? You find that you can play back your message time and time again. We saw in *Volume 1: Science* that in your body cells, there is a tape upon which God has recorded his message. This message is played back every time a new life is created, because its instructions are obeyed to the last letter.

But again I ask, have you ever spoken into your tape recorder and have you either added or altered part of your message? As you know, you can do so. Now I am suggesting to you that God dictated fresh instructions onto his tape recorder, the DNA code or the message of life. He dictated it by the voice of the Holy Spirit into the recording tape of the cell of the blessed virgin Mary. We are treading on holy ground here, so I say all this reverently.

You now know that the DNA tape consists of two ribbons of instructions which twist around each other in helical fashion like a spiral staircase (Fig 9.1). I see no difficulty in one of those tapes being left with the virgin Mary's characteristics of mankind still recorded and the other one being recorded with the character of God by the Holy Spirit. This is similar to recording a new message on the tape of your recorder.

Combining the Human and the Divine

I know I have over-simplified this, but it is an attempt to illustrate how the voice of the Holy Spirit could record the characteristics of God into the DNA code in the virgin Mary's cells. This would combine the human and divine and produce the God-man whom we know as the Lord Jesus Christ.

But what about man's sinful nature. Would that be handed on? The Scriptures tells us 'No'.

The virgin birth was the creation in reverse. In the beginning, God made a woman from the man's cell; at the virgin birth, God made a man from the cell of a woman.

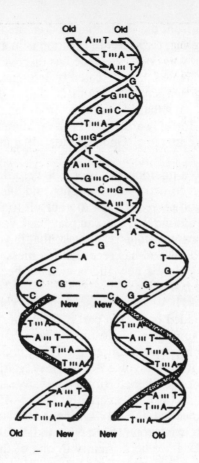

Figure 9.1. DNA strand containing the genes of inheritance. For fuller explanation read *Evidence for Truth, Volume 1: Science.*

THE DNA CODE AND THE INCARNATION

The Scriptures persist that the Word which coded in the beginning became recorded in the virgin Mary at the Incarnation by similar agencies as those at the beginning.

The prologue to the fourth Gospel is a striking application of the phraseology of Genesis 1. It becomes very much more arresting today as we are able to reconsider it in the light of our knowledge of genetic coding. 'The Word' of John 1, known to the Greeks as the Logos, is an application of the repeated expression of Genesis, 'God said'. This is emphasised by other analogies which John makes. The passage is among the best known of the Bible (KJV):

(Continued)

In the beginning was the Word
And the Word was with God,
And the Word was God.
The same was in the beginning with God.
All things were made through him,
And without him was not anything made that was made.

The prologue concludes with a statement demonstrating to us that this same 'Word' who himself coded all life in the beginning, graciously allowed himself to become coded in the DNA of the Incarnation:

And the Word became flesh, and dwelt among us,
And we beheld his glory,
The glory as of the only begotten of the Father,
Full of grace and truth.

God Chose to Use the Mechanisms of Creation

We are not concerned with what God 'could' or 'could not' do by the exercise of supra-natural powers. What we note is that apparently he chose not to work contrary to his original creation, but to use the mechanism he has already placed within that creation to bring about his purpose. He chose a human body of a woman, with its normal cellular constitution. He chose to use the normal nine months' gestation (Luke 1:39–45,56; 2:3–7). He appointed a doctor (Luke), to record it in Holy Scripture. The growth of Jesus Christ to physical, human maturity was also through the natural laws of God's own pre-set engineering, within the normal human experience (Luke 2:40,51,52). It is Luke who tells us how the Word was coded in the DNA of the virgin Mary:

The angel said to her, 'Do not be afraid, Mary, for you have found favour with God. And behold you will conceive in your womb and bear a son – Jesus – Son of the Most High' . . . Mary said to the angel, 'How can this be, since I have no husband?'

The angel then revealed that the conception would be accomplished by two agencies, the Holy Spirit, and the Most High:

The Holy Spirit will come upon you, and the power of the Most High will overshadow you; therefore the child to be born will be called holy, the Son of God . . . For with God nothing will be impossible.

We take the last points first. Why did the Incarnation need two divine agents, the Holy Spirit and the Father? As John has made direct reference to the original creation, we may look there for our clue. We discover that there it was the Spirit of God who was moving upon the face of the waters, presumably to organise the building-blocks of life and the self-replicating polymers. Is it therefore too much to assume that similarly at the Incarnation the Holy Spirit

(Continued)

was active, organising and making available the nucleic acids, with their sugar and phosphate bonds, in other words, the polymers of the DNA strand?

But the instructions to be recorded in code had to be superimposed. At creation this clearly was done by the 'Word', where it is written, 'And God said'. We may also assume, therefore, that when the same Holy Spirit came upon the virgin, he likewise assembled these nucleic acids and bonds which would be already available in the body of the virgin. (We speak with all reverence.) These volumes would be assembled into the 23 chromosomes required to match the 23 in the virgin's ovum, but would include a 'Y' chromosome necessary for a male child. This would be in contrast to the formation of Eve, where the 'Y' chromosome was omitted, and a female resulted.

Contrast with Original Creation

Now comes the contrast with the original creation. Then, the 'Word' evidently gave all the varied instructions into the subatomic particles of the physical world and into the DNA of the biological world. In the case of the virgin, the 'Most High' was the dynamic (Luke 1:35). This might be because it was 'the Word' himself who was being recorded in those nucleic acids, for he was 'begotten of the Father' (John 1:14). The eventual result was that in Christ dwelt 'all the fullness of the Godhead bodily' (Colossians 2:9).

In this way, all the fullness of the Trinity would be involved in those 23 chromosomes prepared for fusion with the ovum of the virgin – the Holy Spirit assembling the DNA code bases, the Father sending forth the Word and the Word himself becoming recorded upon those bases.

Thus far, we have spoken of the divine side of Christ's nature, but we should realise that the physical and spiritual, the human and divine, are not in two watertight compartments. The human side is given more fully by Luke and Matthew. Within the virgin, the ovum to be fertilised would contain the usual 23 chromosomes. There in DNA code would be recorded already an inheritance reaching back to David, Abraham and Eve, with cellular instructions shared with the whole of mankind. Luke therefore records the genealogy of Mary back to Adam.

Was it Parthenogenesis?

There are those who have asked whether the virgin birth may not have been due to parthenogenesis. This refers to a freak case of an ovum being triggered off into separate development. This suggestion does not meet the requirements either of the Incarnation or of biology. If such a child had been born of the virgin Mary, it could only have been a girl, for no 'Y' chromosome would have been available. Also, the child would have genetic material only of Mary's descent, so it would not be a true incarnation – not a complete fusion of the two natures into one.

Also, the question of parthenogenesis appears to be ruled out by the statement in a number of places that the virgin did conceive, but it was without any human male union. It was by the Holy Spirit, so that would be why God is referred to as the Father, and Jesus as the Son of God, and why he is stated to be born holy (Luke 1:25; Matthew 1:20, 25; John 1:14).

(Continued)

> Our knowledge that a foetus receives a complete set of 23 chromosomes from each of its parents gives insight into the oneness of Christ's nature. Those of divine origin and those of the virgin would pair and fuse (in the sense of producing gametes – mature cells), resulting in the one personality, fully divine, fully human, without sin.

In the first case, this would be by subtracting the 'Y' chromosome which contains the male characteristics. In the second case, the 'Y' chromosome would be added by the creating Holy Spirit. Truly, as Mary was told, 'With God all things are possible'. Again, 'That holy being which shall be born of you will be called the Son of God.'

This resulted in the manhood of Jesus becoming that of Adam's before he sinned. Listen to Romans 5:12 onwards: 'By one man [Adam] sin entered into the world (v 15) so by one man [Jesus Christ], life has abounded to many'. This can be taken physically as well as spiritually. And why was he named Jesus – Saviour? Because only a righteous God-man could be offered as your substitute on the cross.

As some would like further particulars, I add material information from the last chapter of my book, *Who Was Adam?*

Replying to Those who Say Incarnation Is Impossible

Insight into the possible mechanics of the Incarnation is a reply to those who contend that the Incarnation of the Lord is scientifically impossible. It is also a help in the difficulties which some in the early centuries and the Middle Ages had in their speculations on how two natures could become one.

Modern genetics reveal that the pairs of genes (alleles) from both parents make one person at conception. The statement 'That which is conceived in her is of the Holy Spirit' shows how God was the Father and the virgin Mary the mother. Also, the fact that DNA is a code demonstrates how the speech, or 'Word', of God, recorded upon the nucleic acids, would form the real genetic contribution from the divine side. We see how Christ was fully and truly man, and yet not two natures, but God-man, not God and man, thus illustrating physically what had been arrived at theologically by earlier divines.

Yet ultimately our only authoritative source for the doctrine of the Incarnation is still the revelation of God in Holy Scripture. We could not discover such things through the medium of science, but having received the revelation of God, we can note that increasing discoveries in science do show how it could come about, and justify the terms of reference, hitherto not fully understood by us, which God's revelation uses.

Science and Theology

The science outlined above does not trespass upon theology, as it refers to the physical mechanism of the Incarnation and has nothing to say concerning what part the Eternal Spirit of Jesus played in this. We certainly have not solved all the problems, for discoveries are still required to complete the picture, and the more true facts science reveals, the more they serve to increase our wonder and worship that God, who is the source of all life, should himself deign to enter that same life as a man, and do so by the very means which he himself had brought into being.

But divine revelation can proceed into an area where science is not competent to speak. From it we learn why the Incarnation was necessary. It was, among other things, in order to reveal the Father (John 14:6; 3:12,13; Mark 9:7), and to make atonement (Mark 10:45). Because Jesus was fully man, he was able fully to represent man when suffering for man's sins on the cross. Because he was fully divine, he was able not to sin and, in suffering as eternal God, his sacrifice was declared completely efficacious for finite men, as well as demonstrating God's love for man. These are merely a few aspects of the theories of atonement (soteriology), but they are sufficient to justify that aspect of the Incarnation reflected in Hebrews 10:5: 'When Christ came into the world, he said, "Sacrifices and offerings thou hast not desired, but a body hast thou prepared me." ' His was a body prepared for complete efficacy in atonement, the ultimate perfection of God's purpose in and for man.

A second Adam to the fight and to the rescue came (Newman, *Praise to the Holiest*).

PREPARATION FOR THE BIRTH OF CHRIST

Love Tussle for Joseph and Mary

Now that we have looked at the scientific possibility, we will come down to human probability by way of a little drama enacted between Joseph and Mary. We can imagine their conversation along the following lines.

'Oh God, help me! How can I take the next step?' The cry of agony came from a girl only just out of her teens. She was in real trouble. How could she tell her loved one to whom she was engaged? No one, not even her fiancé, would believe how it happened.

'It wasn't my fault. I was so in love with Joe; how it will hurt him. It could destroy our coming marriage because he knows that he could not possibly be the cause of my pregnancy. And yet he knows that my whole young life had been absolutely pure. He knows what my principles are. He will be absolutely dumbfounded and yet he will never believe my story. It has been several weeks now. I keep putting it off and putting it off and yet I must tell him.'

She told him.

Joe said, 'I just couldn't believe it. I almost choked in getting out a word. I just had to collapse into a chair to take in what she said. Her words seemed unreal. Did she really say them as they echoed round and round in my head? I felt sick! In fact I rushed to the wash house in case I was. Her story of how she became pregnant is quite incredible. Is she telling lies as a cover up? But she never lies. I can always trust her frank and beautiful truth. Perhaps she could have told a lie to make it easier for me . . . No! no! She wouldn't do it even for that reason. And yet the plain fact is, she's pregnant. Perhaps somebody took advantage of her, and now in shock withdrawal she is suffering delusions. I am afraid that, in my country, I must sue her for breach of promise – well, divorce actually – because the engagement is as binding as the marriage. Our law says that she must be stoned to death for adultery. But I love her. I can't do that! No, I'll do it privately, quietly. I'll just write out a bill of divorce as Moses allowed in the book of Deuteronomy.'

'But Joe, what I'm saying is true. I was in my private room when an angel in shining clothes suddenly appeared in the door and came in. I was terrified. He said, "Don't be afraid. You are favoured above any woman that has ever lived! The Lord is with you!" Well, when I saw him, thoughts rushed through my head. What could such a greeting mean? Angels appeared to Sarah, Abraham's wife, to promise the impossible. An angel appeared to the parents of Samson to promise him. My cousin Elizabeth told me that an angel appeared to her husband to say that she would bear a son even though she was old. He was told he would be the forerunner of the Messiah.

'Messiah! Why there were hundreds of women living in Bethlehem all hoping they would be mothers of the Messiah. They were expecting him about now, because the number of years given to the prophet Daniel come to our times. But they are in Bethlehem and that is where the prophet Micah said the Messiah would be born. I was in Galilee, not in Bethlehem which is miles away to the south; no, it couldn't be that thankfully. I didn't want our love to be disrupted. All these thoughts seemed to tumble through my mind in a moment – no, it couldn't mean me. I was far away from Bethlehem, safely in the north, here in Nazareth.'

Joe replied desperately, 'Well of course it can't be for us! Here am I in Nazareth in a well-established carpenter's business, my own shops and cottage, well settled. I wouldn't go to Bethlehem, even if I wanted to. It's a long time since our ancestors moved from Bethlehem, David's town. Why didn't you tell the angel to go away! Not today, thank you. Try someone else!'

'But the angel said, "Don't be afraid, you have found favour with God!" '

Joe's face flushed. 'Favour with God, eh! What about favour with me. Where do I come in on all this?'

'He gave me no choice. He said, "Behold, you will conceive in your womb and give birth to a son, and you must call his name Jesus. He will be great . . ." '

'That's the trouble with some women,' laughed Joe bitterly. 'As soon as a son is born, their love gets greater for their baby than for their husband. Don't you see! I want us to be close, to always love each other before anyone else!'

'But this greatness was different. The angel went on to say, "He will be called the Son of the Highest and the Lord God will give to him the throne of his father, David." '

'The throne of David; I know we are both descended from King David, but his throne disappeared 600 years ago. The family tree of David has fallen, in spite of God's promise. We are but a sawn-off tree stump left in the ground.'

'That is just what our cousin priest said. He said Isaiah prophesied that we would be just like a tree stump, but that the Messiah would be a shoot springing up out of the stump.'

'Yes,' said Joe, 'but not here in Nazareth!'

'Then the angel said, "He will reign over the house of Israel for ever, and of his kingdom there will be no end." So you see, God has not forgotten his promise to David after all. Well honestly, Joe, I said to the angel that I can't see how this can happen without sexual intercourse and I am not fully married yet. "No problem!" said the angel. "The Holy Spirit will come upon you, and the power of the Highest will overshadow you, so that the holy embryo which will be born from you, will be called the Son of God . . . Nothing is impossible with God, you know!" '

'But did he offer you no option? Was this a rough ride over your whole life? Why didn't you tell him to go away – tell him your first loyalty was to me?'

'But Joe, darling Joe, you know that is not true. Our first loyalty is to God. It was an option. I have free will, so I said to the angel, "See I'm God's servant, his handmaid. If that is how God wants it, go ahead. Let it be to me as God foretold in his Word." '

'In God's Word. Now, you are not thinking of Isaiah chapter 7 are you? The place where it says, "Behold a virgin will be with child"? I can prove to you that that word *parthenos* does not necessarily mean a virgin. It just means a young woman. It need not be you, before we are married.'

'But I have given God my consent. Anyway, I am already pregnant and I assure you, no man has brought it about.'

'So you have made your decision. Well, I will have to make mine to clear my name. I won't get you stoned to death as the law requires because I love you. Oh God, how can you do this to me! Darling, I can't hurt you. I will divorce you privately and quietly.'

Some Days later

'Thank God, he has not left me in the lurch. My beloved Joe has just had a most vivid dream. Ah, here he is.'

'Yes, you can imagine what agony of mind I was in. I was tossing about on my bed. Had I done the right thing? Was it really true that Mary was pregnant? It must be all a terrible nightmare! I fell into an exhausted sleep and then it happened. An angel of the Lord appeared to me. His clothes were bright with glory. His words penetrated my soul. He said to me, "Joseph, Son of David, don't be afraid to marry Mary and make her your wife. She was quite right. The baby which is conceived in her was by the Holy Spirit." '

'Thank God, Oh praise God! He has not left me desolate. What did he say next?'

'Well, it surprised me that he knew it was going to be a boy!'

'He knew that even before he was conceived. He told me it would be a son – Son of God in fact.'

'Ah yes, now about that point. The angel told me, "You were wrong about the word 'parthenos' – it does mean virgin, not just a young woman, that is why the son Jesus – yes, you must call him that – that is why Jesus will be God among you men. But one word more. Don't consummate your marriage, even though she will be your wife, until after the child is born." '

Pre-natal Knowledge

Pre-natal clinics and screening tell us a lot these days about the experience we have all had in the womb. It is now known that a baby can hear all that is going on long before it is born and that it reacts to those sounds.

Elizabeth's baby heard a sound which it recognised three months before he was born. It was a sound which filled him with joy, even though the embryo was only six months old. In fact, that unborn babe was filled with the Holy Spirit. The angel told the father it would be a boy. The angel spoke about joy and gladness and it was with joy that the baby leaped in Elizabeth's womb at that sound.

It is Elizabeth, the mother, who says in Luke 1 what that sound was like: 'Behold, when the voice of your greeting came to my ears, Mary, the babe in my womb leaped for joy!'

Isn't that wonderful? John the Baptist, three months before his birth, felt the joy of the Holy Spirit at the nearness of the Saviour who had only been conceived by the Holy Spirit recently.

Mary, the virgin, had been told by the angel that her cousin Elizabeth was now six months pregnant in old age, 'for with God nothing is impossible'. So, soon after she heard, she hurried to Elizabeth's town. Verse 40 says, 'She entered the house and called a greeting to Elizabeth; and when Elizabeth heard the greeting of Mary, the babe leaped in her womb.' I think that must have been a sweet musical voice of loving greeting by Mary.

The Holy Spirit made Elizabeth cry out loud, 'Why is this privilege granted me, that the mother of my Lord should come to me? Your voice made the babe leap with joy in my womb. Blessed are you Mary because you believed the word of the Lord to you.'

Yes, Mary was a believer and therefore the Lord was her Saviour. She said so, in the Magnificat of praise which burst from her lips (Luke 1:46). She recognised the momentous importance of her virgin conception. 'All generations will call me blessed,' she said. She recognised, moreover, that this was the seed promised to Abraham 2,000 years earlier. 'As he promised to our forefathers, to Abraham and his seed for ever' (Luke 1:55).

Right back in Genesis chapter 12, God promised that all nations would be blessed through the seed of Abraham. Abraham was told he was saved because he believed it; and Mary said the Lord was her Saviour because she believed it. 'My spirit rejoices in God my Saviour.'

God's 100 per cent Success Rate

Did you hear of the man who advertised to expectant mothers? He said that, for ten dollars a time, he would predict whether their baby would be a boy or a girl. Money back if not satisfied. He told everyone who sent in their dollars that their baby would be a boy and, believe it or not, he had 50 per cent success – and 50 per cent profit!

Well, in the Bible, God got it 100 per cent right. He told Abraham it would be a boy. He told Hannah it would be a boy. He told Zechariah it would be a boy. He told Joseph and Mary it would be a boy. Moreover, he told Mary and Joseph that the baby's name was to be Jesus, meaning Saviour.

So then, Luke 2:21 says that eight days after he was born, at his initiation covenant, 'He was called Jesus, the name given to him by the angel before he was conceived in the womb'. Yes, even before he was conceived. Jesus, Saviour.

Oh, how precious is that name, the name which meets my every need; Jesus precious Saviour. Peter wrote, 'To you who believe, he is precious'.

'How sweet the name of Jesus sounds to a believer's ear. It soothes his sorrow, heals his wounds and drives away his fear' (John Newton). What a precious secret God kept until last. In the Old Testament prophecies, he is given many other wonderful names: 'His name shall be called Wonderful, Counsellor, Mighty God, Everlasting Father, Prince of Peace.' That was said to Isaiah about the child to be born, the Son given. His name was to be God-with-us – Emmanuel. His name to Manoah was 'Wonderful'. To David and to Daniel he was to be 'the anointed one – the Christ'.

Mary was told, 'His name will be Jesus'. Joseph was told later, 'You must call his name Jesus for he will save his people from their sins'.

I am glad he saves his own people from their sins, aren't you? For he goes on saving us. He has 100 per cent success. 'None shall pluck them out of my hands,' he promised. Paul wrote in Galatians 4, 'When the time had fully come, God sent forth his Son, born of a woman, born under the law, to save and redeem us who are condemned by God's law, that we might be adopted as his own sons.'

'Jesus will save his people from their sins.' He also saves those who are not yet his people, if they come to him. The promise is in Hebrews 7:25 for 100 per cent success. 'Jesus is able to save to the uttermost, for all time, those who come to God through him.' 'To you who believe, he is precious.' Yes, my Saviour, your name Jesus is very precious, for you have saved my soul.

Simeon's Song

God's guidance made several people converge on the temple in Jerusalem 40 days after that remarkable birth of Jesus. But for the guidance of God, they would all have missed each other.

A week after the birth of Jesus, he was named and initiated in Bethlehem. Then 33 days later, Mary obeyed God's words to Moses and travelled five miles north to Jerusalem to be purified by two sacrifices. Bethlehem is higher than Jerusalem. Its lofty site was 2,550 feet above sea level and was on the main road from Egypt and Hebron, so Mary travelled with Jesus along that limestone ridge guided by obedience to God's Word, to sacrifice two pigeons for her sins. The two others destined to meet them were guided by God's Holy Spirit. They were Simeon and Anna. Simeon had a revelation that he would live to see the Lord's anointed Christ before he died. Led by the Holy Spirit, he went into the temple just before Mary, Joseph and Jesus arrived. At that moment, Luke tells us, Anna the prophetess walked in for her daily prayers.

We have seen before that the Holy Spirit in people gives them sheer delight when they meet Jesus – and still does. Simeon burst out with praise and prophesied even as Elizabeth had done, and Anna too.

Simeon felt his whole life was worthwhile just to take up the Lord's Messiah in his arms. With a full heart he blessed God who had allowed him this precious moment. He burst out with words which were recorded and which Christians have sung down the centuries since: 'Lord now let thy servant depart in peace according to your word. For my eyes have seen thy salvation which thou hast prepared before the face of all nations' (Luke 2:29).

Then he made a remarkable statement for a Jew. It showed he had read the prophecy of Isaiah 49 which says, 'Listen, Oh Isles, unto me, and you nations, for the Lord has called me from the womb of my mother . . . It is the Lord who formed me from the womb . . . I will also give you for a light to the Gentile nations to be my salvation to the ends of the earth.'

And so Simeon concluded with the words, 'A light to lighten the Gentiles, and the glory of your people, Israel.'

Such an important prophecy he must have written down because 50 years later, James, who was chairman of the church council, quoted it. He said, 'Don't be surprised at all these converts coming from the Gentile nations, for that is just what Simeon prophesied when he took up the Christ-child in his arms. Listen to me,' James said, 'Simeon said that at first the church would be mainly from Gentiles. God knew what he is doing from the beginning of history.'

Note that although some modern translations change Simeon to Simon (Peter), I believe the Authorised Version is correct here.

Athlete Stumbles but Wins the Prize

Have you ever hoped that one day you would achieve your life's ambition and then be happy to die? Some gold medallists in sports have felt that, as have some mountaineers. I read a novel about a mountaineer who fell from the Eiger in Switzerland. It was a long time before he was restored sufficiently to speak. 'Did you reach the top?' he was asked. 'Yes,' he said, 'and it made it all worthwhile.'

Simeon knew that in his arms he held the One for whom all history had prepared. He quoted the prophecies given by God in preparation. 'A light to lighten the Gentiles.' 'My eyes have seen your salvation.' 'Known unto God from the beginning of history are all his works.' Simeon held the centre of history in his arms, but he prophesied a warning. 'This child who was sent for blessing will cause many to fall. Indeed, he is the test for many. By their reaction to Jesus, many will either rise or fall. Even his name will be a sign that many will speak against (Luke 2:34).

A famous gold medallist athlete, Kriss Akabusi, said that for many years he thought the name of Jesus Christ was only a swear word. He knew no better until one day at the Commonwealth Games Village, he found a Bible in his room. That Bible led him to find Jesus as his precious Saviour. Instead of a name to stumble over, he found Jesus as the greatest prize in the race of life. Moreover, he said so, openly, to all on the sports field.

Occasionally, you see a sportsman stumble and fall out of the race. Nations have fallen out of the race when Christ has been neglected. Britain is one example, Israel was another.

When James quoted Simeon 50 years later, he said that Simeon understood something which others were afraid to admit. It was this: the Jews would stumble over the Lord Jesus. They would find Christ a rock of offence, a stumbling stone, because salvation was by faith in Christ's complete salvation and not by works, for no one can earn salvation.

For that reason, said James in Acts 15, the church would be mainly a Gentile church at first. Then Christ would return and all the Jewish people would be saved. Paul said this as well. 'Israel will be grafted back in and so all Israel will be saved when Jesus returns to Zion.'

Yes, 'known unto God are all his works from the beginning of history' and Simeon held the centre of history in his arms. So it is also with an individual. If you hold Christ as the centre of your life, he will fill your life with meaning, but if he becomes an offence to you, you will prove the truth of Simeon's words, 'This child is set for the rise or fall of many'. So don't stumble over Jesus. Make him your foundation.

Caesar's Census Found

A newspaper discussion suggested that Jesus was not born in Bethlehem but Matthew and Luke both agree that Jesus was indeed born at Bethlehem, yet some have denied this. Why? – because Mary and Joseph lived at Nazareth.

Luke solves the difficulty by reporting that it was Caesar's census which ordered everybody to register in their ancestral town, so Mary and Joseph had to journey 70 miles south to Bethlehem.

Some denied that Caesar even issued such an edict until the ancient poster bill in figure 9.2 was discovered. Luke says that it was Quirinius who published the order, but some have claimed that Quirinius was governor in AD9, not when Christ was born. However, a document has been found which says he was governor twice. The first time was when Christ was born. This is what Luke tells you.

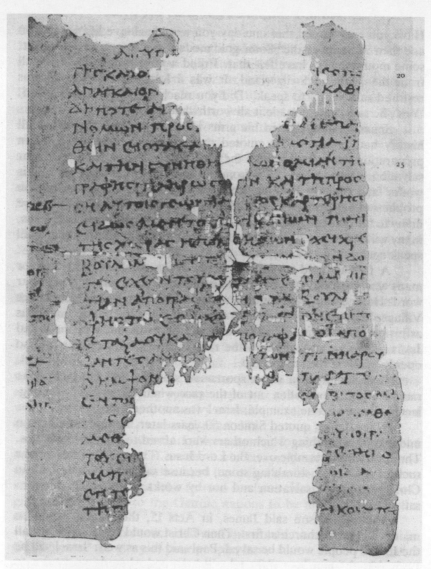

Figure 9.2 Census of Caesar. An example of an edict, 2,000 years old, commanding everyone to return to their native town, similar to the one recorded in Luke 2:1–6 which led to Jesus being born in Bethlehem. Some doubted whether a Roman empire would order their people back to their ancestral town. In answer, this papyrus poster was found in the sands of Egypt. The word for 'enrolment' is exactly the same as is used in Luke 2:1–6. Different words could have been used, but this was not the case. *Translation*: Gaius Bivius Maximus, Prefect of Egypt, saith: The enrolment by household being at hand, it is necessary to notify all who for any cause soever are outside their homes to return to their domestic hearths, that they may also accomplish the customary dispensation of enrolment and continue steadfastly in the husbandry that belongeth to them.

Courtesy: British Museum

SUMMARY

VIRGIN CONCEPTION

A sacred subject, but we must meet difficulties some have by clear explanation.
- In the creation of Eve from Adam's cell, the 'Y' chromosome would have been removed.
- With the Virgin, it would be added by the Holy Spirit (Luke 1:31–35).
- Verse 31 says it was a conception, therefore not parthenogenesis.
- Holy Spirit would supply or re-code DNA for the Word made flesh. Alleles (genetic pairs) from the two sources, human and divine, would become phenotypically one, for one personality to exist, not two natures.
- 'With God nothing shall be impossible' (v 37).
- John 1:1–14 applies, also Gen 1:1–5.

Near-East marriage customs
- Engagement could not be dissolved without a divorce.
- Consummation not allowed until marriage.
- This made possible the virgin conception, then marriage and Christ's virgin birth within wedlock.

Kindred tablets of descent
- Both from the same ancestor by different routes.
- Mary also had a kindred link with a priestly line (Zechariah).
- For Jesus to be born in Bethlehem, Joseph must also be descended from David.

Salvation could be accomplished only by a God-man.

This fulfilled two Old Testament prophecies which looked contradictory: Isaiah 9:1 & 2 said the light of the world would come from Galilee (Nazareth), and Micah 5:2 said that the Eternal One would be born in Bethlehem. Both were fulfilled.

The lesson is obvious. Always stand by Scripture's accounts which are written by truthful men.

10 THE REAL JESUS

THE EVIDENCE FROM MANY SOURCES

Yet another series on TV has attacked the truth of the Gospel accounts of the life of the Lord Jesus. This time it claimed that Jesus was just an ordinary prophet whom the Church a hundred years later made into a Christ whom they depicted as the divine Son of God, namely the Christ or Messiah prophesied in the Old Testament.

It is interesting that one of the promoters of this programme was a Jewish rabbi who, of course, does not believe that Jesus was the Christ. But if it is admitted that the Old Testament does foretell such a person, why is it not admitted that Jesus fulfilled all those scriptures?

Accomplices in this, however, are those in the media who have decided that miracles do not happen. One such critic was introduced in the *Radio Times* as once being a committed Christian, but 'now he believes that because many key events in the Bible are myths', his faith was not based on truth. He is like many others, who are schooled only in the theories of the Higher Critics. The schools and colleges continue to turn them out and are responsible for contributing to the general agnostic outlook of our youth today.

The Jesus of the Gospels Is Real

Is such criticism to be trusted? After giving an initial false report on the Dead Sea Scrolls before all the contents had been properly translated and assessed, one critic wrote a repentant correction 15 years later saying that he jumped to conclusions on pre-existent assumptions and gave a tabloid journalist a sensational type of report.

Rationalists have had a campaign on for many years to smash biblical faith and they have many agnostic allies in the media. They are indeed a formidable pressure group, yet no one is allowed to put on a series of programmes to give all the positive evidence for the truth and accuracy of the Bible. Unfortunately, the result could be similar to the collapse of the Soviet bloc whose failure was due largely to the cynicism which their atheistic systems inbred.

The propaganda is usually the same. It brings up the old theories of the last century and earlier, which they have not allowed to be corrected by factual discoveries.

Since the media do not allow us to reply to all the accusations, I reply in Christian magazines and on Christian radio broadcasts. That is the situation in the UK today. Sceptics are paid millions of pounds for their programmes, but we have to pay for air time to discount their errors. Here then is my reply.

THE HISTORICAL JESUS

Suffered under Pontius Pilate

Have you noticed that God often answers a doubter by someone finding evidence?

There were some who were throwing doubt upon whether Pontius Pilate ever existed. They laughed at the Christians who had repeated all down the centuries these words, 'He suffered under Pontius Pilate'.

Just about then, some archaeologists were digging around the ruins of the Roman Military Garrisons at Caesarea, on the Palestine coast. It was the old headquarters of the Roman governors and would have been Pilate's seat. To their surprise, they dug up an inscribed monumental stone; on it was carved the name of Pontius Pilate, governor of Judea. I have taken a photo of it. Isn't it sad how so many are so quick to doubt God's Word.

Another piece of evidence concerning Pontius Pilate comes from one of the early fathers, Eusebius, who recorded that an early Christian writer wrote to the emperor of Rome. He told him to look up Pilate's report about Jesus. Those early Christian writers were quite sure that Pilate had sent a report about the trial of the Lord Jesus Christ to the emperor.

Now, this is very possible because in the Gospels the Jews threatened to report Pilate to Rome, so Pilate was bound to make his own report.

Pontius Pilate was a typical compromiser. He tried to please everybody. He declared Jesus not guilty, yet he handed him over to the Sadducees. He tried also to please his wife by sending for a basin of water and soap and said he was washing his hands of Jesus.

Have you been to Switzerland? There is a mountain there called Mount Pilatus. It is named after Pilate. Why? The tradition is that when Pilate was dismissed from his job, he retired to that mountain and became demented. He kept wringing his hands round and round as if he was trying to wash off the blood guiltiness.

Many still try to wash their hands of Jesus instead of standing up for the One who was despised and rejected of men.

More Historical than Anybody

I continue to get in letters or see in newspapers the assertion that the picture of Jesus in the New Testament is not a factual one. This is often backed up with the assertion that there is little in history about the man Jesus Christ.

Such statements are completely without foundation. They deceive only the people who have no knowledge of the facts.

The New Testament story of the Lord Jesus has three times more evidence of its accuracy than any other figure of history; three times more than anything about any of the Roman emperors; and many times more written copies of the original accounts. Compared with any event of history, the New Testament has abundantly more reliable documents.

Professor F.F. Bruce of Manchester University says that Caesar's *Gallic Wars* with which many students are familiar, has only nine old copies and the oldest of those is 900 years after Caesar's day, yet nobody questions those. In contrast, the New Testament has 5,000 Greek manuscripts of the New Testament in whole or part. The oldest full copies go back to about AD 330 and part of St John's Gospel which has survived, actually goes back to within a few years of St John's original writing; we also have fragments of St Mark's Gospel and St James' letter and 1 Timothy which are around AD 68.

Of the works of the Roman historian, Livy, of Christ's time, only 20 old copies survive. What a contrast to the 5,000 of the New Testament. The well-known Roman historian, Tacitus, has only four surviving old copies of his *Annals*. What a contrast to the 5,000 old manuscripts of the New Testament.

Concerning the famous history by Herodotus, the oldest copy of the original is 1,300 years after when it was written. Professor Bruce comments, 'Yet no classical scholar would listen to an argument that the authenticity of Herodotus was in doubt'.

He then reviews the wealth of evidence we have for the New Testament and shows what a contrast it is to secular history.

A letter in the press from a sceptic questions whether Jesus Christ really figured in history. The answer is that he did. As many as eight non-Christian historians of the first century refer to Jesus Christ. They were Tacitus, Suetonius, Serapion, Phlegon, Lucian and Josephus, as well as references by Pliny and Thallus. Also, there are nine antagonist references to Jesus in the Jewish Talmud writings. A list of what they say will be given. In addition, the New Testament itself is more than sufficient evidence. Luke says that he wrote down his account from eyewitnesses carefully and accurately. That accuracy was confirmed by Sir William Ramsay. He started by being a sceptic, but he researched all the historical references and dates and incidents which Luke included in his accounts and found them completely accurate to the last detail.

Professor F.F. Bruce writes, 'Attestation of another kind is provided by allusions to and quotations from the New Testament books in other early writings.' The authors known as the Apostolic Fathers wrote chiefly between AD 90 and 160, yet in their works we find evidence for their acquaintance with most of the books of the New Testament.

Evidence of Jesus the Teacher

The New Testament was quoted so extensively by writers and church leaders in the first century after Christ's ministry that a committee at Oxford University in 1905 collected together all the references. They found that nearly all of the New Testament books were referred to by these other writers. The evidence was collected and weighed in a work called 'The New Testament in the Apostolic Fathers, recording the findings of a committee of the Oxford Society of Historical Theology'. If you wish to follow more particulars, here are details from Professor Bruce:

• First take three works dated probably before AD 96, i.e., the Epistle of **Barnabas** AD 70, the **Didache** AD 90, and the Epistle of **Clement** AD 96. These have quotations from the Gospels, Acts, Romans, 1 Corinthians, Ephesians, Titus, Hebrews, 1 Peter and other books.

• Second, in AD 108, **Polycarp** wrote to the Philippians. He was a disciple of St John, and was born in AD 70. He quotes from the Gospels, Acts, Romans, 1 and 2 Corinthians, Galatians, Ephesians, Philippians, 2 Thessalonians, 1 and 2 Timothy, Hebrews, 1 Peter and 1 John.

• Third, in AD 115, **Ignatius** who was born in AD 50 and knew all the Apostles, wrote seven letters during his journey to Rome for his martyrdom there. They included quotations and allusions from the four Gospels, Acts, Romans, 1 and 2 Corinthians, Galatians, Ephesians, Philippians, Colossians, 2 Thessalonians, 1 and 2 Timothy, Titus, Philemon, Hebrews and 1 Peter.

• Fourthly, **Irenaeus** who was born in AD 70, also quotes many scriptures, and he agrees with his contemporary **Papias** that Matthew first wrote in Christ's own native language which was Aramaic-Hebrew. A frequent phrase used by these Apostolic Fathers when making their quotations is, 'as it is said in the Scriptures'.

SECULAR EVIDENCE OF THE HISTORICAL JESUS

Here is a typical question and answer conversation.

Q A Marxist said that Jesus was not a historical character. What do you say to that?

Whoever it was could not know history. We have a number of historians of the first century who refer to Jesus Christ.

These historians were completely secular. They referred to Christ only casually because it impinged on the incident they were writing about. Professor Bruce of Manchester University said that the historicity of Christ is as factual for an unbiased historian as the historicity of Julius Caesar.

Q You said there were secular historians who referred to Jesus. Who were they?

Tacitus is a well-known Roman historian. He was born in AD 52. When writing about Nero, he explained why the tyrant Nero blamed the Christians for the fire of Rome. He said it was because the Christians were a good scapegoat as they were hated. Then he adds this: 'Christ was their founder. He was put to death by Pontius Pilate, who was procurator of Judea in the reign of Tiberius Caesar.' That is clear enough – and we have repeated that in our creed ever since. 'Suffered under Pontius Pilate, was crucified, died and was buried, and on the third day rose again from the dead.'

Listen to the nasty thing Tacitus said about Christians. I quote, 'But the pernicious superstition, repressed for a time, broke out again, not only throughout Judea where the mischief originated, but throughout the city of Rome itself.'

Q Well, that doesn't show much bias towards the Christians! Who are the other contemporary non-Christian historians who write of Jesus Christ?

There are seven or eight others, also several Jewish writings. **Lucian** was one who spoke scornfully of Christ and then said, 'He was the man who was crucified in Palestine because he introduced this new cult called Christianity into the world.' **Suetonius** was a well-known Roman historian. He was a court official under the emperor Hadrian, the one who built Hadrian's wall in Britain. He records that the Jews were making constant disturbances against Christ, so **Hadrian** expelled them from Rome.

Q You said there were several others who refer to Christ in their histories of the time; is there one who was more sympathetic in his history?

Yes, let me quote **Josephus** who wrote *The Wars of the Jews*:

Now there was about this time Jesus, a wise man, if it be lawful to call him a man, for he was a doer of wonderful works, a teacher of such men as receive the truth with pleasure. He drew over to him both many of the Jews, and many of the Gentiles. He was the Christ and, when Pilate, at the suggestion of the principal men among us, had condemned him to the cross, those that loved him at the first did not forsake him; for he appeared to them alive again the third day; as the divine prophets had foretold these and ten thousand other wonderful things concerning him. And the tribe of Christians so named from him are not extinct at this day.

They are not extinct now either, 2,000 years later!

A Roman official named **Pliny** wrote in AD 111 a very detailed report to the emperor of how the Christians met to observe the sacrament of the Lord's Supper. He was seeking counsel from Trajan to take advice on how to treat Christians who refused to acknowledge the emperor as God. He said he made some 'curse Christ, which a genuine Christian could not be compelled to do', even by torture. He says they met on the first day of the week before it was light. They sang a hymn to Christ as to a god and bound themselves by a sacrament not to commit any wicked deeds, never to commit frauds, theft, adultery, never to break their word or deny a trust.

Thallus wrote within 20 years of the cross in AD 52. He tried to explain away the great darkness during the crucifixion which even reached Rome where he lived and was still a talking point. He says it must have been an eclipse. But **Julius**, a Christian, pointed out that an eclipse is impossible during a full moon at the Passover.

Phlegon in the first century wrote, 'During the time of Tiberius Caesar, an eclipse of the sun occurred during the full moon.'

The British Museum has a letter written by a non-Christian named **Serapion** about AD 73. He says that the deaths of Socrates, Pythagoras and Christ were avenged by God. Concerning Christ, he wrote: 'What advantage did the Jews gain from executing their wise King (Jesus)? It was just after that that their kingdom was abolished. God justly avenged.'

Evidence from Jewish Writers

Q You've just mentioned the Jews. You have quoted Roman historians who refer to Jesus in their reports. I would have thought that the Jews would have written something, to say why they rejected him.

They did. They have commentaries on religious observances. In nine of them, they make cryptic references and more open remarks about the Lord Jesus Christ. These are called the Talmudic writings. They are mostly very rude remarks, I'm afraid. I must add that rabbis today are quite different. There attitude has changed. They refer to him in terms of great respect. Some call Jesus their greatest prophet.

Q What sort of things did they write in those early Talmuds?

The Babylonian Talmud says, 'They hanged him on the eve of Passover'. Another Talmud (Baraila) says, 'On the eve of the Passover they hanged Jesus the Nazarene, and a herald went before him, saying, "He has practised sorcery".' (Remember in the Gospels the Jews accused him of using the devil to cast out devils.) Other Talmuds call him illegitimate in very crude words which I won't repeat here. They also make a play upon the words 'virgin birth'. St John's Gospel refers to this jibe when Jesus referred to his father, meaning his heavenly Father. Read it in chapter 8 verse 41. 'We were not born of fornication. We have one Father, even God.' They sneered at Jesus, you see, as illegitimate.

Q Isn't it ironic that unkind remarks made by historians of Christ's time now give convincing proof that Christ was a real historic person?

And that is without all the evidence of the Gospels themselves. We have four separate records of the life of the Lord Jesus in Matthew, Mark, Luke and John. Even without this evidence, when you read the four Gospels, you meet Jesus himself. No one could have invented such a remarkable person. What is more, he changes lives today and gives you new hope and salvation. Paul met him on the road to Damascus when he was hounding Christians to death. Everyone who has been born again by the Holy Spirit feels they have met the living Christ.

PORTRAITS OF JESUS FROM THE EVIDENCE OF THE GOSPELS

But it is the Jewish New Testament writers who give us portraits of the most amazing person that anyone has written about. Let us meet Jesus in them.

Jesus, the Debater

In these portraits of Jesus, we shall see what a mighty preacher he was
with his penetrating rhetoric; what a fascinating teller of stories he
was; but first, look at the Lord Jesus as a superb debater. In the cut and
thrust of debate, he was always the winner. That is because he always
had both **truth and love** in his arguments.

When the police were sent to arrest him, they came back empty-
handed and said, 'No man spoke like this man'. When his opponents
rallied their greatest brains, including the most eminent pontifs, they
were all defeated in argument one by one. Neither did he fall into several traps that were laid so that they could invent a trumped-up charge
against him. The result was that, at the end of a full day of debating in
the country's capital, his opponents shrunk away defeated. Of those
who stayed to the end, was a lawyer paid to argue, but his admiration
was such that he applauded Jesus. 'Well said, Master! What you say is
true!' The debate finished in Matthew 22:46 with this statement: 'No
one was able to answer him a word, nor from that day on did anyone
dare to debate any more questions.'

Jesus loved to turn the question on the debater and this he did to the
end. Indeed, he asked the opposition a most important and clever question. First, it exposed their shallow reasoning and bad motives; secondly, it is a question we must all answer, either for our good or ill. The
question is one upon which turns your destiny. It is this: 'What do you
think of Christ. Whose Son is he?'

Whose Son is he? Is he the illegitimate son of a young woman as
the Pharisees thought, or is he the incarnate Son of God? Do you disbelieve miracles or do you believe that Jesus was conceived in the
womb of the virgin Mary by the creating power of the Holy Spirit? The
debaters only wanted to admit a human origin: 'The Christ is the son
of David!'

Jesus quotes David's Psalm 110, 'The LORD said unto my Lord, "Sit
at my right hand until I make your enemies your footstool".' He saw
that David was inspired by the Holy Spirit to write this. Jesus then tied
them up into knots. He asks how is it that David called him Lord?
Would anybody call his son his Lord? Also how could his son already
exist while he was writing 1000 BC, if he was to be descended from
him? Moreover who was this who was sitting at God's right hand and
called Lord? It could only be a divine person. If David calls him Lord
(Jehovah) how can he be his son?

There was only one answer which the Pharisees dare not give. The
explanation could only be that the Lord whom the Lord God addressed
was his divine Son. He could only become the son of David later in
history through the Incarnation. This would combine his divine origin
with the human origin as David's son. He was thus the pre-existing

Son of God by divine descent who became the Son of Man and the son of David by human descent.

But the Pharisees, by not admitting that Jesus was the pre-existing Son of God who also became the son of David through Mary, found it impossible to answer the question without admitting Christ's divine Sonship.

Only by the virgin conception could the Eternal Lord become man. Only such a God-man could represent man by being his substitute for sin on the cross. An effective atonement could be made only by the incarnate Son of God, son of David.

1 John 4:3 says, 'Any spirit that does not confess that Jesus Christ has come in the flesh is not of God.' So what do you think of Christ? Upon your answer depends your assurance of salvation.

Jesus, the Mighty Preacher

Matthew and Luke give excerpts of the Lord's mighty preaching. Here is a small sample of his rhetoric from his testimony to John the Baptist:

'What did you flock out into the desert to see – a reed shivering in the wind? (No) Then what did you flock out to see – a man dressed in a tailor-cut suit? Behold those in posh clothes and luxury are in kings' courts! What then did you go out to see – a prophet? Yes, I tell you, and more than a prophet! This is he of whom it is written, "Behold, I send my messenger before my face, who will prepare the way before thee!" I tell you' (yes, here is Jesus thrusting home his final point), "I tell you, among those born of women, none is greater than John the Baptist.'

Jesus, the Mighty Healer

Did you know that writers living just after the apostles say that there were still thousands alive who had been healed by the Lord Jesus Christ?

Jesus showed he was the Creator-healer by the miracles that he did. He had made and governed the laws of nature and was able to adjust, supplement or renew as only the Creator could. Limbs began to grow, absent flesh reappeared, empty eye sockets received an eye.

No wonder, as St Luke says, the crowds were so great from all over the country, they trod on one another to push through to get to him. One man was even lowered down through the roof to get to him.

Luke says in chapter 5 verse 17 that people had come from every village and town in Palestine, and the power of the Lord was with Jesus to heal. The same happens in 6:18; people came from everywhere 'to hear him and to be healed of their illnesses and diseases'. Those who were troubled by unclean spirits were cured and all the crowd tried to touch him, because power came forth from him and healed them all. Healed them all! Today, Christians are not so successful in healing everyone, but I have met some marvellous cases of divine healing.

In the crowd before Jesus, there was not a single lame man or blind man who was not healed. 'The mighty power of the Lord healed them all', St Luke says. Luke says he wrote this down from eyewitnesses and Matthew, who was there and made contemporary records, agrees.

The Lord Jesus conveyed this gift of healing to the 12 apostles and later to 70 disciples. I quote, 'He gave them authority over unclean spirits to cast them out, and to heal every disease and every kind of illness.' It was remarked that although in the hundred years after Christ, antagonists disputed many claims, not one denied the healings. They could not. Thousands of healed people were among them.

No wonder crowds flocked to him. Many people value their bodies more than they do their souls, so this was to launch the gospel to the world. And just before Jesus ascended into heaven, he said, 'Go into all the world and preach the gospel to all creation . . . these signs will accompany those who believe. In my name they will cast out demons. They will speak in new tongues . . . They will lay their hands upon the sick and they will recover.'

Jesus, Friend

See how the Lord Jesus valued the affection of friends. Think of that list of enthusiastic introductions in the first chapter of St John's Gospel. After the majestic opening of his creatorship, we see Jesus in great contrast, mixing with friends in their homes. Certainly 'the Word had become flesh and dwelt among us'. It was a series of happy meetings in youthful enthusiasm of friends introducing one another.

At first, John was a disciple of John the Baptist. One day John the Baptist pointed to a man and said, 'Look! There is the Lamb of God!' Immediately John and his brother hurried after Jesus. Jesus looked round and saw them following him. 'Hello,' he said, 'are you wanting me?'

'Where do you live?' asked John, all embarrassed.

'Come along and see,' invited Jesus.

John remembered so well how he first met this wonderful man who was to change and bless him for the rest of his life. He says they went along and stayed with him and his other friends from 4 o'clock in the afternoon until late evening.

John's eyes must have filled with tears as he remembered that this led to a series of introductions. Andy was one. He shot off to find his brother Simon.

Then Phil joined this chatty enthusiastic group. He went and found Nat and so, one by one, they all met as friends, bubbling with enthusiasm, but enthusiasm with a mission. Here were young men looking ahead to life's prospects, wanting to make a better world; and what do you think? They had been lucky enough to bump into the One who was going to do it. He would change lives, and eventually change the world.

For centuries, the Old Testament prophets had foretold all about him. 'We've found the Messiah!' said Andy to Simon. 'We've found the Messiah!' said Phil to Nat. 'You know, the One that all the prophets wrote about!'

'What! No never!' exclaimed Nat, 'Not from that humble home in Nazareth!'

'Come and meet him. You will enjoy being with him. That will convince you.'

It did. In this friendly, homely chatting, Jesus pointed Nat to a glorious future, a vision of things to come. To Simon he gave a nickname and said words which showed that he knew all about him before they had met and how Jesus would change a shaky character into a rock.

To Nat he said, 'I understand your problem which you were wrestling with under that fig tree'.

'How did you know that!' exclaimed Nat. 'You must be all that is claimed.'

Yes, John remembered those first friendly homely days in which just to chat with Jesus opened up a whole new vision for life. John loved him from that moment on.

Jesus, the Master of Conundrums

Quizzes and questions are very popular today. In the Old Testament, the great man for riddles was Samson. In the New Testament, the greatest for conundrums was the Saviour. He was always making people ask, 'What does he mean?' 'What's he getting at?' 'Master, explain to us the meaning of that remark.'

It was all to make people think; to look at themselves; to open their closed minds to receive a new insight, a heavenly truth, or to receive the Saviour himself.

The Lord Jesus illustrated this very graphically once. It was after he had fed miraculously the 5,000 from only five loaves and two fishes. He said, 'That illustrates that I am the Bread of Life whom the Father sent down from heaven. Anyone who eats this bread will live for ever. You must eat my flesh and drink my blood.'

John reports the consternation this caused among the disciples. In John 6:60, he writes, 'Even his disciples said, "This is very hard to understand. Who can tell what he means!" '

Jesus said, 'Does this offend you? I'm speaking spiritually. It is not the eating of oven-baked bread I'm referring to, nor the eating of my physical body; it's my words. They are spirit and they are life. It is the Words of Salvation which give you spiritual life. They lead you to receive me, by believing my words. Actual eating of bread does not save you. The flesh profits you nothing, but when you receive me by believing, you receive eternal life.'

After practice, his disciples began to get better at understanding his conundrums. 'Tell us what you mean by the wheat and the weeds,' they said. But when he had explained, he gave them three more test puzzles without giving them the solution. 'Puzzle them out for yourself,' he said, 'then you will become good expositors of the Bible's precious treasures – treasures new and treasures old.'

What were those three short test stories? The first two were about men finding great treasure. The first found it accidentally. That was like a person accidentally hearing about the priceless jewels of Jesus and his salvation. The next one found a fortune without actually looking for it. He was searching for truth. He was searching for people. Then he found the Pearl of Great Price.

Now, here is a test for you. Did the pearl represent Jesus who is precious beyond all measure to those who find him or did it represent Jesus looking for a lost soul who was very precious to him? Can you look in the Bible for an answer as Jesus advises, to bring out treasures of truth new and old?

Whatever the answers, they show the preciousness of the Lord Jesus. 'To you who believe,' wrote Peter, 'he is precious. He gave up everything for you.' It also illustrates the great joy that a person has when he finds the Lord Jesus Christ and eternal salvation. Both men gave up all that they had to gain that treasure, that pearl. Jesus is so precious that they did it joyfully.

The Authority of Jesus over Nature

In their portrait of Jesus, the Gospels describe the authority of Jesus over nature. 'What kind of man is this,' the disciples ask in awe, 'that even the wind and the waves obey him?'

You know the story of how the Lord rebuked the elements for trying to sink the boat in which they were crossing the turbulent Sea of Galilee. Only once have I seen the terrific storms that can blow up suddenly. It was that same tunnel of air which can rush down the deep valley to the north of Galilee.

Jesus was asleep in peaceful trust after a tiring day. 'Don't you care that we perish?' shouted the disciples. Mark's description, which is a record of Peter's account, is the most graphic. The waves were beating into the boat, filling it full.

Jesus stood up and rebuked the gale and scolded the raging sea and immediately there was a great calm. Then he rebuked his disciples,

'Where is your faith?' he asked.

Jesus showed his power over water again later. It was night. They had left Jesus behind on shore. The disciples were halfway across the inner sea when another gale blew up. To their amazement and horror, they saw Jesus walking on top of the water to rescue them. He must have walked five miles – five miles on rough sea and no water-skis!

They were terrified and thought it must be his ghost. 'Don't be afraid, cheer up, it's me.' 'If it is really you, Lord,' said Peter, 'tell me to walk on the water to you!' Peter clambered out of the boat and started to walk. Then he saw how boisterous the waves were, took his eyes off Jesus and began to sink. 'Save me!' he shouted.

Jesus stretched out his hand, caught him and said, 'Oh you, of small faith. Why did you doubt!' It is the Gospel of Matthew who tells you that when they got into the ship, all the passengers bowed and worshipped him and said, 'It is true, you are the Son of God!'

You are the Son of God! Matthew repeats this, and no wonder. This had followed the creation of enough bread and fish to feed 5,000, all from five loaves and two small fishes.

John reports another creative act earlier; the turning of water into at least 120 gallons of wine – that's about 500 litres! Twelve car tanks full! Here, indeed, is the evidence that Jesus is Lord and Creator; the evidence for John's preface: 'In the beginning was the Word and the Word was with God and the Word was God. He was in the beginning with God. All things were made by him and without him, nothing was made which was made.'

Who is this Word which created all things? The question is answered in verse 14: 'The Word was made flesh and dwelt among us, and we beheld his glory . . . full of grace and truth.'

Jesus' Claim to Divinity

A young man searching for truth told me that the hardest thing for him was to accept Christ's claims to divinity. But it was not only Jesus who said he is divine; there are many others who do so.

Some have asserted that only St John's Gospel claims that Jesus was the Son of God, but this is not so. Let us look at the other three Gospels. In them, we find that:

• The angel Gabriel said Jesus is God's Son;
• Unexpected testimonial comes from evil spirits;
• Peter reaches this conclusion after three years with Jesus;
• The disciples rescued in the storm-rocked boat worshipped him as God;
• The high priest in Matthew's Gospel admitted that Jesus claimed to be God and charged him with blasphemy;

- God the Father himself spoke from heaven and said twice, 'This is my beloved Son in whom I am well pleased'.

These are reported by Matthew, Mark and Luke. All those witnesses are seen in those first three Gospels and of course John's Gospel has many more.

Look at Mark, that very human Gospel. Mark records the evil spirits as crying out in terror. 'We know who you are – the Holy One, the Son of God. We pray you, torment us not.' It is Mark also who records the Roman centurion at the cross as saying, 'Truly, this man was the Son of God.'

Matthew also describes the people mocking the Lord as he hung in agony on the cross: 'He saved others, but he can't save himself . . . Come down off those nails. That's a miracle you could do for yourself . . . Come down and we will then believe you, for you said, "I am the Son of God".' Here is a clear admission from antagonists that they understood that Jesus claimed that he was the Son of God. They must have heard those open statements reported in John's Gospel. The blind man for one said he believed on the Son of God and worshipped him.

John's Gospel makes many references to Jesus being God's Son, until in chapter 14, Philip is startled by Jesus' answer. Philip had said, 'Lord, show us God the Father and we shall be satisfied.' Christ's stupendous reply was, 'Have I been so long with you Philip that you do not know me? He who has seen me has seen the Father!'

Don't you think that is an astonishing statement? That is only understandable if what Jesus told the Jews is true: 'I and the Father are One'. And that could be comprehended only if the many Old Testament prophecies were literal – those who said the future Messiah is God. Take for example Isaiah 9:6, 'His name shall be called, Wonderful Counsellor [that's the Holy Spirit], Everlasting Father, Prince of Peace – Jesus, Mighty God.' In Jesus were all three and yet he is one. As Paul said, 'In Jesus dwells the whole Godhead bodily.'

Jesus never stopped people falling down before him to worship him – a thing strictly forbidden to any but God. Finally, it was John, the beloved apostle, who fell down in worship when he was visited by the risen Christ years later.

Revelation 1:17 says that when he saw his dazzling glory, 'I fell at his feet as though dead, but he laid his right hand on me saying, "Fear not, I am the first and the last"; and again, "I am alpha and omega," says the Lord, "who is, and who was, and who is to come, the Almighty".'

Jesus, Tired and Hungry

Could Jesus have ever felt tired and hungry like us? It was obvious that the Lord had tremendous physical strength, so did he wilt sometimes?

He must have had great strength, otherwise he would not have endured 40 days in the desert with no food. At the end of that fast, he felt very hungry; well, who wouldn't?

He would walk great distances to bring his Good News to others, but when he visited Samaria, we read that Jesus sat on the well-side tired and thirsty, but not too thirsty to tell the Samaritan woman of the 'water of life'.

Many a day, he would have a full day of crowds milling around his feet to be healed from their maladies and disablement. The disciples had to fight to get him free for some rest; even so, he would spend whole nights in prayer.

In spite of his need for sleep and housing, he had no home. To one wanting to follow him in the tough life, he replied, 'Remember, I don't even own a place to lay my head. Foxes have dens to live in and birds have nests, but I, the Man from Heaven, have no earthly home at all' (in the words of the Living Bible translation). He also chose men for similar tough assignments, then whittled them down to a shortlist of 70 (Luke 10).

I remember one of the first men to land on the moon said he was chosen from a shortlist of 500 astronauts. Most of those who passed the test turned out to be Christians. When asked why, HQ suggested that they had faith in the One who had also ascended into heaven!

But though Jesus was tough and chose men who were tough, he had times when he felt exhausted, 'Come aside and rest awhile,' he said to his disciples, so they pushed out a boat for the nine miles across Lake Galilee. Jesus immediately fell into a deep sleep on a sack and, as we have seen, he was so exhausted that even a fierce storm did not wake him.

Even then, when he reached the other side for rest, there was a great crowd waiting for the blessing of his gospel. There must have been at least 15,000 because there were 5,000 men, not counting the women and children. So Jesus did not get much rest after all. The great crowd was so eager to rush round the lake to him that they came without food, except for a boy with his lunch. After two days listening to Jesus, they were all starving, so as you know, Jesus made the boy's lunch multiply into food for the famished.

Yes, it was for others always. Satan had tried to make Jesus change stones into bread after his 40 days' fast, but as starved as he was, the Lord said it was more important to feed on the Word of Life. 'Man shall not live by bread alone, but by every word that comes from the mouth of God.'

The Manliness of Jesus

This happy friendship which Jesus struck up with that group of young men, stood him in good stead in times of stress. Whenever he felt the strain of his task, Jesus called them aside and shared the project with them. On special occasions, he drew aside those first three men who met him in that friendly housegroup. They were Peter, James and John.

As the time for his suffering for sinners drew nearer, he said, 'I feel all pent up until it is accomplished. How I wish it was all over and done with, for this is the reason I came, to give my life a ransom for many.'

Unfortunately, they did not fully understand, but it was a comfort to Jesus to have them near him. This again showed how human he was and, wrote Paul later, 'He is able to strengthen you who are likewise tested.'

Yet the manhood of Jesus was such that he attracted men. They were willing to give up everything and follow him. All sorts too. There was that big, blustering fisherman, Peter. Jesus knew just how to handle him. Impetuous, always banging into trouble, Jesus built him from an unstable personality into a reliable, trustworthy Christian.

Then there was John. No one would have thought that this apostle of Christian love would have started in life with the nickname, 'Son of Thunder'. He was always ready to dive into a rage and call down revenge on anyone who stood in his way. What is worse, he often justified it as righteous indignation, but Jesus said, 'You don't understand in what spirit of love I come.' But he soon did from his daily friendship with Jesus. He saw patient love in the eyes of Jesus; love for that earnest young man who came to him eager for eternal life. He was one who was trying his best, but did not understand that salvation was Christ's free gift – a free gift which cost Christ so much that the thought of the coming cross caused Jesus to sweat great drops of blood.

John was there when those great sweated drops of blood dripped down Christ's garment in Gethsemane's garden. John was one of the three whom Jesus felt he needed nearer to him in his agony. To realise that Jesus was to die voluntarily for people who did not deserve it, gradually changed John from a son of thunder into a son of love – the beloved disciple. That love from Jesus permeated his Epistles, so that he wrote, 'Herein is love, not that we loved God, but that he loved us and gave his Son to die for us.'

It was this same love of God in Christ which made those other men willing to die for Jesus. John says Thomas voiced all their feelings when he said, 'Let us also go up to Jerusalem with Jesus that we might die with him.' Eventually, after a life of witness, every one of those apostles sealed their testimony by their blood.

The Purity and Compassion of Jesus

A striking characteristic of Jesus was his purity. 'Blessed are the pure in heart,' he said in Matthew 5 to the great crowds, 'for they shall see God'.

Yet that purity was not repellent. It attracted people to want to be better. It drew many prostitutes to start a new pure life in Christ. It even rebuked the self-righteous Pharisees who had no sympathy for the fallen and those they spurned. Jesus said to them, 'Go and sin no more,' but to the self-righteous who rejected his gospel of forgiveness, he said, 'Prostitutes and sinners get forgiven and enter into the kingdom of heaven before you'.

There are three accounts of prostitutes who sought him to start a new life. They are three different people because they came to Jesus at three different times in his ministry at three different places, but let's take the one in Luke 7:37, early in his ministry.

She is introduced as a city street woman. Jesus was a guest at the house of a Pharisee and, as was the custom, sat at table half reclined on the couch, with his feet coming out behind him (Fig 10.1).

This prostitute came in unseen and knelt behind him crying her eyes out, sorry for her sins. As she knelt, she poured very expensive ointment over his feet and, to show her feeling of deep worthlessness, used her long hair to wipe away her tears which were flooding over his feet.

The Pharisee was indignant and said to himself, 'Doesn't Jesus know what sort of woman this is?' Jesus could read his thoughts and told him a story to trap him into identifying himself as a callous, hard-hearted man; right living, but with little love either for God or man. If you have bad debts, you will appreciate the story.

One debtor owed the equivalent of 500 days' wages, nearly a year and a half's pay; the other debtor owed 50, nearly two months' pay. The creditor cancelled the debts of both. Which do you think loved the creditor most? Why, the one with the biggest debt. The Pharisee didn't think he needed much forgiveness, therefore he didn't love much. Jesus said, 'This poor woman has washed my feet with her tears of repentance. Her sins were many, her love is great. I have forgiven her.'

Turning to the woman, Jesus said to her, 'Your sins which are many are all forgiven. Your faith has saved you. Go in peace!'

Truly, it was foretold by God to Isaiah that the Messiah would be anointed to preach the gospel to the needy. 'He hath sent me to heal the broken-hearted; to preach deliverance to those enslaved; to release the bruised and battered.' The compassion and sympathy of Jesus certainly fulfilled this prophecy.

How was Jesus so pure and yet so attractive? It was because he knew the true loving purpose which God had when he made man, male

Figure 10.1. Reclining at meal with feet stretched back. This is why the repentant woman was able to pour her expensive ointment over the feet of Jesus and wipe them with her long hair. It was like saying 'I'm only fit for a rag'.

Painting by H.M. Herget, courtesy National Geographic Society and female. He refers to this in two of his talks. Sex was given by God to be a wonderful sacred and pure intimate blessing for man and wife. It was Satan and foul spirits which twisted it and misused and misrepresented it. Those unclean spirits are very active in our world today, even to misrepresent Jesus.

There is another reason why Jesus was absolutely pure and sinless, which is why the New Testament writers emphasise it. It was because only one with no sin could be offered as a sacrifice for sinners. As that beautiful hymn puts it, 'He only was good enough to pay the price of sin. He only could unlock the gate of heaven and let us in.'

VERDICT ON THREE-AND-A-HALF YEARS' MINISTRY

Peter, who knew Jesus for three-and-a-half years, said in 1 Peter 1:19, 'You were redeemed with the precious blood of Christ, as of a lamb without blemish and without spot.' Peter knew him well, and testified that Jesus was spotless. 2 Corinthians 5:21 describes him lovingly as the one who knew no sin, therefore God was able to transfer on to him our sins. 'For God was in Christ, reconciling the world unto himself.'

His Love

Another quite surprising side of Christ's character is his love; his love for people and therefore for you and me.

Perhaps we know about it so well from the Gospel accounts that we have forgotten how surprising it is. Remarkable that he, the Creator, should value a return of love from people, yet in the Old Testament God said, 'Thou shalt love the Lord thy God with all thy heart, mind and soul.'

The Gospel of St John ends with the moving story of how Jesus, even the risen Jesus, wanted to hear that Peter and John and the others loved him. Remember too that these men felt they were failures. They were trying to put their lives back together again, but feeling absolutely drained of emotions. We may feel like that sometimes – failures, worthless, disillusioned. Is it really possible that the Creator, incarnate, should want to know whether we love him? Could we possibly matter to him?

There are these dispirited men back at their old job of fishing and they are even failures at that. They had toiled all night and caught nothing, not even a shrimp. Nearing the shore in the cold dawn, they see a stranger, not near enough to recognise. He had lit a charcoal fire to warm them and cook fish and bread for their empty stomachs. He shouts to them, 'Boys, have you any food?' 'No!' they shout back. 'Then throw in your net on the right side.' They did and a whole shoal of large fishes filled their nets to breaking point. It needed a second boat to haul them all in.

Peter gasped, 'It is the Lord!' Jesus warmed and fed those starving, shivering men before asking the question, 'Do you love me?' Most translations miss the subtle different words Jesus used for love. One means full Christian love and the other just true friendship.

Jesus asked Peter, 'Do you love me more than these?' Peter, smarting from the guilt of his betrayal replies, 'Yes, Lord, you know I am your true friend'. Jesus asks him the second time, 'Do you love me?' Peter says, 'Yes Lord, you know I am your true friend'. For the third time, Jesus uses the lesser word, 'Peter, am I your true friend?' This grieved Peter, who replied, 'Lord, you know everything about me; you know I am your true friend'. He had given up boasting. Jesus said he could show his love by feeding his sheep for whom he loved and died. In John 17, he prayed not only for his disciples, but also for us who would believe on him. He prayed that the love with which the Heavenly Father loved him might be in us.

His Power over Death

Jesus was walking to Nain. The usual great crowd was following. They came upon a funeral procession coming out through the town gate. The funeral undertakers were playing their plaintive music of wailing notes. There was a large number of mourners because it was a teenage lad whose body was carried on the pallet, the only son of a young widow. Yes, she had already lost her husband.

When the Lord saw her, his heart overflowed with sympathy. 'Don't cry!' he said. Then he walked over to the body. The bearers stopped. Jesus touched the young man and said, 'Son, come back to life again!' A gasp of surprise went up and the teenager immediately sat up and began to talk to those around him. Jesus tenderly helped the boy down and gave him into the arms of his joyful mother. You can imagine them flinging their arms around each other in full ecstasy. The only ones who might not feel pleased might be the undertakers who had lost their burial fee! But the rest of the crowd went mad with praise. Here is their reaction: 'Fear seized them all, then they glorified God shouting, "A great prophet has risen among us!" and others sang, "God has visited his people".' This report about the Lord Jesus spread like wildfire throughout the whole of Judea and all the surrounding country.

Christ's power over death was again shown sometime later. He had returned to the west side of the lake and a great crowd was waiting for him as usual. All the first three Gospels tell you, but Mark is the most graphic. Jairus, in great distress, knelt before Jesus and said, 'Please Lord, come quickly, my little daughter aged 12 is at the point of death.'

When Jesus went along, a messenger rushed out. 'Sorry, it's too late. The girl has died'. Jesus said, 'Don't worry Jairus, only believe.' When they reached the house, the undertakers were wailing and playing their death music and making a terrible din.

'What is all this hullabaloo!' said Jesus. 'The girl is not dead, only asleep!' The undertakers laughed. How ridiculous. What nonsense. They were afraid of losing their fee again. They knew she was dead. Jesus pushed them all out and took into the room only the mother and father and Peter, James and John. He said to the dead girl, 'Sweet little girl, I say to you arise.' The girl's spirit returned and she jumped out of bed. 'She is hungry,' said Jesus, 'give her some food.'

That little girl would be one of those who lived on to tell her story to Luke, 28 years later. And still later, the glorified risen Lord appeared to John and said, 'I am the first and the last and I have the keys of death and of Hades!'

The third most startling case of Christ's power over death is the raising of one who had been dead four days. In the two cases earlier, one had been dead less than a day and the little girl had only just died.

Only John tells the story of Lazarus in chapter 11. It was an even greater miracle that Jesus brought to life a man after four days rotting in the tomb. Putrefaction sets in quickly in that hot climate.

Satan had struck at this happy home where Jesus so often stayed and where he valued the friendship of Lazarus and his sisters Martha and Mary. That is why I think Jesus was so vexed in his spirit. It was Satan who had brought death and suffering into the world and into the peaceful home at Bethany.

Jesus was in another part of the country when he received an urgent message from the sisters. 'Come quickly. Lazarus, the friend you love, is dangerously ill.' But surprisingly Jesus stayed on another two days where he was. When asked why, he said, 'It is to glorify God, and that the Son of God might be glorified by it.' He knew, you see, that by raising Lazarus from the dead, it would hasten his own death. It made the authorities plot it more urgently to wipe out the evidence, John tells you.

After two days waiting, Jesus announced, 'I am going to Bethany near Jerusalem to Lazarus.'

'That is asking for trouble,' protested the disciples. 'You know there is a price on your head!'

'I go to awake Lazarus out of sleep,' said Jesus.

'If he is asleep that shows he would recover, so no need to go,' they said.

'Lazarus is dead,' said Jesus bluntly, showing his divine knowledge.

When he reached Bethany, he found that Lazarus had been buried four days. Martha lamented, 'Lord, if only you had come when we called you, Lazarus would not have died.'

'Your brother will rise again. I am the Resurrection and the Life. He who believes in me, though he die, yet shall he live.' Jesus reached the burial cave and said, 'Take away the stone from the entrance!'

'But Lord,' objected Martha, 'After four days, he'll stink!'

'Lazarus, come out!' commanded Jesus. Horrified, the crowd saw Lazarus shuffle to the cave entrance looking like an Egyptian mummy. Even his face was wrapped.

When I visited Bethany, the Franciscans asked me to preach in their church filled with pilgrims. My text was, 'I am the Resurrection and the Life. He who believes in me, though he die, yet shall he live.' Do you believe this?

He Knew the Future

Christ's knowledge of the future is remarkable. For example, he knew all about the details of his coming crucifixion. From chapter 9 in St Luke he prepares his disciples for this coming shock. Verse 51 says he set his face determinedly to go to Jerusalem.

It was the last six months of his ministry, so he plans and organises his last evangelistic campaign to take place on the way through Judea. He chose 70 and sent them in twos to every town and village that he would speak in. 'The harvest is plentiful, but the labourers are few,' he said. 'Pray to the Lord of the harvest to send out labourers into his harvest.'

What a wealth of stories and parables Jesus told on the way, recorded only by Luke. They include some of the most famous – the good Samaritan; the man borrowing three loaves of bread; the rich fool; the fruitless fig tree; the lost sheep; the lost coin; the prodigal son; the unfaithful steward; the rich tycoon and the beggar; the widow and the callous judge and the Pharisee and the tax collector. All these told by Luke led up to the Lord's final devastating revelation. It was about the immediate future. The Lord knew every detail. He spelt it out to the incredulous 12 disciples.

'Look!' he said. 'We are going up to Jerusalem. Everything that has been written about me by the prophets in the Old Testament will be accomplished. I will be delivered to the Gentiles. I will be mocked and shamed and spitefully treated. They will spit upon me, scourge me with metal points in leather thongs. They will kill me, and on the third day I will rise from the dead. Let this sink deep into your ears!' Jesus said.

They looked aghast at him. They just could not take it in. They could not grasp what was being said. But Jesus knew. 'My death,' he said, 'is the purpose of my life. I am to be a ransom for sinners. All the prophets have written about it.'

What had they written? David's Psalm 22 described all the agony of the cross; his cries from the cross; the piercing of his hands and his feet; the gambling for his garments; the preaching of the cross to the ends of the earth and other details.

Then there came the details foretold in Isaiah 53 – that terrible scourging he mentioned; the wicked thieves on either side, and the rich man's tomb in which Jesus' body was to be laid, that he would be wounded for our sins laid upon him; then the resurrection and many being saved by trust in the crucified. Many other prophets had given details.

Yes, Jesus knew all this was in the immediate future. He knew too who would betray him, and that Peter would deny him. He even knew that a cock would crow three times.

THE DIVINITY OF JESUS

Is there an experience that you will always remember? Peter wrote of a soul-shaking experience; he wrote about it years later. It was when he saw Jesus in a new light. It was the glory which shone around Jesus on the Mount of Transfiguration. It was then that he realised that Jesus was the crossroads of history and the meeting-place between heaven and earth.

The glory of it flashed vividly as he wrote in 2 Peter 1:16, 'We have not been telling you clever fairy stories when we described to you the power and coming of our Lord Jesus Christ, for we were eyewitnesses of his splendour and glory. I was there on the holy mountain when he shone out with honour given him by God the Father. I heard that glorious majestic voice calling down from heaven saying, "This is my beloved Son, in whom I am well pleased." '

This radiant revelation happened in the last year of the Lord's ministry. Jesus told his disciples, 'There are some of you standing here who will see the coming of the Son of Man with power in a few days time.' It was this Peter referred to in identical words, 'I saw with my own eyes the power of his coming in splendour and glory.'

All the accounts tell you that six days after Jesus promised this event, he took Peter, James and John up a high mountain, so they were the favoured three he had referred to. Jesus started to spend a whole night in prayer as he often did. It was pitch black with darkness and the three disciples fell asleep. Then suddenly, strange happenings woke Peter. He rubbed his eyes to shake off heavy sleep because a bright light was dazzling him. Jesus' beautiful character was shining through as bright as the sun and his clothing became dazzling white, brighter than any earthly process could make them. And then suddenly two men appeared. They were Moses and Elijah representing the Law and the Prophets, for had not Jesus said that Moses wrote about him and the prophets foretold all about him?

What were they discussing? Peter heard them talking about his exodus – that is the word in the Greek of St Luke's Gospel. They were talking about Christ's exodus at Jerusalem, not about Moses' exodus from Egypt. Yes, that was what heaven was interested in, not the lamb slain in Egypt, but the Lamb to be slain in Jerusalem.

Peter babbled something, not knowing what he said, but it was then that he heard the great voice he mentioned, 'This is my beloved Son, listen to him!' It was the voice resonant with love and pride of the Heavenly Father for his Son, so beautiful in character. Suddenly all went quiet. Peter looked around. Moses and Elijah had disappeared, the light faded, and Jesus stood there alone, the Lamb soon to be slain for sinners at his exodus at Jerusalem.

'Don't tell anyone what you have seen!' said Jesus, 'That is, until I have risen from the dead.'

'Whatever did he mean by that?' whispered the three. They did not know that the Law and the Prophets had also foretold his resurrection.

So you see, because God had created man in his own image, it became possible, by the Incarnation, for the Son of God to be born of a woman and be in the likeness of God. That human being had all the capacity of expressing God. That is why the Lord Jesus was able to say, 'He who has seen me has seen the Father. I and the Father are One' (John 14:9).

'Listen to him!' That majestic voice had said, 'My beloved Son'.

'God has spoken to us by his Son,' the letter to the Hebrews says, 'who is the express image of God, reflects the glory of God and bears the very stamp of his nature, upholding the universe by the power of his word.'

David's Psalm 45 is quoted, 'Of the Son, God said, "Thy throne O God, is for ever and ever".' But was David told this would be by virgin birth? Yes, King David prophesied that this would be through the Incarnation. It is in Psalm 40:6–8 and is quoted in Hebrews 10:5. He said, 'A body hast thou prepared for me.' That was the body of the Lord Jesus Christ brought into being by the conception of the Holy Spirit in the womb of Mary the Virgin. That body which the Holy Spirit prepared in the womb of the Virgin was able to express God's image because God made man in his own image in the beginning. The capacity was there, but only Jesus was able to fulfil it because only he was sinless, and only he was God incarnate. And that is why only he could be the Lamb of God in the exodus at Jerusalem to take away the sin of . . . what did you say your name was?

SUMMARY

EVIDENCE OF THE REAL JESUS

Critics say:
- That Jesus was only a prophet who, in the second century, the Church exaggerated into a miracle-working Messiah. Reason: They thought miracles impossible.
- That Pilate was said to be fiction, but his memorial stone was found at Caesarea barracks; Tacitus, Roman historian AD 115 said 'Executed by sentence of Pontius Pilate, in reign of Tiberius'.

Jesus more historical than anybody:
- Three times more evidence than any other historical figure.
- Caesar's *Gallic Wars* has only nine copies no older than 900 years.
- New Testament has 5,000 Greek manuscripts. Oldest fragment is AD 68.
- Tacitus has only four old copies.
- Herodotus history – oldest copy of original is 1,300 years later.

First-century historians refer to Christ:
- 7 non-Christians (Tacitus, Suetonius, Serapion, Phlegon, Lucian, Pliny, Thallus).
- 9 antagonists (Talmuds).
- 4 Gospels: eyewitnesses, 'accurately recorded' Luke 1:1.
- Quotations by Apostolic Fathers AD 86–108 throughout all New Testament.
- Josephus – fairly full concise summary of Christ.
- Pliny – in a sacrament Christians 'worship Jesus as a God'.
- Thallus – three-hour darkness reached Rome.
- Serapion – fall of Jerusalem because Jews executed Jesus.
- Jewish Talmuds – 'Hanged him on eve of Passover'. 'Illegitimate' and other derogatory comments about Christ.

11 JESUS DEAD OR ALIVE?

LAWYERS SIFT THE EVIDENCE

A most unusual inquest has taken place! The first unusual aspect is that inquests are usually taken by coroners, but in the case in question, the inquest has been conducted by five lawyers. They were five high ranking lawyers too. The second unusual thing was that there was no body!

You can't have an inquest with no body! Well these people did. They could not explain why the body had disappeared, so they said the victim's followers had stolen it, and that in spite of safeguards.

Q What were their safeguards to try to prevent a resurrection?

The body was placed in a cave tomb. They rolled a great stone across the entrance and sealed it and chained it. They also placed a full squadron guard of soldiers against it. But the soldiers came back with a very strange story. They said a great strong angel descended from heaven. His appearance was as bright as lightning. He rolled away the stone. The tomb was empty – the body had gone. They saw no one take away the body. For soldiers to produce a story like this was not typical of Roman soldiers.

The Jewish rulers called an emergency meeting to discuss the crisis. They called the soldier-guard. Such was the strength of their evidence, they bribed them to say that the disciples had stolen the body in order to pretend that Jesus had risen from the dead. Their reaction was quite ironic since the disciples themselves did not believe the Lord Jesus had risen at that point in time!

Q What then happened to the 'missing body'?

This is the question which these five lawyers have asked independently over the last 100 years. Had Jesus swooned and then revived in the tomb?

Call the Witnesses!

That's what one lawyer asked. He 'called' to the witness box the centurion who thrust a spear through Jesus' side. 'Oh, he was dead all right. Blood clot and serum flowed from this deep wound.' The spear entered his heart.

Call the next two witnesses! They said, 'We walked seven miles to Emmaus with the risen Jesus.' Here is their report: 'Jesus showed us all the Old Testament prophecies which foretold that he would die for sins and rise again. We were astonished. Could a man who had been tortured to death walk seven miles on wounded feet torn by nails? It was possible only if he had a new resurrection body. Besides, at the end of the journey he suddenly disappeared.'

No Body to Hide!

Next – call the disciples! Where have you hidden the body of Christ?

'Do you think we would dispose of the precious body of our Messiah and Saviour and never even mark the spot? Do you think we would not venerate the body and visit it like the tombs of Abraham and the patriarchs? When our Master was slain, all our hopes were lost. We were a dispirited, defeated lot, locked indoors for fear of arrest. It was his resurrection which transformed us. He appeared about 12 times to us and changed our defeat into boldness.'

Tell us – where is the body now? Yes, this was the kind of inquest that these lawyers conducted. Most of them were unbelievers, for example, Gilbert West, Lord Littleton and Frank Morison. All of them considered the problem legally and became convinced that Jesus had indeed risen from the dead and ascended into heaven.

GREAT LAWYERS SUM UP THE EVIDENCE

Frank Morison wrote his book *Who Moved the Stone?* which became a bestseller. He tells how his education gave him a sceptical outlook which denied the possibility of miracles. He thought that the resurrection spoilt the matchless story of Jesus, so he set out to write a non-miraculous account of the last week of Christ's life. When he studied the evidence, however, he found he was writing an entirely different book.

His first chapter is headed, 'The book which refused to be written'. He describes it as: 'The inner story of a man who originally set out to write one kind of book and found himself compelled by the sheer force of circumstances to write quite another.' He says:

When, as a very young man, I first began seriously to study the life of Christ, I did so with a very definite feeling that, if I may so put it, his history rested upon very insecure foundations. If you carry your mind back in imagination to the late nineties, you will find in the prevailing intellectual attitude of that period, the key to much of my thought. It is true that the absurd cult which denied even the historical existence of Jesus, had ceased to carry weight. But the work of the Higher Critics – particularly the German critics – had succeeded in spreading a very prevalent impression among students that the particular form in which the narrative of his life and death had come down to us was unreliable, and that one of the four records was nothing other than a brilliant apologetic written many years, and perhaps many decades, after the first generation had passed away. Like most young men, deeply immersed in other things, I had no means of verifying or forming an independent judgement upon these statements. It was the strangeness of many notable things in the story which first arrested and held my interest. It was only later that the irresistible logic of their meaning came into view. Such briefly was the purpose of the book which I had planned. I wanted to take this Last Phase of the life of Jesus, with all its quick and pulsating drama, its sharp, clear-cut background of antiquity, and its tremendous psychological and human interest – to strip it of its overgrowth of primitive beliefs and dogmatic suppositions, and to see this supremely great Person as he really was.

Many other lawyers have been attracted to arguing the case for the resurrection. There are so many witnesses who give their evidence that it appeals to them as a classical court case. **Josh McDowell** gives a list of their verdicts in his splendid book, published in 1983, *Evidence that Demands a Verdict.*

Sir Edward Clark K.C. writes: 'As a lawyer, I have made a prolonged study of the events of the first Easter Day. To me, the evidence is conclusive and over and over again in the High Court I have secured a verdict on evidence not nearly so compelling. Inference follows on evidence and a truthful witness is always actless and disdains effect. The Gospel evidence for the resurrection is of this class and, as a lawyer, I accept it unreservedly as the testimony of truthful men to facts they were able to substantiate.'

Another lawyer is **Lord Lyndhurst.** He is recognised as one of the greatest legal minds in British history, the Solicitor-General of the British government in 1819, Attorney-General of Great Britain in 1824, three times High Chancellor of England and, elected in 1846, High Steward of the University of Cambridge, thus holding in one lifetime the highest offices which a judge in Great Britain could ever have conferred upon him. When Chancellor Lyndhurst died, a document was found in his desk, among his private papers, giving an extended account of his own Christian faith and, in this precious, previously-unknown record, he wrote, 'I know pretty well what evidence is; and I tell you, such evidence as that for the resurrection has never broken down yet.'

Mystery of the Disappearing Body

The disappearance of the body of Jesus is the biggest mystery of all time. It is a problem beyond explanation if you don't accept the evidence that Jesus Christ rose from the dead.

Tell me, if you don't believe that the body of Jesus ascended into heaven, where is it? Where is that body? The three unbelieving lawyers examined the problem as if it were a detective investigation. Three of the lawyers actually set out to write books to disprove the resurrection – to try to show that Jesus did not rise from the dead, but they all reached a very different conclusion. The fourth is a famous lawyer of today who did not start as an agnostic as the others did, but saw the need to produce the evidence on a legally investigative basis.

The first two were the eighteenth-century writers Lord Lyttleton and his friend, Gilbert West. They wrote their books in the early days of the Rationalists, these books are in the Bodlian Library, Oxford. They set out to write for the agnostic Rationalist society to show that Jesus did not rise from the dead. But, to give them credit, they did agree that they must examine the evidence honestly and properly. Lord Lyttleton and his friend, Gilbert West, both wrote independently and came up with the same answer. It was *that the mystery of the disappearance of the body of Jesus can be solved only by his resurrection and ascension.*

Dr Frank Morison, over 35 years ago, started on the same quest as an unbeliever in which his detective style investigation demonstrated that the mystery of the disappearance of Christ's body could be explained only by his resurrection and ascension into heaven. By the time he had finished writing his book, he was a believer.

Professor of Oriental Law, **Sir Norman Anderson**, Director of the Institute of Advanced Legal Studies in the University of London, as a Christian, wrote his book to show that the evidence was conclusive. The body of Jesus Christ disappeared because Jesus rose from the dead and ascended into heaven. This is his legal conclusion.

But first these lawyers considered the other options. If the disciples had stolen the body to pretend that Jesus had risen, where would they put it? Would they keep quiet about it? With all their adoration of the Lord Jesus Christ, would they not want to visit it regularly as the advocates of other religious founders did? Would the women disciples who loved Jesus make no response to Christ's body?

Ladies First with the Evidence

In fact it was the women who were the first to go to the tomb to pay respect and love, and mummify the body of Jesus with spices and wrappings. They witnessed what happened to the body right from the outset. They accompanied the body when it was taken down from the cross by Joseph of Arimathea and laid in his rock-hewn tomb, and it was they who watched and noted how the huge stone was rolled to cover the opening. Pilate, the Roman governor, sealed that stone and posted a bodyguard. In fact that was the problem which confronted the women.

'Who will roll away such a huge stone so that we can enter the tomb to mummify his sacred body?'

When they arrived early in the morning, the stone was already rolled away and the body had gone! They were distraught with grief! Who could have moved it? Who could have taken the body? The soldiers had had the frightening experience of a mighty angel descending from heaven and rolling away the stone. They were flattened with fright, and so were the women when two dazzling angels appeared to remind them that Jesus said he would rise from the dead.

Figure 11.1. Women at tomb.

Where Is the Body?

They rushed to tell the disciples, but they did not believe them. They were too shattered, too disillusioned and were in too frightened a state to have braved the soldiers and to steal the body and, as regards the soldier-guards themselves, they would have been executed if they had allowed the body to be stolen. Besides, where would the disciples put the body – the one whom they revered so much – would they never venerate it?

Had the chief priests stolen the body? They were the ones who had Jesus tortured to death. When the disciples started proclaiming triumphantly that Jesus had risen and ascended, the chief priests would have settled all arguments by bringing out the dead body of Jesus and exhibiting it to disprove the claims. On several occasions, they forbade the disciples to say that Jesus had risen. All Jerusalem had been filled with their triumphant preaching, 'Christ is risen!' they said. 'Just as the Old Testament Scriptures foretold'.

'Oh no, he has not!' the high priests would say. 'Here is the body. Bring it out for everyone to see!'

Another excuse was that the soldier-guard had fallen asleep and the disciples stole the body. The Pharisees bribed them to say this.

Strict Security and Discipline

The whole guard falling asleep on duty! It must have taken a heavy bribe to make them risk their heads. The disciplines and penal ties for such a thing were severe. Here are some of the military rules set out in Josh McDowell's book, *Evidence which Demands a Verdict*.

George Currie, in speaking of the discipline of the Roman guard, says,

The punishment for quitting post was death, according to the laws *(Dion. Hal, Antiq. Rom. VIII. 79)*. The most famous discourse on the strictness of camp discipline is that of Polybius, which indicates that the fear of punishments produced faultless attention to duty, especially in the night watches. It carries weight from the prestige of the author, who was describing what he had an opportunity to see with his own eyes. His statements are duplicated in a general way by others.

Professor Currie documents the following examples from the annals of Roman military history which reflect the type of disciplinary measures employed in the Roman army: 'In 418, standard bearer lagging in battle, slain by general's own hand; in 390, asleep on duty, hurled from the cliff of the Capitolium.'

What was the temple guard? **Alfred Edersheim** in *Life and Times of Jesus the Messiah* (Longman, 1920) gives us the following information concerning them:

At night, guards were placed in twenty-four stations about the gates and courts. Of these twenty-one were occupied by Levites alone; the other innermost three jointly by priests and Levites. Each guard consisted of ten men; so that in all, two hundred and forty Levites and thirty priests were on duty every night. The Temple guards were relieved by day, but not during the night, which the Romans divided into four, but the Jews, properly, into three watches, the fourth being really the morning watch.

Edersheim also gives us this description of the tight discipline under which the temple police worked:

> During the night, the captain of the Temple made his rounds. On his approach, the guards had to rise and salute him in a particular manner. Any guard found asleep whcn on duty was beaten, or his garments were set on fire – a punishment, as we know, actually awarded. Hence the admonition to us who, as it were, are here on Temple guard, 'Blessed is he that watcheth, and keepeth his garments' (Rev 16:15).

The **Mishnah** (collection of rabbinical traditions) shows the treatment given anyone found asleep during the watch:

> The officer of the Temple Mount used to go round to every watch with lighted torches before him, and if any watch did not stand up and say to him, 'O officer of the Temple Mount, peace be to thee!' and it was manifest that he was asleep, he would beat him with his staff, and he had the right to burn his raiment. And they would say, 'What is the noise in the Temple Court?' 'The noise of some Levite that is being beaten and having his raiment burnt because he went to sleep during his watch.' R. Eliezer b. Jacob said: 'They once found my mother's brother asleep and burnt his raiment.'

Mystery of the Grave Wrappings

Dr John Stott discusses another aspect of evidence. It is what St John saw as he looked at the grave clothes left on the ledge of the tomb. He realised the significance of what he saw, and believed.

What did he see? It was that the body of Jesus had passed through the grave wrappings without unwinding them. The head wrappings were separated from the body wrappings by an empty gap where the neck would have been.

> The body cloths under the weight of 100 lbs of spices, once the support of the body had been removed, would have collapsed . . . When the apostles reached the tomb: the stone slab; the collapsed graveclothes, the shell of the headcloth and the gap between the two. No wonder they 'saw and believed'. They were like a discarded chrysalis from which the butterfly had emerged.

Another line of evidence is that the Lord Jesus declared to the confused and uncomprehending disciples that he would be crucified and rise again the third day. This he said over 12 times. As they got nearer to Jerusalem on that last journey, we read in Luke 18:31–34:

> Jesus took the twelve aside and told them, 'We are going up to Jerusalem and everything that is written by the prophets about the Son of Man will

be fulfilled. He will be turned over to the Gentiles [Romans]. They will mock him, insult him, spit on him, flog him and kill him. On the third day he will rise again.' The disciples did not understand any of this. Its meaning was hidden from them, and they did not know what he was talking about.

He said that he must fulfil the Scriptures. The Old Testament had foretold it all. In *Volume 3: Prophecy*, we will look at the evidence of prophecy concerning the Messiah.

THE RISEN LORD JESUS

The first to see the risen Lord Jesus was Mary Magdalene. The first to witness his gaping wounds were the disciples. The first to be invited to thrust his fist into the Saviour's gaping side was unbelieving Thomas. The first to rush into the tomb and see and realise that the body had risen straight through the grave wrappings without disturbing them, was John.

Moreover, the body of Jesus had passed through the rock of the tomb *before the angel moved the stone*. That body of Jesus had also passed through the wall of the upper room to appear to the disciples. It was the same body because they saw and touched his wounds. It was the same body because the risen Jesus ate food with them. It was not the ghost or spirit of Jesus only, because Jesus ate food with them and said: 'A spirit or ghost does not eat food. It really is me!'

Atomic Change in the Body?

Yet that same body had a resurrection change. It did not need blood. His blood had been shed for sinners – for you and me. He stood there with gaping wounds, but no haemorrhage. His life support was not by blood.

Science now knows that the same body could be changed in its atomic particles from protons and electrons into neutrons, but only the Creator could do this. In such a case, the body could pass through solid rock and wall as Jesus had done. Later, Paul said that at the resurrection our bodies would be changed 'atomically'. That is the actual word he uses in the Greek of 1 Corinthians 15:52: we shall all be changed 'in atom', just as Christ was. It was an atomic change of the same body.

It was the appearance of the risen Christ to Paul that changed him from a murderer of Christians to the Church's most successful evangelist. And only the resurrection can explain how the shattered, defeated, fearful disciples suddenly became triumphant, bold, proclaiming evangelists, refusing to keep quiet, braving the threats of the authorities and facing death gladly.

The Impact of the Resurrection

McDowell records yet another investigation into the resurrection. It was by **Simon Greenleaf**. He was the famous Royal Professor of Law at Harvard University and succeeded Justice Joseph Story as the Dane Professor of Law in the same university, upon Story's death in 1846. H.W.H. Knott says of this great authority in jurisprudence: 'To the efforts of Story and Greenleaf is to be ascribed the rise of the Harvard Law School to its eminent position among the legal schools of the United States.' Greenleaf produced a famous work entitled *A Treatise on the Law of Evidence*, which 'is still considered the greatest single authority on evidence in the entire literature of legal procedure'. In 1846, while still Professor of Law at Harvard, Greenleaf wrote a volume entitled, *An Examination of the Testimony of the Four Evangelists by the Rules of Evidence Administered in the Courts of Justice.* In his classic work, the author examines the value of the testimony of the apostles to the resurrection of Christ. This brilliant jurist's critical comments contend that only the resurrection of Christ, their Master, could explain the change which came over their lives. From defeated, disillusioned disciples, they were changed into victorious, brave witnesses before the cleverest legal, political and religious authorities of their day.

They Knew where the Body Had Gone

The disciples had witnessed that risen body speaking to them for hours over a 40-day period, pointing out the prophecies of the Old Testament which said that Jesus must die for sins and rise again. At least 12 times, possibly 16 times, he had appeared to them or to individual members. They had seen that risen body ascend into heaven. The Bible says 500 people at one time had seen him (1 Corinthians 15:6). They knew where the body had gone. The risen, glorified Jesus was now in the presence of God with power and authority. They knew the prophecies also which said that one day soon all the world will see Jesus descending from heaven to save the world from destroying itself. They would see the very wounds in his hands and feet, the prophecies said, when he comes to judge everyone who rejects him as Saviour.

This can only mean close-up television coverage of the returning Lord. Only news coverage of close-up shots will reveal such details, confirming the prophecies that every eye of the world's inhabitants will see his wounds. Everybody will know then where the risen body of Jesus went, but it will be too late for them then if they hide from him now in doubt, instead of responding in faith.

SUMMARY

LAWYERS' INQUEST ON THE RESURRECTION

Three lawyers set out to prove Jesus did not rise:
- Frank Morison, *Who Moved the Stone?*
- Gilbert West and Lord Lyttleton, both Rationalists.
- Examined evidence by legal methods. It proved the resurrection.

Two eminent Christian lawyers give their legal findings:
- Prof Norman Anderson. 'Empty tomb stands, a veritable rock of evidence.'
- Sir Edward Clark K.C. 'Evidence is conclusive.'

Other lawyers:
- Lord Lyndhurst, 'Such evidence has never broken down.'
- Simon Greenleaf, 'No possible motive for fabrication.'

The disciples and followers:
- The empty, hollow, mummy-like grave wrappings made John believe when he saw them.
- Changed into victorious, brave witnesses.

Prophesied:
- In Old Testament: Ps 16:8–11; 22; 110:1; 118:22–24; Job 19:25; Is 53:10.
- By Jesus: Matt 12:38; 16:21; 17:9; 17:22; 20:18; 26:32; John 2:18.
- But they could not understand it.

When he had risen: 'He opened their understanding that they might understand the Scriptures, and he said to them, "Thus it is written and thus it behoved Christ to suffer, and to rise from the dead the third day" ' (Lk 24:45).

12 THE RESURRECTION JIGSAW PUZZLE
EVIDENCE OF JESUS AFTER HIS RESURRECTION

What excitement and confusion on that first day of the resurrection! There was running about, reporting the empty tomb, seeing angels, seeing Jesus. All this was mixed with incredulity turning into amazed belief. In the confusion of reports coming in, it was not easy to sort out the order of events.

All the accounts from the four Gospels and Paul's list in 1 Corinthians 15, are like a jigsaw puzzle. I have found it fascinating to put the pieces together – and I want to tell you this – they all fit! Yes, there is harmony in the accounts.

THE APPEARANCES OF JESUS

There are 16 jigsaw pieces to the complete picture. They are 16 separate accounts of 12 appearances of Jesus. It is because some Bible scholars have reduced the pieces to only half that number that they could not fit them together.

Do you see what I mean? Because, say, two of the jigsaw pieces or incidents are nearly the same shape or detail, they regarded them as one and tried to fit them in the same gap. Now, if you do that with a jigsaw puzzle, it will never complete its picture. Many bits are almost the same, but if you try to force two slightly different pieces into the same gap, you will get into a mess.

Well, I have cut out all the pieces, so to speak, the 16 incidents, from the four Gospels and 1 Corinthians 15. I find they fit into a complete and thrilling picture of the Lord's miraculous resurrection.

Imagine about 20 individuals rushing around giving their report of what they had seen and then five writers trying to piece the evidence together – that is what we get in the five accounts – by Matthew, Mark, Luke, John and Paul. Their eyewitness reports show individuals and groups rushing around confused, alarmed, bursting into tears, amazed with joy, disbelieving, seeing an empty tomb, reporting what the angels said, what the soldier-guard said, and yes, eventually what Jesus said – for they had met the risen Jesus alive and well, walking around with gaping wounds in his hands and feet and side. It was only individuals who saw him first, then it was whole groups of people.

Do you know, now that I have fitted the jigsaw together, I find that the risen Lord Jesus appeared on that first day of resurrection as many as five times! The fifth time was in the evening of that day when he appeared to all the apostles in the upper room – that is, all except Thomas. During the next 39 days, he appeared another seven times. That makes 12 times in all and the crowd got bigger and bigger each time.

The Opening Drama

Isn't it exciting piecing together this jigsaw of all the resurrection incidents and seeing the living risen Christ speaking out the message of life to us? We can fit these 16 accounts or incidents together because various reports in the Gospels and Paul's report say this was before that, and that was after this.

Now, Mary Magdalene was the first actually to see the risen Lord Jesus, John tells us that. But there were several events before that wonderful occasion. Mary met her Saviour after the stone had been rolled away and after she had seen that the tomb was empty, but Matthew starts the story before the stone was rolled away.

Two women had reached the tomb while the soldier-guard was still there. The great circular stone still stood immobile and sealed against the entrance when suddenly a great strong angel descended from heaven. His face flashed like lightning and his garment glistened like snow. The soldiers fell flat on the ground, helpless to stop the angel. He pushed back that huge stone, tons in weight, just as if it were a matchbox. The chains and seals snapped off like threads. The soldier bodyguards got up and ran for their lives to tell the authorities.

Were those women scared? Well, would you be? The angel spoke kindly to the women. 'Don't be frightened. You seek Jesus who was crucified. Well, he's not here!'

Q Why on earth did the angel roll away the stone if Jesus was not inside?

To prove that the body was no longer there! 'See, look, he's not here!'

Well, how did he get out? That great stone was blocking the way and the soldier-guard was outside and Jesus was dead anyway.

The angel explained, 'He is risen! He has come alive – don't you remember he said he would?'

Well, how did he get out? Ah – it was no earthly body, not mere resuscitation. It was a resurrection body. The same body, but changed in a moment, in the twinkling of an eye, a body which could pass through the rock tomb and through anything.

So then, angel, why go to all this bother and drama of rolling back the stone?

The angel said to the women, 'Come and see where his body was and then go and tell his disciples.'

Yes, the stone was not rolled away to let the Saviour out. He had gone already. It was to let the witnesses in. And he will let you into the secret of the resurrection if you will believe.

Ladies First

Now, as I said, on that resurrection morning, there was quite a lot of running around, panic and tears, unbelief and amazement. Luke reports what the various women reported to the apostles. First, it was one or two women, then it was a group of them. Really, the men didn't know what to believe and record.

Matthew and Mark agreed that it was two women who first visited the tomb – Mary Magdalene and Mary who was James' mother. They were the ones who witnessed those terrifying incidents of the mighty scintillating angel flattening the soldiers and freeing the stone. It wasn't until later when Mary Magdalene was alone that she met Jesus.

Luke says in chapter 24 verse 10 that it was as the various women came in with their story that they had to piece it together. Luke says he is only recording the jumbled reports of the women. I quote, 'It was Mary Magdalene and Joanna and Mary, mother of James and other women which told these things to the apostles, but they did not believe them. Their words seemed like idle gossip.'

That is just what those first two women anticipated; so at first they told no one, in spite of the angel's instructions. It is Mark who gives us this clue. You can imagine their feelings. 'Those men will say it is just a tale.'

From Mark's clue, we can piece together the events, but he never actually puts his notes into narrative form in chapter 16. After an attempt in the first few verses, he gives it up and just includes the original notes which Peter gives him.

That is how I see it. You can imagine Peter saying to the various women as they came in. 'Pull yourself together woman! Stop jabbering, calm down and get the facts straight! Now what happened next? Stop sobbing and shouting – take it slowly!'

Well, Peter never got it sorted out, so Mark just left his notes as a summary attached to the end of his Gospel, all because the women couldn't be logical. Remember Professor Higgins' lament in *My Fair Lady?* 'Why can't women be logical, calm and unemotional, straightforward and rational, so superbly controlled like men!'

Well, thank God he didn't make women that way; and that is why he arranged 'Ladies First' at the tomb. The women had to prepare the men for the news gradually, otherwise the men would have cracked up under their own logic. In their disillusionment they couldn't take in anything that was beyond rational explanation. And I can recall to mind some in today's media who still can't! Anything outside the small compass of the human mind which requires faith and acceptance and honest reporting by Spirit-filled men is dismissed. But it is dismissed at the peril of the soul because God says, 'It is by faith you are saved'.

Incredulity of the Disciples

Here is the likely order of events, when the various reports of the women came in to get sorted out.

Everyone agreed that it was Mary who first actually saw and spoke to the risen Lord Jesus, but before that, various things happened in the rush and panic.

The two Marys got to the tomb while the guard was still there and the tomb still all sealed up. The mighty angel, bright as the sun, flattened them and rolled the stone away and sat on it! He told the two women to tell the disciples that Jesus had risen from the dead, but at first they were afraid to, so they just ran to Peter and John and told them the body was missing. Peter and John ran to see.

The women were very confused, so Mary Magdalene turned back to check. She could hardly believe her eyes. Was it only a vision, had the body really gone. She met one she thought was the gardener. 'The body's missing,' she sobbed. 'Do you know who's taken my precious Lord?'

'Miriam!' The stranger used the pet name that Jesus always used for her. It could only be Jesus.

'Oh, my dear master!' she exclaimed.

'You must do as the angels said, tell the apostles that I have risen from the dead.'

So Mary catches up with the other Mary again. 'We must tell them the whole story,' she says. But the second Mary still has not seen Jesus. It is only Mary Magdalene's tale, so first they find all the rest of the women who mourned for Jesus. On the way to do this, Jesus met them, to give a message to the apostles. 'They must meet me in Galilee,' he said. 'That is another part of the angel's instructions you forgot.'

The second Mary was now a second valuable witness of the living Jesus. They each tell the rest of the women who then in turn flood back to the tomb to see for themselves, while the two Marys go on to tell the apostles.

Meanwhile, the risen Lord had a special very private interview with Peter, who was a broken man. His denial had left scars and needed restoration and healing. So he was the third person to see the risen Lord (Luke 24:34). But the rest of the apostles, except John, just would not believe.

It was incredible.

Later that same evening, the two Emmaus disciples had hurried back making a 14-mile round trip to tell the apostles of their own amazing incident. Jesus had walked with them all the way to Emmaus explaining from the Old Testament that it was all foretold in Scripture that he would die for sins and rise again from the dead. So they were the fourth party to see Jesus that day.

The Growing Assembly

Now the apostles were beginning to believe. 'He has also appeared to Peter!' they exclaimed (and Paul tells us later that Jesus had also appeared to James, his half-brother). Thus, by seeing all those individuals first, the risen Lord had prepared their minds for the final shock. He suddenly appeared in the midst of all of them in the upper room – and with the doors all locked too. They were truly amazed! Things happened as he stood amidst the dumbfounded group of the apostles.

Jesus was actually standing in the middle of that upper room, in the middle of those apostles – ten of them. They were locked inside the building in fear of the authorities who had crucified the Lord. Then Jesus began to talk and make some astonishing demonstrations. The account is given in detail by Luke and John. At first they thought they had seen a ghost. They were startled, some were terrified. 'It's a ghost,' someone shouted.

Then Jesus actually opened his mouth and spoke. He said gently, 'Peace be with you – I'm not a ghost. Does a ghost have flesh and bones as you see that I have? See, it really is me, I myself. Touch me, feel my muscles and bones.'

Then, horror of horrors, he began to show them his hands, those hands which had blessed and healed. There were the gaping wounds where the nails had torn through the flesh. There were the great gashes in his feet. He showed them those and then . . . oh! his side. He showed them that – a great gaping wound where the soldier's spear had been thrust through to his heart. Flesh and bones all right, but he did not mention blood, did he? No wonder. There was no blood in him. He had shed it all on the cross. The gaping wounds did not bleed. All his blood had been poured out for sinners, to cleanse away their sins.

Here then, they gazed on him. Here he was, without any obvious means of life support. The gaping wounds did not bleed and yet he smiled, he talked, he demonstrated and . . . yes, he was going to eat.

They still disbelieved. 'Why do questions arise in your heart? Does a ghost eat? Here, give me some food and I will show you that it really is me in my changed resurrection body.' So they gave him some cooked fish. His torn hand took it and he ate it all. They watched the fish disappearing into his mouth. Then he spent hours with them turning up the sections of Scripture, showing the prophecies of that very day. So what an end to a day full of staggering unbelievable events.

As the evening closed and palpitating hearts quietened, peace stole in. It was true. There was hope yet. The kingdom mission was not over. It is still not over. In fact, it's over to you! What do you think?

A Packed Refresher Course

Thirty-nine days were to follow in which Jesus appeared and disappeared – five-and-a-half weeks in which they never knew when he might appear again; when he would appear to give them further instructions and insights into the Scriptures and an understanding of the purposes of God for the world; nearly six weeks in which their own hearts were to be examined, in which they were to see their weaknesses and be prepared for the Lord's new miraculous strength.

Jesus appeared in different places at different times. A whole week passed before he appeared in the midst of them again in the upper room, on the following Lord's Day; a whole week in which to think and meditate upon those six appearances the Sunday before. Seven days had passed in silence since resurrection day. And then?

'Thomas, stretch out your hand and thrust your fingers into my wounds!'

The voice – that well-known voice – came from the middle of the room, and there he was, looking at Thomas, and there Thomas was, staring at Jesus. His jaw dropped at the sight of Jesus. You see, he was not there the previous week when Jesus appeared. He had uttered foolish words of bitter unbelief.

'Let me thrust my fingers into his wounds; let me thrust my fist into that gaping side you talked about! That is not very likely. I won't believe if I don't see!'

Jesus knew all about what he had said. He must have been there, invisible, when Thomas said it. So now he says, 'Come on Thomas, do what you said. Thrust your fingers and fist into my wounds. They were inflicted for you. Did not the prophets say that I must suffer for you – for your sins; and that was so that repentance and forgiveness might be preached to the whole world . . . and starting with you Thomas.'

Thomas wished he could have eaten his words. He made no attempt to touch the wounds, so in the end, he did not need the tactile evidence which his companions had. He just fell to his knees and croaked hoarsely, 'My Lord, and my God'.

'You have believed,' said the risen Jesus, 'because you have seen. Blessed are all those to whom you will preach who will not see and yet they will believe!'

What prophetic words! Later, Thomas made his way to India, and there to this day is the church of St Thomas, spread throughout a province. Down the centuries, Indian Christians have believed and faced persecution and shunned idolatry and survived, even though they never saw with the physical eyes of their founder, Thomas. Jesus is real and alive in their midst today, but they need reviving even as Thomas needed restoration.

I found it a moving experience to visit the site of Thomas' martyrdom in Madras. The monument is on a steep hill. It tells you that he visited India in AD 51 and was knifed while kneeling in prayer in AD 68.

ENCOUNTERS IN GALILEE

Now that all the apostles were convinced that Jesus was truly risen, alive and well, they could be reminded to go to Galilee. They had been told to do this at the outset and at last they were beginning to assemble. John makes the entry in his account that this was the third time that they met Jesus as a group.

Only seven of them so far had reached the shore of the lake and they were not expecting the others until the morning. They were feeling the vacuum aftermath, the reaction to unearthly events. Then, with all the rest coming, the women too, they must get some food together, so Peter announced, 'I am going fishing'.

'Right, we are coming too!' But as they worked hard all night, they caught nothing – except perhaps a cold! Disappointed, as day was breaking, they neared the shore. There was a man on the shore and he shouted, 'Hello boys! Have you caught any fish?'

'No!'

'Then cast out your nets on the right side of the boat!' Who was this telling them how to fish? Well, anyway, here goes; so they flung out those circular throw nets that you can still see in Galilee today, and immediately shoals of fish couldn't wait to jump into them! When they dragged their nets to shore, this man had made a fire and already had fish on it – so he didn't need theirs, but still he accepted their fish and added to the cooking.

Jesus Grills the Fish – and Peter, Too!

Now, before this, Peter had realised that it was Jesus as soon as the miraculous catch was made. He jumped into the sea clutching his short fisherman's jacket to him, impetuous as usual to reach Jesus first. It was after they had eaten the grilled fish and been refreshed that Jesus continued his sensitive restoration work on Peter.

'Do you love me more than these?' Jesus asked.

Peter remembered his boast and his failure at the trial of Jesus.

'Lord', he replied, 'You know that I am your true friend', he said.

'Show that by feeding my lambs'.

'Peter do you love me?'

'Lord, you know that I am your true friend.'

'Then take care of my sheep!' The third time Jesus said, 'Peter, am I your true friend?'

Peter was saddened that he had used this lesser term of affection and he said, 'Lord you know everything about me. You know that I am your true friend.'

'Then feed my sheep!'

Isn't it wonderful that the Lord Jesus, Creator of the universe, wants your deep and full love, not just affection!

Figure 12.1. Galilee Lake (south end) 200 metres below sea level.

Why to Galilee?

As I read the accounts of the 12 resurrection appearances, I notice that two of them were in Galilee. One was by the Lake of Galilee and the other on a mountain in Galilee. One is recorded by Matthew and the other by John. I notice, too, how urgent it was for them to go to Galilee. Three Gospel stories tell the disciples to go to Galilee, the angels told them to go to Galilee and, when the women failed to deliver the message to the disciples, the Lord Jesus met two of them and reminded them to instruct the disciples to go to Galilee.

Jesus said he would meet them there, so it was a divine appointment. After they met him there, he sent them back to Jerusalem to stay there and meet in the upper room until a new power came into them. It seems then, that the Lord gives special messages or commissions at certain times in certain places.

To tempt Jesus to get a kingdom the easy way, the devil took him up into a high mountain. To get Christ's kingdom, the hard way, Jesus took his disciples up into a mountain in Galilee.

It was home ground, but why there? Did they need to be taken back in memory to where it had all started? It started by the lake when some were fishing and Jesus promised to make them fishers of men. What a reminder of that when the seven had gone back to fishing. They were waiting for the others to assemble. Another miraculous catch reminded them that it was only the miracle-working gospel that could catch unwilling fish. That experience for those was a recommissioning in itself.

The Divine Commission

Then, when all eleven apostles were gathered upon the mountain in Galilee, and they were uplifted above their traumatic experiences to look into the distance over the fields and plains into far countries, Jesus said (Matthew 28:16), 'Go into all the world to preach the gospel, make disciples of all nations. All authority in heaven and earth has been given to me. Behold I am with you every day until the end of the age.' That was the commission.

It was like Jacob of old who had to be brought back to Bethel to renew his pledge with God. It was when he came back to the old place that he began to see things differently, he began to understand the plan God had for his life. He rededicated himself to the task and became a new person with a new name.

It must have been the same with the disciples. They had misunderstood the message. They were too earthbound. It was a material kingdom which had been their ambition, but now they were beginning to see and understand.

FINAL DAYS ON EARTH

Back to Jerusalem

Now, restored in the quietness and memories of Galilee, the apostles returned to crowded Jerusalem. They obeyed their Lord's instructions and secluded themselves in the upper room which had been the scene of so many dramatic events. The Lord's mother and brethren had joined them. There were now 120 of them, Luke tells us in Acts 1:15. Those who have been in that restored room know how spacious it is. It would take 120 comfortably.

In that room, the risen Lord Jesus commenced his regular Old Testament studies and showed his followers how to use them effectively in their preaching. This is how I read the words of Luke in Acts.

The actual appearances of Jesus to individuals and groups number 12 or even 13, but I gather from the phrases of Luke's language that a number of regular visits followed in which he completed his training for the final commissioning. My own translation of Acts 1 brings this out rather well:

> He was taken up into heaven after giving instructions through the Holy Spirit to the apostles he had chosen. After his suffering he continued to show himself to these men and gave many convincing proofs that he was alive. He continued to appear to them over a period of 40 days and spoke about the kingdom of God. On one such occasion, while he was eating with them, he gave this command, 'Do not leave Jerusalem, but wait for the gift my Father promised.'

Now, on the occasions reported in the Gospels of his teaching in the upper room, in none of them does Jesus mention this subject of waiting for the Holy Spirit, so it would be on subsequent visits, especially as verse 4 implies, that he continued to come and eat with them and teach them throughout that 40 days; and especially when you remember that Luke's resurrection accounts continue into the book of the Acts. Luke shows Christ's methods. He went through the Old Testament from beginning to end and showed that he was anticipated in all the Scriptures.

The apostles adopted this as their method ever after. This is God's way of convincing people, so make it yours. Christ was foretold in the Old Testament and fulfilled in the New Testament. Always argue this with your Bible open and marked. Peter and Paul usually did it this way.

500 Witnesses

Imagine the excitement which brought together 500 people. They crowded around a dead man who had come alive. Paul tells us in 1 Corinthians 15:6 that, after the risen Lord Jesus was seen by the apostles, he was seen by as many as 500 brethren on one occasion. We are not told where this was, but we are told that it was before Jesus had his private talk with his half-brother.

When Paul was writing this about 15 years after the resurrection and said that most of those 500 people were still alive, you could have gone to any one of those 500 people to ask them, 'Did you see a man who had been tortured to death, mutilated, scourged, a spear thrust through to the heart, drained of his blood, and then who had come alive again?'

Any one of that 500 would have said, 'Yes! Yes! I could hardly believe my eyes, but there he was, inviting people to touch him and examine his gaping wounds! He preached to us from the Old Testament. He went through prophecy after prophecy from Moses to Malachi proving that this was all foretold. God had prepared for this for 2,000 years so that we could be saved.'

Then you might have asked any one of that crowd of 500, 'How long did this go on?'

'It went on for five-and-a-half weeks, then suddenly it stopped. We saw him no more!'

Nationalist Mindset a Hindrance to the Gospel

We have noted that in addition to the 12 appearances of the risen Jesus, Luke hints that Jesus made his visits to the upper room regularly during those 40 days after the resurrection. I quote, 'He appeared to them over a period of 40 days and taught about the kingdom. On one such occasion, while he was eating with them, he commanded them not to leave Jerusalem until empowered . . .'

We noticed that this is presented as a regular feature throughout the 40 days. What were they taught 'about the kingdom'? Surely they had had plenty on that throughout the previous three-and-a-half years? Yes, but they could never grasp that it was a spiritual kingdom to be won in people's hearts by preaching and persuasion. 'Go into every nation and . . . and what?' Use military weapons? Kill with the sword? Fire bullets? No, conquer people's hearts and minds by preaching and teaching the truth of the gospel.

You can see that that did not appear very exciting and attractive to some of them. They asked, 'Lord, will you restore the kingdom to Israel now?'

They were still nationalists. They still could think only of weapons, swords and guns. Some of them had joined Christ's band originally just as nationalists. There was Simon the Zealot, for example. He is mentioned as still with them in the upper room. The Zealots, you remember, were those militants who rose up against Rome 40 years later and brought down the whole nation of Israel in ruins.

Jesus' kingdom was to be established with the power of love and forgiveness. Only his way brings peace and happiness. In any case, they were to use words not weapons. They were to win souls, not kill bodies.

Now, Judas Iscariot was smart enough to see earlier what Jesus was getting at, so he opted out and became a double agent, but some of the others were so set in their minds that they still preferred politics to preaching. That is, until the Holy Spirit came at Pentecost and changed their hearts and filled them with the fire of love.

Many are still like that today. Sunday School teaching and church teaching can only prepare them, but they will still be earthbound until they receive Christ into their hearts and the Holy Spirit into their brains!

T. E. McCally tells how he attended Sunday School and then church, but then his thinking was taken up with man-made philosophy. His faith died. Then, 'One day,' he said, 'I stopped fighting inside and surrendered and turned my life over completely to Jesus Christ. Within an instant, I was flooded with the love and forgiveness of God. Jesus Christ was suddenly very, very real. I had just met him.'

Explaining to James

Another misunderstanding Jesus needed to explain was to his half-brother, James. Paul said he appeared to James privately after the 500. Why?

Imagine how confused James and his three brothers would be. Here was this elder brother Jesus. He had grown up with them in the carpenter's cottage. Then, at the age of 30, he suddenly seemed to take leave of his mind (Mark 3:21), leaving home, gathering huge crowds and making fantastic claims. No wonder 'none of his brothers and sisters believed on him'. Who did he think he was! What has he got that we haven't! He seems to think that he is different!

So it would be explained to James how and why Jesus was certainly different. Perhaps James heard the village whispers that Christ was illegitimate – those sneers which the Pharisees and the Jewish Targums (records) repeated again later. Yes, James certainly needed to hear the facts – the facts of the Incarnation when the Word was made flesh and dwelt among them – dwelt with them for 30 years!

What a testimony, that James in his letter calls Jesus 'Lord of Glory'. What a piece of evidence that Roman historian Josephus should refer to James, that he was so respected by the Jerusalem populace, that they attributed the destruction of Jerusalem to be judgment for James' martyrdom by the high priest.

THE ASCENSION

Come with me in imagination to Jerusalem. The old city itself is in the mountains on a hill. Surrounding this hill are others. There is a higher one on the east side called the Mount of Olives and a valley runs between Jerusalem and the Mount of Olives. It is called the Valley of Kidron.

On the last visit of the risen Lord Jesus to the upper room in Jerusalem, he led those 120 men and women disciples out, down into Kidron Valley, past the Garden of Gethsemane, up the hill to the top of Mount Olivet. When all had got their breath, he gave them their final instructions.

We read from Acts 1:6–11:

> So when they met together, they asked him, 'Lord, are you at this time going to restore the kingdom to Israel?' He said to them, 'It is not for you to know the times or dates the Father has set by his own authority. But you will receive power when the Holy Spirit comes on you, and you will be my witnesses in Jerusalem, and in all Judea and Samaria, and to the ends of the earth.' After he said this, he was taken up before their very eyes, and a cloud hid him from their sight. They were looking intently up into the sky as he was going, when suddenly two men dressed in white stood beside them. 'Men of Galilee,' they said, 'Why do you stand here looking into the sky? This same Jesus, who has been taken from you into heaven, will come back in the same way you have seen him go into heaven.'

It had become a thrilling experience meeting the risen Jesus day in and day out for 40 days. They must have thought that this was going to continue indefinitely, but now came the final shock. He was going to leave them.

'But Lord,' they said, 'Aren't you going to restore the kingdom to Israel now?' (v 6).

You can imagine their thoughts, 'Isn't your next move going to be marching up to the Jewish Council and telling them to get hopping? Aren't you going to the Roman Governor, Pilate, at the Military Fort at Caesarea to tell him to make himself scarce? Aren't you entering Herod's palace to tell that usurper to get his foxy body off that throne, because that is where you are going to sit!? Lord, we are right behind you, ready to march! Nothing can stop you. You appear and disappear at will. They will have the daylights scared out of them. You have got the power!'

'No,' said Jesus, 'I am going to give you the job, not by your own force but by the power of the Holy Spirit. He will descend upon you with a new power in a few days' time. I am leaving you to spread the kingdom. It will be the power of words – words of the gospel; words of witness; penetrating words by which the Holy Spirit will change hearts all over the world. It will be a strange message. It will be the word of the cross; of a Galilean on the gallows, giving life to believers throughout the world. I am leaving you to do it. Wait for that power – you will understand then.'

Then, to their astonishment, he began to ascend into the sky as he blessed them. They stared up into the blue sky at his disappearing figure. They couldn't believe it. At the very peak of triumph, they were on their own. It was over to them.

Now it is over to you.

S U M M A R Y

RESURRECTION JIGSAW PUZZLE

Fitting in 12 appearances of the risen Jesus

Jesus appeared five times on the first Resurrection Day:
- Two women saw stone rolled away, Mary Magdalene and Mary, James' mother. 'Men will only think it's a tale.' Told no one, but 'body is missing'.
- Mary stays and sees Jesus. (Appearance 1)
- Mary catches up with other Mary and both see Jesus. (2)
- Christ's personal interview with guilty Peter. (3)
- Two walking to Emmaus. Tell apostles who exclaim, 'He's appeared to Peter'. (4)
- Sunday evening to all in upper room. (5) They had been prepared by reports.
- 'I'm not a ghost!'
- Old Testament foretold it all.

Next 39 days, another 7 times (fulfilling Old Testament prophecies):
- Next Sunday in the upper room to all, especially Thomas, John 20:16. (6)
- At Galilee lakeside as reminded by the angel. 7 disciples, John 21. (7)
- On a mountain in Galilee to all 11 apostles. Recommissioning, Matt 28:16. (8)
- 120 including Holy Family and holy women in upper room, Acts 1. (9)
- 500 brethren in one gathering, 1 Cor 15:6. (10)
- Then to James, half-brother of Jesus. (Christ's origin needed explaining), 1 Cor 15:7. (11)
- The Ascension from Mt of Olives with promise to return. (12)

13 THE DEAD SEA SCROLLS 'COVER-UP'
EVIDENCE FROM THE CAVES OF QUMRAN

The discovery of the Dead Sea Scrolls has given valuable evidence for the truth of the Old Testament. It has confirmed that all the ancient Scriptures were copied from the original writings very accurately down the fifteen centuries from Moses to Malachi.

The discovery has also proved that the prophecies about Jesus were written down centuries before he came; they were not added as some suggest. The Dead Sea sect had started making copies of the Old Testament books two centuries before Christ came, and then preserved them carefully. This explains why the Jews were all expecting the Messiah to come in Jesus' time. All the Gospels speak of this expectancy: 'Are you the Christ?' or 'Are you Elijah who is to come before Christ?' One Dead Sea record expresses disappointment that he had not yet arrived, as his time was due, according to Daniel's 490-year prophetic dating – no one, it adds, except 'this Nazarene'.

The very fact that Daniel's date of chapter 9:24 was getting near seemed to have created the Dead Sea sect. They were preparing for his coming, but got confused by combining the characteristics of his two main events into one. They did not want to see that he would first come to be rejected, crucified for our sins, and later return with almighty power. 'This Nazarene' was not the worldwide ruler they wanted.

All the books of the Old Testament were found in the caves of Qumran except the book of Esther. These prophecies concerning Christ from Genesis to Malachi, written over a period of many centuries, described all the details of the Lord Jesus whom God was to send as our Saviour: his virgin birth, his prenatal eternal origin, his childhood, his ministry, his sinless character, his atoning death by crucifixion, his resurrection, his ascension into heaven, and his second coming to judge the world, and to bring in peace on earth.

Unfortunately, the media is often ready to seize on statements by a sensationalist if he knocks the Church or the Bible.

There have been several instances of this concerning the Dead Sea Scrolls. It has given the public the impression that they expose Christianity as something invented by those who wrote the scrolls from 130 BC to AD 68 and they go on to accuse the Church of trying to cover up these things. The accusation is laughable for anyone who knows even a few basic facts. The scrolls actually are a great testimony to the accuracy of our Bible text.

Instead of there being an attempt to prevent the scrolls coming to public attention, it was prominent clerics and scholars of the Church who rescued many copies and bought them so that they could be translated for all to read.

NO COVER-UP

Five of the scrolls were found in Cave 1. The Archbishop of the Syrian Orthodox monastery in Jerusalem bought them and, as he could not read Hebrew, he told the American School of Oriental Research about the find, hoping that their scholars could translate the scrolls, so there was no cover-up there.

By the Lord's providence, John Trevor was director and also a good photographer. He photographed each column of the great scroll of Isaiah which was 24 feet long and 10 inches high. In great excitement, he sent some of the prints to Dr W.F. Albright, Director of the American School of Oriental Research. Albright replied immediately:

> My heartiest congratulations on the greatest manuscript discovery of modern times . . . What an incredible find! And there can happily not be the slightest doubt in the world about the genuineness of the manuscript . . . I date it around 100 BC.

He meant that it was about the year that this copy was made from earlier copies. These in turn went back to when Isaiah wrote the original during a period around 740 to 722 BC.

The importance of the discovery was that it proved the great accuracy of the copyists over a period of 1,000 years, because before this discovery, our oldest copy was made in the tenth century AD.

Gleason Archer states that it 'proved to be word-for-word identical with our standard Hebrew Bible'. There were only a few variations which were no more than slips of pen and variations in spelling. It supported the fidelity of the Masoretic system of copying.

Edmund Wilson was one who wrote the first report of the discovery in 1955. Later in 1969, he wrote a review in which he admits that, as a journalist, he and others gave a tabloid sensational type of report on the origins of Christianity. These journalists assumed that Christ got all his ideas from the Dead Sea Scrolls. It was to his credit that he wrote a re-assessment 14 years later.

He tells us that he had no affiliation with any church. To me, this explains why, when he read in the Dead Sea Scrolls some phrases that Jesus used, he thought that Jesus got his teaching from the scrolls. Only one who did not know that these phrases were in the Old Testament prophecies concerning the Messiah, would misunderstand.

What were those phrases? Jesus described himself as 'The Son of Man'. Where did Jesus get this expression from? It was from Daniel's prophecy about him in chapter 7 verse 13. Was this invented by the scrolls? Of course not. They came much later.

'I saw in the night visions, and behold, with the clouds of heaven there came one like the Son of Man . . . and to him was given dominion and glory and kingdom.'

This is why Jesus replied to the high priest at his trial (Matthew 26:64): 'Hereafter you will see the Son of Man seated at the right hand of Power and coming on the clouds of heaven'. He was quoting that same prophecy of Daniel. The Dead Sea Scrolls echo this prophecy too.

Another phrase was about 'The Teacher of Righteousness' who would be 'favoured with divine revelations'. Was this invented by the scrolls? No, it was a prophecy of Moses in Deuteronomy 18:15–19, Isaiah 42:1–4 and other prophecies.

A third phrase was, 'The new covenant' or New Testament. Was this invented by the scrolls? No. Any Christian familiar with the Old Testament knows that this was foretold by God to Jeremiah in chapter 31 verses 31 to 34:

> Behold the days will come, says the Lord, when I will make a new covenant [or New Testament] with the house of Israel . . . I will write it in their hearts . . . they shall all know me from the least of them to the greatest of them, says the Lord, for I will forgive their iniquity and remember their sin no more.

That is why the Lord Jesus at the last supper took the cup and said, 'This cup is the new covenant in my blood which is shed for you.' It is through trusting in the cleansing blood of Christ that our sins are forgiven and anybody can come to know God personally from the humblest to the greatest.

A scroll about a spiritual warfare between the sons of light and the sons of darkness says, 'The Teacher of Righteousness shall divide the world after the last judgment and save the elect.' Was this an invention by the scrolls? No. The prophets Joel, Isaiah, Ezekiel, Daniel and Zechariah were told this by God from eight centuries BC onwards. The Lord Jesus confirms this in Matthew 25:31:

> When the Son of Man shall come in his glory, and all the holy angels with him, then shall he sit upon the throne of his glory; and before him will be gathered all nations; and he shall separate them one from another, as a shepherd divides his sheep from the goats.

The Dead Sea Scrolls in Perspective

Geza Vermes, who wrote in the early days about the scrolls, also corrects false statements in his *Dead Sea Scrolls: Qumran in Perspective*. In Chapter 8, he writes:

> In the opening phases of scrolls research, the adjective 'revolutionary' was on everyone's lips. Today, such an emotive word is out of place . . . through more mature assessment.

He finds, as others have done, that the scrolls reveal how accurately the original scriptures had been copied. The book of Isaiah, for example, had collected very few mistakes – they were mainly in punctuation – and none which altered any doctrine. They had their own system of checking to maintain accuracy.

Figure 13.1. Scroll of Isaiah. This scroll was found by a goat-herd boy and sold for one shilling (5 pence). It was later purchased for £20,000. It proved that all our modern copies are faithful and accurate copies of the original by Isaiah. It also confirms that the 66 chapters of Isaiah were written by one author, namely Isaiah himself. This scroll would have been copied from an original copy around 150–200 BC.

A thousand years later, in AD 1008, Aaron-ben-Moses-ben-Asher invented a new system of copying, which was nearly foolproof. It included counting every line, word and character horizontally and vertically, as well as adding pointing for the vowel sounds. This system is called the Masoretic text. It was made error-proof by the scribe checking it with his master copy. Every letter and word had to be accounted for and in the same place.

When our Hebrew Bibles of the twentieth century are compared with scroll copies originating two centuries before Christ, the accuracy is amazing. There is no evidence of careless work or of tampering with the original text: there are no insertions or deletions 'of convenience or prejudice'.

> The excitement of the Dead Sea Scrolls is that they fill a thousand years' gap of missing scrolls, with a testimony of accuracy for our present Bible copies.

So what does Geza Vermes write in *Qumran in Perspective*? He says, 'The cave manuscripts have not affected any significant understanding of the Bible message . . . They have completely supported the Masoretic text and with this Millar Burrows agrees' (another expert, who wrote *The Dead Sea Scrolls*, Viking Press, 1955).

He gives other information which disproves sceptical liberal theologians who said that, because God could not foretell the future, there must have been two or three different Isaiahs, some writing after the events they prophesied. But this scroll of Isaiah copied in the second century BC showed it was one book from one writer (i.e. Isaiah 740 BC). The writer of the scroll of Ecclesiasticus said that Isaiah was written by one single prophet, and the Septuagint also showed that all 66 chapters are one book from one writer.

Those of us who have seen the Isaiah scroll know that what is now our chapter 39 ends one line up from the bottom of the scroll column. The next line at the very bottom starts what is now our chapter 40, which continues onto the next column. (See Fig 13.1.) Some thought this was by a different author, but obviously if another author was writing, a fresh column would have been started.

As I have said, it demolishes the theory of two Isaiahs. There is obviously no concept of an ending and starting of a new work by someone else. Also, see my additional evidence for the unity of Isaiah in Chapter 18 of *Volume 1: Science*.

The critics denied that it could be one work and written as early as 722 BC because they did not believe that there was a God who could reveal his future plans. They quote those passages in Isaiah which speak of Judah's return from Babylon through the help of Cyrus the Persian emperor. Yet this is the very test point of the proof that God is God:

> Remember the former things of old, for I am God and there is no one else. I am God and there is none like me; declaring the end from the beginning, and from ancient times the things that are not yet done, saying, 'My coun-

sel shall stand and I will do all my purpose, calling a ravenous bird from a far country [Cyrus].' Yes, I have spoken and I will bring it to pass. I have purposed it and I will do it (Isaiah 46:9–11).

Cyrus is actually named by God in Isaiah 44:24–45:6 as much as 200 years before he is emperor:

> Thus says the Lord . . . I am Jehovah who makes all things . . . that frustrates the tokens of the liars, and makes diviners mad, that turns clever wiseacres backwards, and makes their knowledge look foolish . . . that says of Cyrus, he is my shepherd and will perform all my pleasure, even saying to Jerusalem, 'Thou shalt be rebuilt,' and to the temple, 'Thy foundation shall be laid.' Thus says the Lord to his anointed to Cyrus whose right hand I have upheld to subdue nations before him. I the Lord have called you by name. I am the God of Israel . . . I am Jehovah, there is none else. There is no other God but me. I equipped you even though you did not know me.

Josephus tells us that this prophecy was shown to Cyrus and that is why he brought the exile to an end, after 70 years, as God also told Jeremiah. It explains why Cyrus made the following proclamation in Ezra 1:2: 'Thus says Cyrus, king of Persia, Jehovah God of heaven has given me all the kingdoms of the earth.' (He is actually quoting Isaiah 45:1.) 'And he has charged me to build him a house which is in Jerusalem, in Judah . . . Jehovah God of Israel, he is God.'

God emphasises his knowledge of the future again in Isaiah 48:3–5: 'I have declared things from the beginning . . . even from the beginning I declared them to you because I knew you were obstinate.'

It Is the Sceptics who Cover Up the Truth

There has been no one more obstinate than the Higher Critics. An editorial in the *Church of England Newspaper* said that those who claim to be liberal critics are often the most resistant to factual discovery.

So you see, God bases the proof that he is the Creator on his ability to foretell to the prophets his future plans. Yet most of the postdating by critics of prophetic passages is on the assumption that God cannot plan and foretell the future! God makes it clear that this is a very serious attitude.

Hebrew scholar, Yigel Yadin, thought it was significant that the scrolls would be made public at the very time that the creation of the State of Israel was announced.

Critics have been very quiet about the evidence from the Dead Sea scrolls of Isaiah on its unity, and instead still continue to propagate their second Isaiah theory. That is their 'cover-up'.

Another testimony to the unity of Isaiah is the phrase typical only of Isaiah. It is, 'The Holy One of Israel'. This phrase occurs 30 times and it is almost equally divided between chapters 1–39 and 40–66. Outside Isaiah, it occurs only six times and that is in the written history for which Isaiah is responsible. (See *Volume 1: Science*, Chapter 18.)

There is no real cover-up. Eleven caves have yielded something from every book of the Old Testament except Esther, about 200 manuscripts; 70 of them are of the Pentateuch (the Books of Moses, or the Torah). There are also many commentaries by the Essenes who lived at Qumran on the Dead Sea.

Who were these Essenes who were responsible for writing the scrolls during that 200 years from about 150 BC to 68 AD? The journalistic writers said they were a new discovery shedding new light, but this is not correct. The Essenes were well known by Origen (AD 185–254) and others who wrote about them. Origen had even found some scrolls in a cave near Jericho. These Essenes were withdrawing from the world to purify themselves to get ready for the Messiah, but were as uncertain about details as the people were in John 7:40. 'Some said this is the Prophet, others said, this is the Messiah, but some said, shall the Messiah come from Galilee?'

The only cover-up seems to have been by a certain critic whom journalist Wilson describes as an 'angry young man', who had lost his faith and had fantastic ideas, so a television company seized upon his jaunty style.

In fact, Edmund Wilson says that the critic argued from an unpublished text which he was reluctant to divulge. Here is what Wilson writes on pages 166–168 and then page 174 of *Dead Sea Scrolls:*

At a conversation tape-recorded in December 1966, critic A was confronted by Professor Y. Yadin of the Hebrew University, Professor Geza Vermes of Oxford, and Canon E .F. Carpenter of Westminster, who challenged him to defend his thesis. He had made a good deal of what he calls, 'a little document', in which, he says, occurs a Semitic word which must underlie the significant name Cephas given by Jesus to Simon Peter. The Essenes, according to the critic, deemed it a rather special word (meaning the 'ability to read men's minds'). Therefore Peter was an Essene overseer.

Here again, says Wilson, critic A is arguing from a text that has not been published and Professors Yadin and Vermes keep asking him what it is. Professor Vermes reminds him that it has been the habit . . . first to publish scholarly papers before making any public statement. The critic says he has not got the document.

'What is the document?' he is asked.

'It is this little clinical record.'

'I don't find your argument about that word Cephas convincing at all,' said Yadin.

Later a reporter enquires, 'Are you saying the prophets were on LSD?' 'Yes, indeed,' says critic A, 'or something very like it . . . The origins of Christianity can be seen against this . . . The Priests and Prophets were dope-pushers.' (!)

But who was doing the cover-up and who seemed most doped? Wilson comments: 'His utterances are coming to sound more and more fanciful.'

A Message from the Scrolls

In contrast, the fulfilment of prophecies are far from fanciful as the following will show.

I found it very thrilling to read Yigel Yadin's book *Message of the Scrolls*. Yadin is the son of Professor Sukenik who bought the first three scrolls for the University of Jerusalem. He wrote on page 14:

> I cannot avoid the feeling that there is something symbolic in the discovery of the scrolls and their acquisition at the moment of the creation of the State of Israel. It is as if these manuscripts have been waiting in caves for two thousand years until the people of Israel had returned to their home . . . the first three scrolls were bought by my father for Israel on 29th November 1947, the very day on which the United Nations voted for the re-creation of the Jewish State in Israel after two thousand years.

Then Yadin quotes on page 73 of his book a very significant statement in one of the Dead Sea Scrolls. It was written by one of the Dead Sea sect. The scroll is called, 'The Assumption of Moses', and the writer is actually instructing the preservation of some of the scrolls. He writes:

> Preserve the scrolls which I shall deliver unto you . . . anoint them with oil and put them away in earthen vessels . . . until his (God's) name should be called upon, until the day of repentance, in the visitation wherewith the Lord will visit them *in the consummation of the end of days*.

Was the writer thinking of Jeremiah 32:14?

> Thus says the Lord of Hosts, the God of Israel . . . put them in an earthenware vessel, that they may last for a long time . . . Ah Lord God! It is thou who hast made the heavens and the earth by thy great power. Nothing is too hard for thee. I will gather them (Israel) from all countries whither I have driven them and I will bring them back . . . I will plant them in this land' (vv 37, 41).

Another Scroll Fantasy

Another resurgence of scroll fantasy has been published in the daily papers. It was distressing to read the heading: 'Jesus was a divorced father of three, claims scholar'. It is even more distressing to read that the author teaches Divinity at Sydney University. She claims to get her ideas from the Dead Sea Scrolls, but as Professor G. Vermes, the scrolls' expert, says, the scrolls were written before Christ and so are irrelevant to such a claim.

So where would she find this irrelevant theme? It seems obvious to me that she read the scroll's copy of Hosea. This prophet sired three children from his prostitute wife. He divorces her for further adultery. God says this illustrates his own pain over unfaithful Israel whom he divorces, but will take her back in the latter days. This is significant today as Israel returns to the Holy Land (*Volume 3: Prophecy* enlarges on this).

What are the opinions of others on the irrelevant claim? Professor Sir Henry Chadwick, Master of Peterhouse, Cambridge, said, 'It's bosh!' Dr Peter Cotterell, a former Principal of London Bible College, said, 'I see no evidence for scepticism of what the Gospels say. I think people who question the Scriptures are simply venting their personal prejudices.'

Only in these days of widespread ignorance of the Scriptures could such fantastic accusations get a hearing. Satan's tactics at this time seem to attack the beautifully good character of the Lord Jesus Christ. Two films in the last decade have done this, the last being Thorsen's 'Jesus' film which has been banned in Britain for its blasphemy. 'All kinds of things will be said against the Son of Man,' said Jesus.

Indeed, you can actually use this as evidence that prophecy is being fulfilled. You can quote 2 Timothy 4:3,4:

> The time will come when people will not endure sound teaching, but will look for teachers who will tell them just what they want to hear. They won't listen to what the Bible says but will follow their own misguided ideas' (Living Bible).

Why the Scrolls Were Deposited

Q What caused the scrolls to be deposited in the Dead Sea caves?

It was the outbreak of the 'Wars of the Jews', to give Josephus' name to the conflict. The Roman military might had decided to wipe out Jewry in Palestine. The campaign to do this started in AD 66 and lasted three-and-a-half years to the fall of Jerusalem in AD 70. A

Figure 13.2. Caves of Qumran. The Dead Sea Scrolls were found in caves such as these in 1947.

description of the wars and the reason for the outbreak are described in the next chapter and are foretold by the Lord Jesus Christ in Luke 21.

Jesus had told the Christians that the first warning sign would be that Jerusalem would be surrounded by Roman armies. They would then withdraw. This would allow the Christians to escape before a major campaign was launched. The Christians obeyed and escaped.

Did this convince other Jews that the sacred Scriptures needed rescuing and placing in a safe, secret place? This is a question which I have not seen raised, but something must have impelled the action taken, because in AD 68 cave 8 was sealed with its safely preserved Scriptures inside. Scores of Scriptures were placed in jars and their tops sealed. Other caves were used also, bringing the number up to 11.

The question is, what alerted the Qumran community to the fact that Jewry and Jerusalem were doomed? In contrast, the majority of the Jews thought that their rebellion and resistance would be successful and rejoiced in the initial retreat of the Romans in AD 66.

So what connection had the rescue of the Scriptures by the Qumran community with the Christians who obeyed Christ's warning?

To fill 11 caves by AD 68, it must have taken some time before to collect all those 200 manuscripts, seal the jars and transport them to selected caves. Whatever the answer, it preserved nearly all those ancient copies for discovery in our modern times and gave valuable testimony to the accuracy by which they had been copied down over a period of 2,000 years. The Scroll community had also preserved other scrolls about the rules of their community and of their expectation of the prophesied Messiah.

Fragments Establish Exciting Connections

Among the fragments discovered in cave 7 was a piece of St James' general Epistle, a section of Paul's first letter to Timothy (3:16 to 4:3), and a fragment of St Mark's Gospel, that is if Professor O'Callaghan is correct. They were fragments because, after this cave was discovered in 1947, the scrolls became scattered.

These fragments must indicate interest in the New Testament message, and it is especially significant that James' Epistle was there. Now Josephus, the historian, tells us that James was greatly venerated by Jew and Christian alike. When we read of his actions in the Acts, we find that he did all he could to stop a split between Christians and Jews.

'You know dear brother,' James said to Paul, 'how many thousands of Jews have also believed and they are all very insistent that Jewish believers must continue to follow the Jewish traditions. Go with four men to the temple to fulfil the Levitical vow of purification.'

Figure 13.3. First cave of Dead Sea Scrolls. It is sited near the top centre of the picture. The walls of the Qumran sect dwellings are seen in the foreground.

Perhaps that is why he addressed his letter to all the 12 tribes of Israel and not to Christians alone. So perhaps it was through him that Qumran connections were told of Christ's warning and that 'not one stone of the temple or Jerusalem would be left standing'.

How the Scrolls Were Found

The discovery of the scrolls is a fascinating story. In 1947, a Bedouin shepherd boy named Muhammad was looking for a goat which had strayed away. He thought it might have disappeared into a hole in the cliff on the north-west side of the Dead Sea. He threw a stone into the hole and to his surprise, heard the stone shatter some pottery. He climbed into the cave and to his astonishment saw on the floor many large jars. Their tops were sealed. Inside he found leather scrolls wrapped in linen cloths. The scrolls had been preserved in excellent condition for 1,900 years since AD 68.

The scroll of Isaiah was 24 feet long and 10 inches high. It was sold for a shilling but later it was sold for thousands of dollars. Expert archaeologists tested the scroll for style of writing and age of material and dated the time it was copied to be about 125 BC.

Examination of the many books of the Old Testament revealed how carefully and accurately scribes had made copies of the Bible down the centuries. Millar Burrows, who is quoted in *Evidence which Demands a Verdict,* by Josh McDowell, says:

> It is a matter of wonder that through something like a thousand years, the text underwent so little alteration. As I said in my first mention of the scrolls 'Herein lies its chief importance, supporting the fidelity of the Masoretic method of copying.'

The two copies of Isaiah discovered in Qumran cave 1 were 1,000 years earlier than the oldest copy known up to that time which was AD 980.

Fred Kenyon of the British Museum explained that the reason why earlier copies before AD 980 had not been preserved by the Masoretics, was because their methods of copying were so accurate and could be relied upon. Other scriptures showed similar accurate copying. Dr Basil Atkinson, Under-Librarian of Cambridge University, said it is 'little short of miraculous'.

DEAD SEA SCROLLS: USEFUL LIST OF EVIDENCE

1. Scrolls prove the accuracy with which our Scriptures have been copied and handed down. They were copied for over 1,000 years without an intervening copy surviving until the Dead Sea Scrolls were found.

2. They support the claims of the Masoretic method to ensure accurate copying.

3. Sir Frederick Kenyon, former Director of the British Museum, says that Bible copies are three times more reliable than the secular classics such as Shakespeare, Marlowe, or Greek and Roman history which nobody bothers to question.

4. A fragment of St James' Epistle was found in cave 7. This must have been copied from James' original some time before the jars were sealed in AD 68. This cave also contained a fragment from Mark's Gospel.

5. The scrolls support the claim that Isaiah was written by the one prophet Isaiah in about 740 BC, showing that God did foretell his future plans. 'I am God and there is no-one else . . . declaring the end from the beginning, and from ancient times the things that are not yet done . . . I will fulfil all my purpose' (Isaiah 46:9,10).

6. The scrolls got their anticipation of Christian phrases from the prophecies of the Old Testament:

(a) 'New Covenant' from Jeremiah 31:31, 500 years earlier;

(b) 'Son of Man' from Daniel 7:13 about 500 years earlier;

(c) The 'Righteous Teacher' who would judge the world from Deuteronomy 18:15–19 (1400 BC) and Isaiah 42:1–4 (750 BC) and other prophecies.

(d) 'Bread and Wine' – Genesis 14:18 and Psalm 110:4.

7. The three sections of Old Testament Scripture are summed up as complete, just as Jesus did in Luke 24:44, i.e. The Torah, The Prophets, and the Psalms, which all foretold the Messiah Jesus.

SAMPLES FROM THE DEAD SEA SCROLLS

Translated by Theodor H. Gaster
The Scriptures of the Dead Sea Sect
Published by William Clowes and Sons Ltd

The Manual of Discipline

Of the Commitment

Everyone who wishes to join the community must pledge himself to respect God and man; to live according to the communal rule; to seek God; to do what is good and upright in his sight, in accordance with what he has commanded through Moses and through his servants the prophets; to love all that he has chosen and hate all that he has rejected; to keep far from evil and to cling to all good works; to act truthfully and righteously and justly on earth and to walk no more in the stubbornness of a guilty heart and of lustful eyes, doing all manner of evil; to bring into a bond of mutual love all who have declared their willingness to carry out the statutes of God; to join the formal community of God; to walk blamelessly before him in conformity with his various laws and disposi-tions; to love all the children of light, each according to his stake in the formal community of God; and to hate all the children of darkness, each according to the measure of his guilt, which God will ultimately requite.

All who declare their willingness to serve God's truth must bring all of their mind, all of their strength, and all of their wealth into the community of God, so that their minds may be purified by the truth of his precepts, their strength controlled by his perfect ways, and their wealth disposed in accordance with his just design. They must not deviate by a single step from carrying out the orders of God at the times appointed for them; they must neither advance the statutory times nor postpone the prescribed seasons. They must not turn aside from the ordinances of God's truth either to the right or to the left.

Of Initiation

Moreover, all who would join the ranks of the community must enter into a covenant in the presence of God.

The Zadokite Document

Of God's Vengeance and Providence

Now listen, all right-minded men, and take note how God acts: he has a feud with all flesh and exacts satisfaction from all who spurn him.

Whenever Israel broke faith and renounced him, he hid his face both from it and from his sanctuary and consigned them to the sword. But whenev-er he called to mind the covenant which he had made with their forebears, he spared them a remnant and did not consign them to utter extinction.

So, in the Era of Anger, that era of the three hundred and ninety years, when he delivered them into the hand of Nebuchadnezzar, king of Babylon, he

(Continued)

took care of them and brought to blossom alike out of the priesthood and out of the laity that root which had been planted of old, allowing it once more to possess the land and to grow fat in the richness of its soil. Then they realised their iniquity and knew that they had been at fault. For twenty years, however, they remained like blind men groping their way, until at last God took note of their deeds, how that they were seeking him sincerely, and he raised up for them one who would teach the Law correctly, to guide them in the way of his heart and to demonstrate to future ages what he does to a generation that incurs his anger, that is, to the congregation of those that betray him and turn aside from his way.

The period in question was that whereof it is written, 'Like a stubborn heifer, Israel was stubborn' [Hos 4:16]. It was the time when a certain scoffer arose to distil upon Israel the waters deceptive and to lead them astray in a trackless waste, bringing low whatsoever had once been high, diverting them from the proper paths and removing the landmarks which their forebears had set up.

Proof-texts of the Messianic Era

Extracts from Dead Sea Commentaries

[Genesis 49:10]. 'Ne'er shall the sceptre from Judah depart, nor the ruler's staff from between his feet, until [in the end] one who owns them shall come and claim the subservience of peoples.'

[This means that] the wielding of sovereignty will [never] be diverted from the tribe of Judah. So long as Israel possesses a government of its own, occupancy of the throne shall not be dissociated from [the line of] David. For the word mehoqeq [commonly rendered 'ruler's staff', is connected with hoq, 'statute, stipulation', and thus] refers to the covenant (sworn by God) regarding the kingship, while the 'feet' denote the clans of Israel.

[The words, 'Until one who owns them shall come' mean:] Until the coming of the legitimately anointed [king], the Scion of David. For it was to David and his seed that the covenant was given regarding kingship over his people for eternal generations [that covenant] which [the Lord] has indeed kept and maintained and now consummated with the members of [this] Community, expression, 'the subservience of peoples' referring to the church of the members of [this] Community.

[2 Samuel 7:11–14.] 'Moreover, the Lord hath told thee that he will build thee a house . . . "I will set up thy seed after thee . . . and I will establish the throne of his kingdom for ever. I will be to him for a father, and he shall be to me for a son".'

'He' is the Scion of David who will function alongside of the Expounder of the Law, i.e. the man who will expound [it] aright at the end of days, even as the scripture says, 'I will raise up the tabernacle of David that is fallen down' That tabernacle denotes the Law [Torah] which has fallen into neglect. Subsequently, however, [that man] will arise to bring salvation to Israel.

S U M M A R Y

A COVER-UP ON THE SCROLLS?

11 Caves, 200 manuscripts covering:
- every OT book (not Esther).
- fragment of James' Epistle.
- Essene commentaries.
- Essenes described by Origen AD 185–254.

Not a cover-up by the Church. Clerics and scholars rescued them, e.g.:
- Yigel Yadin significance, son of Prof Sukenik.
- Yadin quotes 'Assumption of Moses' which instructs scroll preservation. Also Jer 32:14.
- Syrian Orthodox Archbishop.
- American Oriental School of Research.
- John Trevor sent photo of Isaiah to Dr W.F. Albright.
- Prof Sukenik bought three scrolls for University of Jerusalem the day State of Israel created.

Cover-up was by sceptics:
- They misrepresented them before they had been read.
- Critic A's dope accusation. Later challenged by Yadin, Vermes and Carpenter.
- Critic W 14 years later confessed to sensational inaccuracy.
- Geza Vermes and Albright correct false statements of others as 'emotive' and say 'not affected Bible message'.
- Supported accuracy of copying.
- Millar Burrows, Dead Sea Scrolls expert, agrees.
- Demolishes 'second' Isaiah theory. God proves he is God by foretelling Cyrus and Exile. Josephus agrees.
- An Australian writer in 1992 probably misinterprets Hosea's experiences as reference to Christ.

Essenes did not invent Christ, neither did Jesus get his ideas from them.
- They were quoting Old Testament prophecies describing Christ.
- 'The Son of Man' from Dan 7:13.
- 'Teacher of Righteousness' from Deut 18:15–19, etc.
- 'He is to judge the world and save elect and divide between sons of darkness and sons of light', from Dan 12:2,10 and Joel, Isaiah, Ezekiel, Zechariah.
- 'The New Covenant' from Jer 31:31–34.

14

JOSEPHUS AND HIS HISTORICAL RECORD
EVIDENCE OF THE FALL OF JERUSALEM

Have you noticed that often God gets a man of the world to record the fulfilment of prophecy? Nearly 2,000 years ago, Josephus wrote a detailed history which showed how Christ's prophecies were fulfilled. Imagine the scene as recorded by Josephus the eye witness.

James Executed

Jews were gathered in huge crowds in Jerusalem. They whispered to each other in hushed tones. A foreboding of ill darkened the brow of every Israelite. It is AD 63, that is over 30 years since the Lord Jesus Christ foretold the events about to happen. Imagine one Israelite voicing his fears:

'The high priest Ananias has executed James! To slaughter such a good man is bound to bring disaster.' The crowds murmur agreement.

'Which James is this?' asks a visitor to the city. 'I thought James the brother of John was killed 20 years ago – killed by that tyrant King Herod.'

'No, this other James was the half-brother of Jesus Christ. He was head of the church in Jerusalem and was also widely respected. He was venerated by all the Jews, not only by the Christians. In fact, James tried to keep both together, all the Jews whether Christian or not. Even his Epistle he addressed to all of us, not the Christians only. He addressed it to all the twelve tribes. He hung on to the hope that the big split between Jew and Christian would never come. He emphasised holy living like his brother – well, they suppose it's his brother – Jesus, whom he had grown up with all his life. His Epistle is an echo of his brother's Sermon on the Mount. It urges us to have beautiful characters like that he had seen in his brother right from childhood.'

The visitor interrupts. 'Could he find no fault in Jesus then, even from boyhood?'

'No, and the Jerusalem Jews could not fault James either. They absolutely adored him. They thought he was a real saint. Even Josephus, our national historian, concedes that. Only the ambitious high priest hated him and now he has seized the opportunity. The Roman Procurator, Festus, died. We are waiting for a new governor in his place. In this absence of authority, the high priest arrested James and killed him.'

The visitor would watch the Jews wailing and throwing earth on their heads. How strange that James, a Christian, should be so venerated and mourned by everybody.

'Doom will come upon us,' wailed the crowds. 'Our arbitrator of peace has perished. He kept the factions together. Did he not write: "Wisdom which is from above is first pure, then peaceable, gentle, open to reason, full of mercy and good fruits . . . the harvest of righteousness is sown in peace by those who make peace".'

A man stands up and shouts, 'What James the Just said would happen will happen now. He wrote, "The cries of defrauded labourers have reached the ears of the Lord of Hosts . . . the coming of the Lord is at hand. Behold the Judge is standing at the door." Jerusalem would be destroyed. Woe upon us. Lord have mercy!'

God did have mercy on those who obeyed Christ's prophecies. They escaped before the Roman invasion shattered the land.

Florus Provokes the Jews

Did you know that King Agrippa and Queen Bernice of Acts chapter 25 figure in historical writings? Did Paul's testimony to King Agrippa and his queen have any good effect on them?

'Almost you persuade me to be a Christian,' replied Agrippa to Paul. Perhaps it almost persuaded Queen Bernice as well. We learn from three historians of Paul's day that Bernice was only a teenager, aged 19 years, but already she had married three times. She had married, but had forsaken two kings before she married Agrippa, who was her brother, so she was a sister-wife.

Did Paul's testimony soften her attitude to people? Josephus says that she went to the wicked Roman governor to plead for Jews who were being massacred in the temple market. She did it at the risk of her own life. Who was the Roman governor? His name was Florus. He had been appointed by Nero and it was he who whipped up Jewish rebellion by his outrageous greed. Josephus tells you that 'he marched hastily with an army of horsemen and foot soldiers into Jerusalem and called out aloud to the soldiers to plunder the upper-market place' and to kill men, women and children, to steal their goods; 3,600 were murdered that day.

It was then that Bernice came to the wicked Florus barefooted to plead for the Jews. The governor Florus took no notice. He was greedy and coveted the rich temple treasures and the next day made a plot.

Let us imagine a worshipper telling you what happened. 'We were bringing our money, our tithes, to put into the collection boxes and to bring our sacrifices. Thousands of us were quietly waiting for the procession of the priests and musicians.

'The silver trumpets sounded and out came hundreds of priests carrying the golden sacred cups and vessels and ornamental vestments. There followed the huge orchestra with the harps and musical instruments and then an enormous choir. I had been noticing hundreds of strange men in cloaks. Suddenly, they threw their cloaks aside. They were Florus' soldiers with swords. They rushed at us worshippers, trampling us down and killing many. They wrenched our money from us and stole the treasury boxes and the golden holy chalices. Thousands of us were killed. I escaped by pretending to be dead.'

'Did not the Army commander at Caesarea protest?'

'Yes, he did, but that liar Florus told him that it happened because he was putting down a rebellion. It was nothing of the sort! He was robbing the temple of its riches.'

It was this ruthless robbery and sacrilege which sparked off the war of the Jews with Rome and the destruction of the temple and Jerusalem.

Listen again to what Jesus said. If Israel had accepted Jesus as Saviour, it would have been avoided. That applies also to my nation and yours. Restoration comes from revival.

Agrippa and Bernice Weep

When Paul gave his testimony before King Agrippa and Queen Bernice in Acts 26, he did not know that soon the royal couple would witness that tragedy.

The historian Josephus tells how Agrippa and Bernice wept. The Jews had rushed to tell them of the slaughter that Florus had plotted in order to rob the temple and worshippers of their riches.

Josephus says, 'Both Agrippa and Bernice wept' when they heard the news 'and by their tears repressed a great deal of the violence threatened by the people in revenge'.

'Tell Nero that it was Florus who began this violence,' the people shouted. 'We would not fight against the Romans but against your governor Florus!'

King Agrippa pleaded, 'But that would still look like war against the Romans, for you have not paid the taxes due to Caesar, and you have besieged the Roman garrison! Don't pay taxes to Florus, pay them to Rome!'

But this did not satisfy the furious mob. They burnt the palace of Agrippa and Bernice and massacred the Roman soldiers in the local Jerusalem garrison. They captured their weapons – 300 dart-throwing machines and 50 heavy catapults.

THE OMINOUS YEAR OF AD 66

News of this reached the Roman general Cestius and he marched his troops to within six miles of Jerusalem and encamped. The furious Jews attacked the camp suddenly and scattered many soldiers, but the swerving manoeuvres of the horsemen put the Jews to flight and Cestius pursued them to Jerusalem.

Soon the rhythm of military feet could be heard in Jerusalem. The earth trembled at the rumbling of heavy catapult machines; the air carried the neighing of hundreds of horses, then the smell of their manure reached the nostrils of the citizens. Cestius surrounded Jerusalem for five days and his troops battered at the walls. Even the Christians in the city were apprehensive. Had not Luke recorded the words of Jesus years earlier, 13 years before in AD 53? It warned the Christians to evacuate Jerusalem when armies surrounded it. (Matthew and Mark had not recorded that bit about the armies.) What did it mean? How could they escape if armies were all around the walls?

The deep valleys around the east, south and west of Jerusalem made the walls impossible to attack, so Cestius attacked from the north. The Christians wondered even more how they could obey Christ and escape. They watched as Cestius demolished part of the northern wall. But the counter-attacks by the Jewish factions were so fierce and fanatical that General Cestius decided that he needed more troops from Rome, so he ordered a retreat and withdrew back to Caesarea.

Josephus then adds these significant words: 'He (General Cestius) retired from the city, without any reason in the world.'

But there was a reason! Can you guess it? Jesus had prophesied to the believers, 'When you see Jerusalem surrounded by armies, then know that its destruction is near. Then let those who are in Judea fly to the mountains, let those who are inside the city depart, and let not those who are out in the country enter the city.' This particular warning was recorded only by Luke.

Josephus says, 'The Jews, after they had beaten General Cestius, were greatly encouraged by their unexpected success.' But he says, 'After this calamity had befallen General Cestius, many of the most eminent of the Jews swam away from the city as if from a ship when it was going to sink.' Who were these people?

It is Hegessippus, another historian, who tells us that those who forsook the city were the Christians. They read an oracle left by Christ. Now what oracle was that? It was recorded only in Luke's Gospel. Here is evidence that Luke wrote well before AD 66. Indeed, Luke's Gospel had been written 13 years earlier.

Do you look at world events and see them 'without any reason in the world' or do you ponder the words of Christ who says, 'If only you had known that this was your fatal hour and repented, but you would not, and so now you are left desolate'?

Imagine a Christian family inside Jerusalem. The father reads Luke 21:19: 'In your patience, possess your souls.' 'That means keep your heads,' says a son. Father nods and reads on: 'When you see Jerusalem surrounded by armies, know that destruction is near. Let those in the province of Judea escape to the mountains and those in the city evacuate it and don't return.'

'The Lord has spoken,' says the mother. 'We must not only evacuate Jerusalem, but migrate even outside the country. Look, the words of Jesus are so precise!'

'Oh no!' cry the children.

'We must obey Jesus,' said Father, 'otherwise we shall perish. Jesus said so in Luke's Gospel.'

History tells us why. Although the Zealots thought they had victory, the Christians knew better and evacuated the whole country. They took refuge in the Mountains of Pella, east of the Jordan River. It was well that they did, as we shall see.

Woe unto Bethsaida!

The fall of Jerusalem itself was three-and-a-half years later in AD 70, so why must Christians flee the whole country so early?

It is that contemporary historian Josephus who again reveals the reason. The tyrant Nero was so furious at the humiliation of General Cestius and his troops that Nero raved. 'The whole of Jewry must be wiped out,' he shouted. 'The demolition must start in the north in Galilee and work down southward through the country until the armies reach Jerusalem.

Had not Nero already executed Paul by the sword – that impudent leader who would dare to suggest that there was another ruler to whom he must bow – Jesus Christ? Was he not from Galilee? That was a hotbed of hot-headed Zealots anyway!

So Nero's foremost commanders were sent. They were General Vespasian and his military son, Titus. Can you imagine Nero stamping around his palace in a rage? 'I'll show them!' he would shout. 'Who is King around here! I'll wipe out this Galilean! I'll wipe out Galilee itself.'

And where did they start? Josephus tells you. In the north, in Bethsaida and Chorazim, in Capernaum of Galilee. Little did Nero know that he was fulfilling the very words of that same despised Nazarene:

Woe unto you Chorazim! Woe unto you Bethsaida, for if the mighty miracles I did in you had been done in Tyre and Sidon, they would have repented long ago. And you, Capernaum, proud and exalted up to heaven, shall be brought down to hell, for if my mighty miracles done in you, had been done in Sodom, the Sodom sinners would have been spared.

The Christians reading these words in Matthew's Gospel, would realise that they had fled the whole country just in time. Great Roman armies were marching up to the north, led by the famous generals, Vespasian and Titus. Messengers from the area brought the shocking news to the Christian refugees in the Mountains of Pella, east of Jordan. Truly Rome meant business.

How graphically the warnings of Jesus were being fulfilled! The Christians already had Matthew and Mark's Gospels which recorded his words against Capernaum, Bethsaida and Chorazim. How realistically was it to be shown that people's spiritual response had political and military consequences! How many wars would have been avoided if whole populations had repented and believed the gospel?

THE WARS OF THE JEWS

Imagine a Christian family living in Judea, halfway between Galilee in the north and Jerusalem to the south. 'Surely, we'll be safe here!' the wife and children would wail.

'No,' replies the father, 'Jesus said fly to the mountains. We must pack all we can on the donkeys and carts and make for the mountains of Pella on the other side of Jordan.'

All the towns around the Lake of Galilee were now a burning heap of ruins. What was once the most thickly populated area of Palestine was a scene of desolation. The smoke ascended to the skies and the inhabitants were either massacred or dragged off into slavery.

Methodically, the Roman armies moved south town by town, village by village, wiping them out one by one. The horrifying details are described by the historian Josephus. 'These are the days of vengeance', just as Jesus had foretold.

Christ's call to his nation to repent was not popular. It never is popular for a Christian to urge his own nation to fear the judgment, to fear hell and to turn to Christ.

It is not popular, yet Jesus did it out of kindness. He knew that when people fear judgment day and begin to live God-centred lives, they can avert calamity. The overruling authority of God can change the whole situation.

A society full of crimes and murders can become a happy prosperous community. The history of the Jews proves this, and so does the history of your own country and mine.

A Tax Collector's Terrible Warning

Recorded history proves the Gospels' accuracy. Imagine this conversation.

'We are Christians from Capernaum. We were well-known to Matthew 40 years ago because he was the government tax collector. He knew all about us too, because we were on his tax lists. The Roman tax collectors were expected to write down our dues in our native tongue and then to translate them into Greek to report to Rome. Yes, he knew all about the change in our lives when we followed Christ.'

But here is Matthew. Let's ask him.

'What about the change in your life, Matthew, when Jesus said to you, "Follow me!" You did not give up your note-taking, did you? You adapted it to taking notes of all that Jesus said and taught. Now tell us Matthew, did Jesus warn us that a calamity would fall on Capernaum? You must have that in your notes, especially as you lived in Capernaum.'

Matthew unrolled his notebook and said, 'Jesus did indeed warn Capernaum of the consequences of rejecting Christ's salvation. Here are his words. I wrote them down in Aramaic as he said them. "You, Capernaum, proud and exalted up to heaven, shall be brought down to hell, for if my mighty miracles done in you had been done in Sodom, Sodom would have repented and been spared." '

We can imagine another saying to Matthew, 'Jesus also warned the other towns around the lake of Galilee – Chorazim and Bethsaida.'

'What did he say? We are from Bethsaida. Let us see his words you have written down in this Aramaic dialect which Jesus spoke.'

'Here,' Matthew replies, pointing to his original notes.

'Woe unto you Chorazim! Woe unto you Bethsaida! For if the mighty miracles I did in you had been done in Tyre and Sidon, they would have repented long ago.'

The listeners pale with alarm. One shouts, 'The judgment is coming. Rome's strongest armies are marching up to us. Can it be true that we must do what Luke's Gospel tells – fly from the whole country, or is there time for us to urge Capernaum to repent? If we repent, could God stop Rome's military might?'

'The prophets say he can,' says Matthew. 'Jeremiah said 580 years ago, before Jerusalem was destroyed, that God could stop even the armies of Babylon already on the march, if the Jews repented. Our God is all-powerful. He can overrule even military movements.'

Stopped by Prayer?

Can prayer stop the world's greatest armies? Listen to the evidence of history.

Josephus, the historian, tells us how mighty were the forces that Rome sent to wipe out Israel. As he was a military commander himself, he had first-hand experience of all he recorded. He tells you that there were three legions – the 5th, 10th and 15th. These were accompanied by 31 cohorts, 6,000 archers and thousands of horsemen. The total army numbered 60,000.

In his prophecy, Jesus was worried that such a massive army might attack Jerusalem in winter. What could stop them? 'Prayer,' said the Lord. 'Pray that your flight from Jerusalem may not be in the severity of winter. Alas for mothers with babies.'

But this army reached Jerusalem in the winter. In the three years from AD 66, they devastated the whole country north of Jerusalem.

Josephus writes, 'Vespasian was returning to Caesarea and getting ready with all his army to march directly to Jerusalem.' How would you feel if you were living in Jerusalem?

Let's imagine one receiving news of the Roman forces. He says, 'What can we do to stop this mighty invasion in winter?' What a help it is to have the advice of Jesus written in the two Gospels, Matthew and Mark. What was that advice? Here it is in Matthew 24:20. 'Pray that your escape be not in winter or on a Sabbath day.'

Some people in the city must have prayed very hard. Imagine their agonised prayers. Then the news came through, 'The invasion has been halted!' Josephus tells you why: 'Vespasian was informed that Nero was dead, therefore he put off (delayed) his expedition against Jerusalem.'

'Thank God!' the Christians would cry. 'Thank God as well that Matthew wrote Christ's words during his ministry, and Mark wrote down Peter's memoirs. That was 25 years ago now, so that we all knew them and knew what to do. But what did Jesus mean by saying, "Pray that your flight be not on a Sabbath?" Does that have a significance we have yet to see?'

Vespasian, the New Emperor

When news reached the Roman army in Palestine that Nero had died, they all proclaimed Vespasian to be the next emperor of Rome. So Vespasian departed for Rome, and left his son Titus to attack Jerusalem.

Titus now waited for the spring, the time of the Passover. Perhaps it was the Passover which drew some of the traditional Christians back to the capital. Furthermore, the rebels in Jerusalem mistook this lull for a change of plans, so they renewed their attacks on one another.

Simon the brigand had 15,000 rebels, John the Zealot had 8,500 Zealot fighters and Eleazor, the high priest, led a faction to protect the temple from the rebels and Zealots. All these started fighting each other again, also killing innocent citizens. Josephus says, 'They even burnt the corn which would have enabled Jerusalem to withstand a siege for many years. That was so that their rival faction could not get it. They even continued fighting each other as the Roman troops were arriving to attack Jerusalem.'

At the time of unleavened bread, Eleazar opened the gates of the inmost court for the worshippers, but John's Zealots crept in with them, their armour covered by cloaks. They then beat and killed and trampled the worshippers to death.

During these disasters inside Jerusalem, Titus' army had levelled all the area between Mount Scopus and the city walls. They took only four days to do this. It was then that the Christians in the city realised what Christ's prophecy meant: 'When you see the desecration, don't wait for the Sabbath, don't even go down into your houses to collect goods, make your escape immediately. Jump from rooftop to rooftop.'

The sign of the sacrilege by the Zealots had just been committed. Tomorrow was the Passover Sabbath, so the Christians jumped from rooftop to rooftop and over the walls.

They were the last to escape. Titus having levelled the ground, now closed in on the city. His army was posted seven deep all around to stop any escape. Josephus says they were a nation of three million people sealed off as in a prison. Over a million had come up for the feast.

Truly the warning by Christ was fulfilled. When he wept over the city, he said, 'If only you had known and accepted me, it would have ensured your peace, but the days will come when your enemies will build up banks around you, and hem you in on every side, because you did not recognise your opportunity of my visit to you' (Luke 19:42–44).

That is true for all people who fail to accept Christ. Don't blame the Jews. Jesus said to us in Luke 13, 'Do you think they were worse sinners than all the others? I tell you, no, for unless you repent, you will all likewise perish.'

THE FALL OF JERUSALEM

How literally were the words of Christ fulfilled about the fall of Jerusalem. All those who read his words in Matthew, Mark and Luke and obeyed them escaped. When Jerusalem fell in flames and blood, not one Christian who obeyed Christ's words was there.

Christ's words were in those three Gospels and in circulation years before and thoroughly read: Matthew, 30 years earlier; Mark, 25 years earlier; and Luke, 16 years earlier.

How literally Titus fulfilled Christ's prophecy. His army carted earth and wood from 11 miles around Jerusalem. With it, he built rows of encircling banks and even three towers 75 feet high from which to

shoot missiles into the city. Citizens gazed out in fear to see the surrounding legions on every side, foot soldiers in front, archers behind
them and the horsemen in the rear.

Simon, the brigand in the city, had 340 catapult engines mounted on
the walls to fire stones and darts at them, but they were beyond range.
Read again that accurate prophecy of Christ in Luke 19:43. He wept
over the city and said, 'Your enemies will cast up a bank around you,
surround you and hem you in on every side, and dash you to the ground
. . . and will not leave one stone upon another.'

Inside the city, the factions continued to slaughter priests and people until there were none to offer the daily sacrifice.

The sacrifice ceased just as Daniel 9:27 had prophesied. No sacrifice has ever been offered since to this day. History testifies that the
sacrifice of Jesus was sufficient for all times.

Eventually, the Romans battered their way in through the temple
end. The temple gates went up in flames. Titus ordered the temple not
to be burnt, but the soldiers were so infuriated that they fired the temple. A great groan went up from the Jews as they saw their precious
golden, jewelled temple burnt to the ground. Nearly three million Jews
died; 1,100,000 who went up for the feast never returned. Titus was
shocked to see all the valleys around Jerusalem filled with rotting bodies.

Caesar ordered the demolition of the whole city. Oxen and ploughs
harrowed over the rubble, just as the prophet Micah had foretold. Only
the western wall and towers were left standing. No wonder Jesus wept
over the city 40 years before. Forty years in which to hear the gospel
and repent.

How long has God given for your nation and mine to repent and
believe in Jesus? Only a gospel revival saves and uplifts a nation from
corruption.

Is God's hand behind history? Why do you think Josephus wrote
such a detailed eyewitness history of the fall of Jerusalem in AD 70?

If you have formed a habit of looking for God's hand behind history, you will see that God provided this man, who was not a Christian,
to witness that Christ's prophecies were fulfilled. Jesus described
beforehand all the details of what would happen before his generation
died. Josephus recorded the fulfilment.

With such graphic details, how are we to know that the words of
Jesus were not written after the event? We must answer that question
because sceptics have suggested it.

The reason that Jesus made the prophecies was to forewarn the
Christians to escape before the judgment of God fell. We know that the

Gospels have the genuine words of Jesus because the Christians did escape. So the warnings of Jesus were known long beforehand. For both stages, Jesus said, 'Escape!' and many did.

Evidence in Rome

The Lord Jesus prophesied that after the fall of Jerusalem, 'They shall be led away captive into all nations' (Luke 21:24).

Josephus again unknowingly records his eye-witness account of the fulfilment of Christ's words. He gives detailed figures which showed that nearly three million Jews perished and 97,000 were taken away as prisoners. Here are Josephus' words: 'Of the young men [Titus] chose out the tallest and most beautiful, and reserved them for the march of triumph (in Rome later).'

There is still a carved panel in Rome on the Arch of Triumph. It shows Rome actually celebrating that victory. The Roman soldiers are depicted carrying the seven-branched lampstand from the temple. All the details of that lampstand are exactly as described in Exodus 25 in the time of Moses, nearly 3,500 years ago.

Now to return to Josephus' description, he continues, ' . . . as for the rest of the multitude, those who were about 17 years of age, he put into chains, and sent them to the Egyptian mines. Titus also sent a huge number into the provinces as a present to them; but those who were under 17 years of age, he sold for slaves.'

Doesn't it tear your heart to think of them! And those Jews who were captured in the countryside beforehand were also led as slaves into captivity. No wonder Jesus was distressed when he prophesied, 'Alas, for there shall be great distress in the land, and wrath upon this people; and they shall fall by the edge of the sword, and shall be led away captive into all nations.'

The Times of the Gentiles

But thank God, that is not the end of the story. Jesus said 'Until' – that important word. It was only to be until. Until what? 'Until the times of the Gentiles are fulfilled.'

Q What is meant by 'the times of the Gentiles'?

If you read all the Scriptures, you will find it means all the centuries since Christ during which Gentile rulers have governed Jerusalem. The exciting thing is this, that Gentile rule ended in 1967. In 1967 the Israelis entered and governed the old city of Jerusalem for the first time since Jesus uttered those words. (In Volume 3: Prophecy, I will give you many more amazing details.)

Now, whatever you think of the situation today in Jerusalem, and whether it is right or wrong, doesn't alter the fact that the Lord Jesus Christ said that such a happening is a sign that his second coming is near. He will descend from heaven to judge the world. But first he will come for his own. I do hope and pray that you belong to him.

Figure 14.1. Romans carrying the seven-branched golden lampstand, part of the spoil from Jerusalem (bas-relief on the Arch of Titus, Rome). Note its design. It is exactly as recorded by Moses 1,500 years earlier in Exodus 25:31. This demonstrates the accuracy of Exodus writings.

SUMMARY

JOSEPHUS' HISTORY

1. **Jewish non-Christian** wrote history for Romans as observer.
   - His record showed how Christ's prophecies were fulfilled, AD 66–70.
   - High priest Ananias executed James when Festus died.
   - Festus also features in Acts 25 and 26.
   - King Agrippa and Queen Bernice in Acts also figure in history.
   - Florus slew 3,600 Jewish worshippers to steal treasure: this sparked revolt.
   - Mob massacred Roman garrison and took their war machines.

2. **Cestius** surrounded Jerusalem in AD 66.
   - Luke, 13 years earlier, recorded this (21:20,21) as the sign to flee whole country. Josephus said certain ones fled.
   - Jesus knew this would start three-and-a-half years' war over the whole land.
   - Bethsaida, Chorazim, Capernaum would suffer. 'Woe unto you', wrote Capernaum's converted tax collector, Matt 24:20.

3. **Vespasian and Titus** in winter of AD 69 prepare attack on Jerusalem.
   - 'Pray that your flight be not in winter.'
   - Campaign postponed. Nero had died.
   - Rebel Zealots and temple guard renewed in-fighting.

4. **Titus marched up as Passover approached.**
   - Sacrilege committed by Zealots warned remaining Christians to flee.
   - Jesus had wept 'Your enemies will make a bank and hem you in'.
   - 3 million Jews were trapped.
   - Sacrifices ceased for ever as Dan 9:27 prophesied. None necessary after Christ's sacrifice, Heb 10:1–22.

5. **'Captives into all nations'** Lk 21:24
   - Titus sent best young men for march of triumph.
   - Depicted on Rome's ancient Arch of Triumph with the seven-branched lampstand of Exodus 25.
   - 17-year-olds sent in chains to Egyptian mines.
   - Under 17-year-olds sold as slaves around the empire.

6. **'Until Gentile rule ends in Jerusalem'** Lk 21
   It ended in 1967 with Israel back in Jerusalem city.

15 THE BIBLE SPEAKS FOR ITSELF
ACCURACY OF THE NEW TESTAMENT

New Testament means new covenant. That there would be a new covenant was anticipated by Moses (Deuteronomy 18:18,19), and Jeremiah 31:31 says, 'Behold, the days are coming, saith the Lord, that I will make a new covenant with the house of Israel and with the house of Judah.'

We come now to the remarkable story of the inspiration and preservation of the New Testament. 'God, who in times past by various means at different times spoke unto us by the prophets', has finally 'spoken unto us by his Son whom he appointed heir of all things, by whom also he made the worlds' (Hebrews 1).

'Heaven and earth shall pass away,' said Jesus, 'but my words shall never pass away.' The words of the Saviour will actually judge each one of us when we appear before God for reckoning (John 12:48). Like the Highway Code, it is an additional offence not to have read and understood them.

The New Testament falls into three sections – Historical Section (Fourfold Gospel and Acts), the Letters of Paul and the Letters of other Apostles.

HISTORICAL SECTION – FOURFOLD GOSPEL

The life, death and resurrection of Jesus are so important for our salvation that a fourfold account is given. They all purport to be either written by eye-witnesses or taken down from eye-witnesses. It would be remarkable if having made preparation throughout the pages and history of the Old Testament, God had not made provision for a reliable record of the climax in his Son. Luke writes in his prologue:

Whereas many have taken in hand to set forth in order a declaration of those things which are most surely believed among us, even as they delivered them unto us, who from the beginning were eyewitnesses, and ministers of the word; it seemed good to me also, having had perfect understanding of all things from the very first, to write unto you in order, most excellent Theophilus, that you might know the certainty of those things wherein you have been instructed.

'I saw all this myself,' wrote St John, 'and have given an accurate report so that you also can believe. The soldiers did this in fulfilment [unknowingly] of the [Old Testament] Scripture that says, "Not one of his bones shall be broken" and "They shall look on him whom they pierced"' (John 19:35, Living Bible).

In spite of such assurances, there are those who, while never questioning secular classics which have only a third of the evidence for their veracity, ask cynically, 'Yea, hath God said?' like the serpent of old. An instance of their scepticism being proved wrong is John's mention of 'The Pavement' in chapter 19. They said this never existed because no other historian had referred to it. It has now been unearthed eight feet below the present surface. It had been covered up ever since AD 70 at the fall of Jerusalem.

The Real Jesus

Can the ordinary person be certain that Jesus really is as portrayed in the Gospels and Epistles?

Michael Green of Oxford (former Principal of St John's College, Nottingham) in an article on the Real Jesus, tells us he is exactly as portrayed in the Gospels and Epistles. This was to counter the assumption of one Bible critic who described himself as an atheist priest(!), and who has been widely featured on television. He claimed that the Gospels reflected the later-developed thought of the Church of the second century. In so thinking, he accepted the assumptions of the German Tübingen school of over a century ago, before we had as much documentary evidence as now.

Can the ordinary churchman decide whether his faith is well founded upon what he reads in his New Testament, i.e. whether the accounts are factual or whether theology has changed the image of a naturally-born prophet into a divine Son of God, who was conceived miraculously and resurrected miraculously? He can, because the text itself tells us the principles which governed their writing.

We will analyse Luke's statement about his methods in his prologue both to his Gospel and the Acts. He declares:

1. That he obtained his information from eye-witnesses.
2. That he had complete understanding from the first.
3. That he wrote in order of events.
4. That many others he knew had written down their experiences.
5. That there were many infallible proofs of the whole life and miracles of Jesus.

We conclude from this that Luke's object was to record events as they happened, not as embellished by non-eye-witnesses in the second century.

Luke had three great opportunities to collect his eye-witness reports for his Gospel and Acts. John Wenham points out that Luke was absent according to the Acts of the Apostles between AD 51 and 56. He suggests Paul refers to Luke's Gospel in the second letter to the Corinthians written in AD 56, 'whose fame is in the gospel' (2 Corinthians 8:18). So Luke could have written his Gospel as early as AD 54. His next opportunity was Paul's imprisonment in AD 57 in the garrison where Peter had rehearsed his Gospel eight years earlier to Cornelius. Many had already written anecdotes of Jesus (Luke 1:1). Luke also had access to Philip's four prophetic daughters who had first-hand information according to early church writers (Acts 21:8,9), and Paul knew of 500 living who had seen Christ after his resurrection (1 Corinthians 15). Luke then wrote his sequel, the Acts of the Apostles, up to date in AD 62.

We can therefore have the reassurance of ample evidence that the Gospels were written early enough to come from living witnesses, and so were not later records of myth and legend.

Clues to Dates of Writing

Professor F.F. Bruce of Manchester University has pointed out (*New Testament Documents*, IVP, 1979) that a clue to the date of the completion of St Luke's Gospel is the date of the end of Acts which is a sequel to it. It is obvious that Acts ends unfinished. It was written up to date. Paul was a prisoner in Rome awaiting trial before Nero. If it was written after that trial in AD 62 or after the second trial and execution in AD 64, Luke would surely have recorded it. We can safely conclude then that Acts was written before AD 62 and Luke's Gospel a reasonable time before that.

What testimony have we to Matthew and Mark? A Christian writing as early as AD 100 was a disciple of St John. His name is Papias, yet his information is ignored by many scholars.

Concerning Mark's Gospel, Papias says that Mark was Peter's companion and 'wrote down accurately all that Peter mentioned, whether sayings or doings of Christ . . . for he paid attention to this one thing, not to omit anything that he heard, nor to include any false statements.'

So the inference is that it came from Peter's own lips, recorded by Mark. So accuracy can again be claimed. The accounts are represented as factual and neither fictional nor even a theological embellishment of later church thought.

Of Matthew's Gospel, Papias said, 'Matthew compiled the sayings in the Hebrew Aramaic tongue (the language of Jesus) and everyone translated them as best he could.' Now, it is significant that it is in Matthew's Gospel that we have the longest sections of 'sayings'. We shall see later how it is probable that Matthew, who was used to recording for Rome as a tax collector, continued his note-taking when he followed Jesus.

Dr F.F. Bruce says that 'it can be shown that one and the same Aramaic original underlies the variant Greek renderings in the first three Gospels'.

Dr B. Chilton of Sheffield University, in a most scholarly article ('Profiles of a Rabbi', Atlanta, 1989), demonstrated how the actual Aramaic words of Jesus underlay the three Greek-varying translations of a verse by the synoptists, Matthew, Mark and Luke. The verse contains the words of Jesus before the transfiguration about the kingdom of God coming in power (Matthew 16:28; Mark 9:1; Luke 9:27). This again testifies to the record being factual rather than an attempt by later thought to put into the mouth of Jesus what was an evolution of church thought.

It would seem that the materialist mind will go to all lengths to avoid confrontation with the real Jesus – the miracle-working, truth-speaking Son of God, faithfully recorded by honest writers.

Was John's Gospel Written before AD 70?

St John adds another dimension to the word-portrait. Can we judge whether it is idealised or actual? In answer, we note that John also states his objects and methods. He declares:

1. That he was an eye-witness and closest companion: 'I saw all this myself,' he said, 'and have given an accurate report so that you can believe' (19:35);
2. He affirms the absolute truth and accuracy of his writing;
3. He wished to convince his readers of the Messiahship and deity of Jesus (20:31);
4. The writer was the disciple closest to Jesus (21:20–24);
5. His Gospel was intended to be supplementary. It can be shown from what John omits and includes that he had the Synoptists before him.

St John records Christ's promise to bring back to his memory all that Jesus had said (14:26). It was thought that John wrote in his old age, but Dr John Robinson challenges this, showing that the Gospel must have been written before AD 70. He says that the Judaistic type of Christianity was utterly shattered by the wars of AD 66–70. There is no sign of this in John's Gospel: 'One of the oddest facts about the New Testament is that the single most datable and climactic event of the period – the fall of Jerusalem AD 70, and with it the collapse of institutional Judaism based on the Temple – is never once mentioned as a past fact' – it is only predicted.

As with C.F.D. Moule, 'It was hard to believe that a Judaistic type of Christianity would not have shown the scars' in writings after AD 70.

For example, the threat of excommunication mentioned eight times in the New Testament would not apply after the crash of Judaism. Far from it being second-century developed thought, it would not even have had post-AD 70 relevance.

The Pool of Bethesda is written of as existing at the time of writing; after AD 70, it was hidden under 15–40 feet of rubble and only rediscovered in recent years. Similar topographical notes give support.

Furthermore, a comparison with the Dead Sea Scrolls shows John's Gospel to be pre-Gnostic in language according to Reiche; and Dr J. Schonfield, the Dead Sea Scrolls expert, thinks that dialect changes reveal that all the Gospels were written within 25 years of the crucifixion. Obviously, if John wrote to supplement Matthew, Mark and Luke, the latter three, called the Synoptics, were written even earlier.

The Significance of Jesus' Prophecy of Jerusalem's Fall

Jesus warned Christians about the coming destruction. This must have been broadcast well in advance in order to make escape possible. Dr J. Robinson agrees that it must have been written down beforehand, otherwise certain wording would have been coloured by knowledge after the event; e.g. Matthew does not mention that sacrifices ceased forever. Yet this appears in Daniel's prophecy to which he alluded (Daniel 9:27). He would certainly have alluded to this staggering blow to fourteen centuries of Jewish sacrifices, and inferred that the cross had superseded them.

> Critics are very free with accusations that the Gospel writers fraudulently wrote history after the event as if it were a prophecy before the event.

If we can show that the Christians actually did flee on recognising the prophet's sign, then we prove that the prophecy was genuine. This we can show through two historians outside the New Testament who gave a full record.

It is not realised by most scholars that Jesus made two prophecies of two separate events. Hitherto, critics thought that the Gospel writers confused reports of the same event. The first was the sign to flee the country before the wars of the Jews started in AD 66, the other immediately before the actual fall of Jerusalem AD 70. Luke records the first and Mark and Matthew record the second, and both are testified to by independent historians.

So the first sign was that Jerusalem would be surrounded by

Roman armies as recorded by Luke 21:20. As we saw in the previous chapter, this was fulfilled in AD 66 when the commander Cestius surrounded Jerusalem to quell the rioting Jewish Zealots. Cestius did not know that the victory was his and in the words of Josephus, the contemporary historian, Cestius withdrew 'for no reason in the world'. Jesus had foretold the reason! It was to enable the Christians to escape. 'Many distinguished Jews abandoned the city as swimmers desert a sinking ship' wrote Josephus. 'They were commanded by an oracle given before the war,' said Hegessippus, the other historian.

The remainder did not flee, but rejoiced at the unexpected relief. The Christians, we are told, escaped to Pella which was on the east side of Jordan. Thus they obeyed the Lord in fleeing not only from Jerusalem, but also from the surrounding provinces. 'Stay not in Judaea or in the country,' Jesus had said (Luke 21:21).

The reason for this was soon to be seen. Nero sent Vespasian and Titus to commence a three-and-a-half year war on the Jews starting in Galilee, where Jesus commenced his ministry, and ending at Jerusalem, where Jesus gave the nation its last chance, at the Passover.

So within that generation, as Jesus had warned, the nation was judged at the same places over the same time period of three-and-a-half years, during which Jesus implored those areas to repent and believe the gospel.

The second sign was the abomination in the sacred temple. This sign was recorded by Matthew (24:15–18) and Mark (13:14–16). The Lord urged the need of speedy escape from Jerusalem. They were to jump from housetop to housetop to get out in time which even in the Jerusalem of today is a credibly quick way to travel. The memoirs of Hegessippus tell of the fulfilment. Titus reached Jerusalem when it was crammed with pilgrims up for the Passover – perhaps many Christians had returned for the feast, too.

We have seen how the Zealots committed a terrible sacrilege in the temple. This sign was recognised and the Christians fled. Within hours, Titus closed in on the city and not one escaped after that. Eventually all, except youths taken for slavery, were crucified around the walls of Jerusalem. The Romans had put up earth barricades all around to prevent escape (Luke 19:41–44).

Jesus had said, 'Pray that your flight be not in the winter.' Josephus tells us how Vespasian and Titus were preparing to assault Jerusalem in the winter, but were halted by news of Nero's unexpected death. Vespasian was proclaimed Emperor and returned to Rome.

Also as foretold by Jesus, the Romans completely flattened Jerusalem and ploughed Zion so that 'one could not tell if anyone had lived there'.

Thus the evidence is indeed that the prophecy was given before the event for all to read. Yet Bible critics want us to believe that Matthew did not write his Gospel – in spite of his story of his own conversion and baptismal name (Matthew 9:9, cf. Mark 2:14). Critic C actually goes farther than many sceptics and suggests that the writer of Matthew invented the character of Jesus from the messianic prophecies of the Old Testament! But at least he admits the reality of those Old Testament prophecies describing the Messiah who was to come.

The Synoptic Puzzle

The interdependence of the four Gospels is a fascinating subject. The relationship between the writing of the first three is called the synoptic problem. As G. T. Manley says (*Bible Commentary*, IVF, 1947), the contents shared by the synoptists derives from apostolic preaching, especially as uttered by Peter and written down by Mark, also the apostolic teaching (the sayings of Jesus) written down by Matthew.

It is interesting that Peter's preaching to the Roman centurion at the garrison of Caesarea, within a few years of the cross (Acts 10:34–43), is an epitome of St Mark's Gospel and may be the reason for the Latin explanation of Jewish customs in that Gospel, seeing that the first Gentiles were Latin soldiers and their families (as well as the evidence that Mark wrote it while in Rome). St Mark's Gospel is full of action and vivid descriptions and Peter's involvement is reflected in a number of personal touches. This internal evidence bears out the statement reported by Papias, a disciple of John the apostle, that Mark was Peter's companion and 'wrote down accurately all that he mentioned'.

Most of Mark's material is shared with Matthew and Luke's Gospels, so it was thought that St Mark could have been the first Gospel in writing, but now it seems there was a common Aramaic source here also, which would confirm Matthew to be first. In addition, we have the sayings of Jesus such as the Sermon on the Mount shared by Matthew and Luke only. This accords with the statement of Papias in AD 100 who had been trained by St John, that 'Matthew compiled the sayings in the Hebrew Aramaic tongue and everyone translated them as best he could'. These sayings would be those recorded at the time of utterance or soon after by Matthew who, as an ex-civil servant, would be used to making entries on the spot. Hence, the reason why they were taken down in the language Jesus actually used. Later Luke himself would be one of those who had access to Matthew's notes and translated them into Greek. Matthew himself would also translate these notes of his when he came to write his own Gospel in Greek.

Luke had a third source. About half of his material is not found in the others. When he was in the Holy Land during Paul's visit to Jerusalem in AD 57 and two years' imprisonment at Caesarea on the coast, he must have interviewed witness after witness. For instance,

Mary, the mother of Jesus, and others concerned with the circumstances of the Lord's birth, with their early Christian songs such as the
Magnificat, also Philip the Evangelist and his four prophetic daughters
(Acts 21:8), plus over 500 witnesses of the risen Christ (1 Corinthians
15:6), not to mention the thousands still alive whom Christ had cured.

Luke, as a scholar, had the gift of accurate reporting linked with
historic data, as Sir William Ramsay discovered. 'Luke's history is
unsurpassed in respect of its trustworthiness. He should be placed
among the very greatest of historians.' Luke, as a doctor, loved Christ's
compassion for the underprivileged and unfortunate, hence he records
the famous parables of the Good Samaritan, also the Rich Fool, the
Prodigal Son, the Insistent Widow, etc.

All four Gospels give a large proportion of space to the death and
resurrection of Jesus. This is because, unlike any other man, Jesus was
the only one whose main purpose was to die an atoning death for the
human race. 'The Son of Man has come to give his life a ransom for
many,' said Jesus, as recorded by all the synoptists. 'God so loved the
world that he gave his only begotten Son,' says Jesus in John's Gospel.
'As Moses lifted up the serpent in the wilderness, even so must the Son
of Man be lifted up on the cross . . . that whosoever believes on him
should not perish but have eternal life.'

THE FOUNDING OF THE CHURCH (ACTS OF THE APOSTLES)

It is only the work of 'Acts of the Apostles' which tells us of the
Church's beginnings and of the spread of the Good News of Salvation
to Jew, Samaritan and Gentile. First, Luke records the coming of the
new Pentecostal power for believers, followed by the first 12 chapters
which centre on Peter's ministry in the Holy Land. From then on, the
scene switches to Paul's mission to the Roman empire, in three itiner-
ant tours which 'turned the world upside down' (Acts 17:6).

This is Luke's sequel to his Gospel account and he sends it to the
same person, opening thus, 'The former work I have made, O
Theophilus, of all that Jesus began both to do and to teach . . . he
showed himself alive after his passion by many infallible proofs.'

Acts of the Apostles Unfinished

We have mentioned that it is by this work that we are able to give a
close date to when St Luke's Gospel was written and therefore Mark's
Gospel before it. Those reaching the end of Acts for the first time often
exclaim, 'But the story isn't finished! What happened after this? Did
Paul appear before Nero? Was he released or was he executed?'

The explanation is self-evident. The Acts of the Apostles does not
supply the answers because the record was written up to date, which

was before Paul's release, re-arrest and execution around AD 63. While Paul was two years captive in Rome, Luke completed the account up to that time. Evidence substantiating this is given by Professor F. F. Bruce briefly as follows:

> After the careful and detailed account of the events leading up to the trial, we are left in ignorance of the trial itself . . . Had Luke written after Paul's death, the note upon which Acts ends would not have been so confident . . . The attitude to the Roman power throughout the book makes it difficult to believe that the Neroian persecution of Christians in AD 64 had begun. (Paul had appealed to Caesar for justice.) There is no hint throughout Acts of the Jewish War of AD 66–70 or of the fall of Jerusalem . . . Prominence is given to subjects which were of urgent interest in the Church before the fall of Jerusalem, but which lost their practical importance afterwards.

It is only from Paul's second letter to Timothy (2 Timothy 4:6–8,16–18) and the sub-apostolic writers that we learn that Paul was released then two years later was again brought before Nero and executed. This means then that Acts was finished between AD 60 and 62. Luke must have been compiling material for Acts as well as for the Gospel during that two-years' imprisonment of Paul at Caesarea in Palestine AD 57–79 (Acts 23:23 and 24:27), and then bringing it up to date during the Roman imprisonment. Information for the early chapters of Acts, which involves Philip (especially Acts 6:5 and 8:5–40), would have come from Philip the Evangelist and his prophetic daughters who lived at Caesarea (Acts 21:8–10). Also from the Caesarean garrison would come the important events surrounding the presentation of the gospel to the Gentile soldiers (Acts 10 and 11), the first Gentiles officially to be admitted to the Church by Peter.

As St Luke's Gospel would have been completed by AD 57, since Acts was its sequel (Luke 1:1–3 and Acts 1:1–3), it is possible that the Gospel was partly written in Achaia in Northern Greece, as Papias seems to imply that it was written even earlier than AD 57, indeed John Wenham dates it as AD 54.

The scholarly book by John Wenham in 1991, *Re-dating Matthew, Mark and Luke*, establishes even earlier dates, for Matthew by AD 40, Mark by AD 44, when in Rome with Peter from AD 42 to AD 44. Probably that is why Paul took Mark on his first mission in AD 47. The new churches would need his Gospel. More than eight early church writers from AD 90 onwards testify to that order of Matthew, Mark, Luke and then John.

Q When then did modern critics ignore all the information given by writers soon after the apostles had died?

They assumed that Christ's miracles were impossible and therefore the Gospels were later folklore in spite of their claims to veracity and eye-witness reports.

Wenham shows that many events paralleled in the Gospels looked like individual reporting, not copying, because of the sprinkling of a great number of insignificant word differences throughout the text which would be pointless for copyists to make. Wenham identifies 'The brother famed for the gospel' in 2 Corinthians 8:18 as Luke. Paul wrote that in AD 56. Therefore Luke's Gospel would be about AD 54. We have seen already that John's Gospel was a supplement to the others, but written before the events of AD 66–70.

Acts Vindicated by Archaeology

Sir William Ramsay was one who started by assuming that Acts was written too late to be accurate, but his archaeological discoveries and his knowledge of Roman history compelled him to revise his opinion. This was partly because the detailed descriptions and titles of the officials Paul met in various provinces were completely accurate. This knowledge of Luke must have been contemporary with the events because the titles of the provincial governors changed suddenly at times if the status of provinces changed. Yet Luke always uses the correct title of which there are about eleven occurrences.

At Cyprus, it was a proconsul; at Philippi, it was magistrate, praetors and rod-bearers; at Corinth, they were proconsuls of Achaia; at Ephesus, the Town Clerk, or on the Isle of Malta, the Chief Man. Luke thus showed both contemporary knowledge and accurate diary recording.

The account of Paul's sea voyage to Rome, with its storm and wind systems, its seacraft and shipwreck are, according to Holtzman, 'one of the most instructive documents for the knowledge of ancient seamanship'. Bruce says that the accuracy of the voyage narrative of Acts 27, was vindicated by James Smith of Jordanhill. In my own voyages around the Mediterranean in the interests of archaeology and anthropology, I have been surprised at the frequency of storms created by unrelenting gales blowing down from the Black Sea and through the Aegean.

Luke's accuracy derives from his methodical mind and classical training in medicine. As his trustworthiness has been vindicated in all points where he can be checked, we should assume his accuracy elsewhere.

LETTERS TO THE CHURCHES

St Paul's Letters

The third body of writings in the New Testament is the 14 letters of Paul. They were first circulated separately, then as a combined work with the letter to the Hebrews at the end, and named the Corpus Paulinus.

Their order is not chronological, but rather is in an order to develop the subject spiritually for the reader. The letter to the Romans comes first, because this is the most comprehensive statement on the way of salvation. It demonstrates that a righteous God could forgive us only if he could do so righteously, and that he can do so only through Christ's sacrifice which meets all his just requirements. God can accept us, therefore, only if we plead guilty and accept the penalty paid for each one of us by the sinless Son of God.

The actual chronological order of Paul's letters is as follows.

Galatians, written after Paul's first missionary journey to save his new converts in Turkey from being deceived by Judaisers. They said that the full redemption of Christ was not sufficient to save, without works. This letter was specially necessary to refute the error, as the first council of the Church had not yet met. It met in Jerusalem soon after in AD 50 to issue its support of this gospel of Paul and Peter (see Acts 15). We have to beware of similar false teaching today from those who have failed to trust in the finished work of the cross for their eternal salvation.

Then were written two letters to the persecuted but rejoicing Christians in that great port **Thessalonica** on the North Aegean Sea, won to Christ on Paul's second missionary journey. These are especially helpful for new Christians experiencing their first opposition.

The letters of Paul to **Corinth** on his third missionary journey deal with a church full of problems arising out of their permissive and sceptical cosmopolitan city. The letter to the **Romans** follows, then the letters from prison – **Colossians, Philemon, Ephesians, Philippians.** On his release he writes to Timothy and Titus, then while imprisoned again, his **second letter to Timothy**. 'The time of my departure has come. I have fought a good fight . . .'

Paul was given direct revelation on many issues (2 Corinthians 12:2–4), but on transitory things he gives his sanctified advice (1 Corinthians 7:25; 1 Corinthians 11:14–16).

All these letters speak to us today as God's voice in similar situations. They were regarded as Scripture immediately they were written, according to 2 Peter 3:16 (Living Bible), 'Our beloved brother Paul has talked about these same things in many of his letters . . . there are people who . . . have twisted his letters around . . . just as they do the other parts of the Scriptures.'

The General Epistles

The last letters of the New Testament were from other living witnesses of Christ: James, Peter, John and Jude.

James was the half-brother of the Lord. He did not believe in Jesus during his ministry, but the shock of the crucifixion and surprise of the resurrection brought about his conversion. The risen Lord Jesus had a special interview to explain things to him (1 Corinthians 15:7). Josephus the historian tells us that he became the most revered figure in Jerusalem, as a great example of love and just dealing. His letter is a reflection of Christ's Sermon on the Mount, very practical, as you would expect from one who had lived with Jesus. His graphic illustrations also reflect Christ's style. He unhesitatingly supported Christ's claims and the authority of his Word and calls him the Lord Jesus Christ, the Lord of Glory, in 2:1. When the high priest had him murdered in AD 65, the Jews said that the calamities which started the next year, leading to the fall of Jerusalem, were God's judgment for killing such a holy man.

Peter was reliant upon his scribe, consequently his style changes a little according to the scribe who takes down his two letters. This gave sceptics the opportunity to question whether he wrote the second letter. There are many characteristic phrases which come out in both letters. One is his phrase 'ages of the ages' meaning eternity. It appears in both Epistles. Other words and phrases rarely found in other writings are the words 'precious', 'virtue', 'love of brethren', 'without blemish' and 'without spot', 'Jesus the spotless Lamb'. Likewise, both letters speak characteristically about the judgment of the Flood, and rather mysteriously about the spirits in prison in the underworld awaiting judgment. There are biographical references too. In his second letter, he says he was the one who saw the glory of the Lord Jesus Christ on the Mount of Transfiguration. He refers also to what Jesus said in John 21:18.

Jude, the half-brother of Jesus, shows in his letter that it was common knowledge among the apostles that in these last days there would be scepticism and a breakdown of morals.

John's letters also record the warnings which Jesus gave of unbelief arising in the Church itself. In fact in 1 John 2:18,19, he infers that even antichrist(s) can arise from within the Church. This work of unbelief is the work of the arch-liar, Satan, but those who are anointed by the Holy Spirit will not be deceived by those satanic deceptions. The same Holy Spirit who inspired the Scriptures brings about the new birth of the believer and enables the believer also to understand God's Word.

THE BOOK OF REVELATION

This book is a personal message to us from the Lord Jesus himself – risen, glorified and coming again. 'Write what you see, what is now and what is to take place after this.'

I have likened the visions given to John, the writer of Revelation, to a triumphal arch on which are four panels. Each one shows prophesied history leading to Christ's victory and has seven symbolic pictures. These symbols foretell history from St John's day to Christ's second coming, followed by judgment and a cleaning up of the world that had been spoilt and ruined by sin and Satan. The snake, Satan, is banished to hell and no longer deceives the world (Revelation 20). The saved rejoice after their persecution on earth. Thus the themes which were started in Genesis are finalised in the book of Revelation.

The last chapter of Revelation ends with loving invitation. 'I Jesus have sent my angel to you with this testimony. Let him who is thirsty come . . . and take the water of life without payment', and the whole Bible ends with his words, 'I warn everyone who hears the words of the prophecy of this book, if anyone adds to them, God will add to him the plagues that are written in this book and, if anyone takes away from the words of the book of this prophecy, God will take away his share in the tree of life and in the holy city.'

QUESTIONS ON THE AUTHORITY OF SCRIPTURE

Here are a number of additional questions which are sometimes asked.

Q Who decided where Scripture should finish?

In the case of the New Testament, the writing of Scripture ceased when the living witnesses of Christ had all died. Jesus had said, 'You are witnesses of me. The Holy Spirit will bring back to you all the things which I have spoken.' With the life, atoning death, resurrection and ascension of Christ, the gospel was complete and became the final revelation 'once and for all time delivered unto the Christians' (Jude 3).

In the case of the Old Testament, Scripture ceased when the preparation for the first coming of the Messiah was complete and the spirit of prophecy was withdrawn 400 years before he came. Thus it was acknowledged in the Apocrypha and by Josephus that no prophet had arisen since that time, and that the time was anticipated when prophecy would again be given, because as Peter said, 'Prophecy did not come in old times by man's willing it to, but men spoke from God as they were borne along by his Holy Spirit' (2 Peter 1:21).

Q Who decided what should be included in Scripture?

We see from above that the Holy Spirit of God decided it. 'All Scripture is given by inspiration of God and is profitable for doctrine, reproof, correction, instruction in righteousness, as a complete provision for the man of God' (2 Timothy 3:16).

It should be said that the bringing together of the Scriptures into one book is quite a different question from that of divine inspiration. Some confuse the two issues. It was not the publication of a list of accepted books by some Jewish or Church Council which made them inspired. They were inspired by God the moment he gave his message to the prophet, scribe or disciple (2 Peter 3:16) and, as regards the Gospel writers, it was a matter of accurate recording of what the living witnesses heard and said of the Word made flesh (John 21:24).

Before ever such a list (or canon) of books was made, each work was written and sent to various individuals or churches and circulated separately. The first complete volume was the Torah or Pentateuch which circulated down the centuries as one complete volume. It was divided into five books only at the time of the Greek translation of it at Alexandria in the third century BC. As other books of the prophets were written, they also circulated individually (Daniel 9:2) and later kept in the synagogues. This was so even in Christ's lifetime. When Jesus came to the Nazareth synagogue, he stood up to read the lesson and the book or roll of the prophet Isaiah was given to him to read (Luke 4:17). That book was just as inspired as when bound in one volume with others, for Jesus said, 'This day is this scripture fulfilled in your ears.'

At first, a list of inspired books was acknowledged, before ever they were combined in one volume. That list of the Old Testament Scriptures, in its three sections, was recognised when completed in the time of Ezra and Nehemiah in the fifth century BC and authorised by the risen Jesus in AD 30 (Luke 24), long before any Jewish Council approved the list in AD 98 at Jamnia.

Likewise, the New Testament was at first circulated in separate books. The first volume containing several books was the writings of St Paul (Corpus Paulinus) containing his Epistles Romans to Hebrews. The Synoptic Gospels circulated separately until John had written his. Then they were circulated together as the fourfold Gospel (Evangelion).

In the case of the New Testament, as it has been said, when the living witnesses died, the canon of Scripture closed, so it became the task of the early Christians to exclude from that list all that was written after. Writings afterwards were merely helpful works, but not Scripture, and so it became the task of the Christians, following the time of the apostles, to exclude all subsequent writings. Only scriptures which had sufficient evidence that they were written by or were records of the living witnesses were accepted. Lists began to appear soon after the last apostle died, and a final list was drawn up in AD 397, after all the evidence was thoroughly reviewed by a Council of the whole church at Carthage. It was the need to exclude spurious writings which called for a Church Council in AD 397 to authorise a list. This was not to declare them inspired but to exclude any writings which did not originate from the living witnesses of our Lord.

Q A further question is about the reliability of the text and translations.

The Old Testament was written in Hebrew because that was the language of the prophets, and the New Testament in Greek because that was the universal language, appropriate for the gospel which was to be preached to all nations. Accurate copying became a principle from the first and various systems were developed to ensure this. Consequently, in the words of Sir Frederick Kenyon, former Director of the British Museum, we have a text three times more reliable than the secular classics such as Shakespeare or Marlowe or the Greek and Roman classics which nobody bothers to question.

Where a copying error crept in, in one locality, it could be eliminated by copies from other localities. Indeed, a family tree of copies was drawn up which corrected one another. Thus it can be said that practically nowhere is the meaning of the text in doubt and, what is more important, nowhere is the truth of Christian teaching in doubt.

The Dead Sea Scrolls revealed how accurately scriptures had been copied. The book of Isaiah had been copied in the Hebrew for over 1,000 years without an intervening copy surviving, until the copy found in the Dead Sea cave. It revealed that the copying had been carried out down the thousand years with unbelievable accuracy. See also Professor F. F. Bruce, *Are the New Testament Documents Reliable?* (IVP, 1968); Sir Frederick Kenyon, *The Bible and Ancient Manuscripts* (Eyre and Spottiswoode, 1939); Dr. J. W. Wenham, *Christ and the Bible* (Tyndale Press, 1984); F. F. Bruce, *The Books and the Parchments* (Pickering & Inglis, 1968).

Q What is the oldest discovery of surviving Scripture manuscripts?

It was not at first possible to bind all the writings into one volume until scrolls gave place to paged books (codex), but the Muratorian fragment written in AD 170 lists all the New Testament except the Epistle of James and John's third Epistle. It also says that an allegory called, 'The Shepherd of Hermas' is not Scripture, but may be read in churches for edification.

The oldest discovery of Old Testament books is the Dead Sea Scrolls, 100 BC–AD 70. The oldest discovery of a Bible is the Chester Beatty Papyri, discovered in Egypt in 1930. Copies date between AD 200 and 250. Various pages are missing, but the coverage is the whole Bible, Genesis to Revelation.

The oldest pieces of New Testament are the 'Magdalen' Matthew fragments of 50 AD and Ryland's fragment of John 19. O'Callaghan (papyrologist) reports three fragments dated AD 68 of Mark 6:52 concerning Gennesaret, and 1 Timothy 3:16–4:3 (written by Paul in prison only six years earlier) and James 1:23, 'If anyone is a hearer of the word and not a doer, he sees his reflection but forgets what he is like', from Cave 7 Qumran sealed in AD 68 (cf. John Wenham's *Re-dating Matthew, Mark and Luke*, Hodder, 1991).

There are in existence over 3,000 Greek manuscripts of the whole or part of the New Testament, going back to about AD 350.

In addition to actual old copies still existing, we have quotations from the New Testament in the works of early church writers from as early as just after AD 70 and into the next century. Practically all the New Testament is quoted. The evidence is collected and assessed by the Oxford Society of Historical Theology in *The New Testament in the Apostolic Fathers*.

Sir Frederick Kenyon, former Director of the British Museum and leading authority on ancient manuscripts said, 'The interval between the dates of original composition and the earliest existing evidence becomes so small as to be in fact negligible, and the last foundation for any doubt that the scriptures have come down to us substantially as they were written has now been removed' (*The Bible and Ancient Manuscripts*, British Museum, p 288).

Q Are there conflicting accounts in the Bible?

When advocates of the documentary theory disrupt a Bible story (in itself harmonious) and reassemble it to suit that theory, it sometimes creates conflicting accounts. Therefore they manufacture their own contradictions. In other cases, I have not found a supposed contradiction which has not arisen out of careless reading or lack of systematic investigation. Actually, the Bible is a wonderful harmony of truth, and although having over 40 human authors spanning 15 centuries, its consistency can be accounted for only by divine authorship. *It states truths largely unacceptable to fallen man.*

SUMMARY

THE BIBLE SPEAKS FOR ITSELF

Testimony of Early Church Writers AD 70–170

Matthew AD 30.
- Aramaic notes during ministry.
- Papias b. AD 60.
- Aramaic underlies Greek translation – Bruce, Chilton, Howard.
- Note-taking prevalent in Christ's time.
- 'Certain Matthew passages more original than Mark's' (Blomberg).

Mark (St. Peter's).
- Probably written in Rome AD 44 after Peter's escape, Acts 12.
- 'Wrote down accurately . . . paid attention not to include any false statement'
- Papias b. AD 60.

Luke AD 54 or 57.
- William Ramsay's archaeological research finds Luke very accurate. Luke gives his methods:
- Information obtained from eye-witnesses.
- Complete understanding from the first.
- Wrote an order of events.
- Others he knew had written their experiences.
- Infallible proofs of Christ's life and miracles.

John AD 65 says:
- He was eyewitness (19:35).
- Confirms truth and accuracy.
- Closest companion to Jesus. (21:20–24).
- Gospel supplementary to Synoptics, but before 'Wars of Jews'.

Other:
- Significance of prophecy of fall of Jerusalem.
- Warnings useless if written afterwards.
- Luke warned of armies surrounding Jerusalem AD 66.
- Matthew and Mark warned of fall in AD 70.
- James, half-brother of Jesus, very significant, as Josephus refers to him.

16 SUPPRESSING THE EVIDENCE
CONFLICT OVER THE DATING OF THE GOSPELS

The life and atonement of Jesus is the centre of all Scripture. Therefore God has given four confirmatory accounts of this in the Gospels. Some incidents are reported in two, three or even in all four Gospels.

However, Bible critics often try to give supposed examples of contradictory comparisons in the reports of the same incident. We must therefore spend some more time looking at the evidence for truth that confirms the reliability of Scripture.

Why do critics look for contradictions? Why do they do this? The reasons stated are as follows:

1. the Gospel writers (supposedly) inherited different versions;
2. they were (supposedly) not true to the tradition, or at any rate not bound by it;
3. we (supposedly) cannot be sure of the original form of the event or dialogue.

A supposed example is then given. It may be a parable which Jesus told. But we may find that the parable was given at two different times in the ministry. Preachers often tell the same story at different times, but with variations in the details.

An example given is the story which Jesus told of the invitation to the big feast. One is given in Luke 14:16–24 and the other in Matthew 22:1–14. Then comes a typical ploy to undermine the Scriptures. The student is asked to compare the two and note the differences, but they are not informed that Jesus gave the parable on two different occasions at two different times in his ministry.

With Luke, it is when Jesus was invited to dinner in the house of a ruler, which was during his evangelisation campaign in Peraea (east of Jordan). With Matthew, a similar story was told nearly a year later, to the Pharisees in the temple courts, a few days before the crucifixion, but with big differences suited to the occasion.

Thus it was not a case of Matthew and Luke reporting the same parable rather inaccurately, but reporting two different occasions, in two different situations, with two different objectives.

'I Have Told You this Before'

A similar attempt to suggest contradiction is made concerning Christ's reference to his second coming as going to surprise the unprepared like those before the Flood of Noah and those of Sodom.

On what separate occasions did Jesus teach this? Luke 17:26–37 says Jesus taught this 'as he was passing between Samaria and Galilee' (v 11), but Matthew 24:37–41 says it was as Jesus sat on the Mount of Olives during the week before his crucifixion.

Now, it should be obvious that Jesus would often repeat his teaching, both to his learning disciples and to the changing crowds. Indeed, in Mark 13:23 he says, 'I have told you this before'. Significantly, it is not Mark, but only Luke who records this earlier instance.

The Lord's prayer is another example. He gave it to his disciples early in his ministry in the Sermon on the Mount as an example of prayer; but much later, in the third year of his ministry, they wanted a prayer to repeat in John the Baptist style. They had forgotten the teaching of two years earlier.

Two Different Blind Men

Likewise, the details of the healing of the blind man at Jericho are slightly different in Luke 18:35–43 from those by Mark 10:46–52. But notice that they were two different men. Luke says it was a beggar sitting at the roadside before Jesus reached Jericho. Mark tells of blind Bartimaeus who was on the other side of the town when Jesus was leaving it (v 46). There were always many beggars at every city gate in those days.

So learn to criticise the critics. Their attitude is wrong, always looking for supposed faults, often manufacturing them by pulling them out of context. Unfortunately, they teach a wrong attitude to God's Word.

In fact, there is more behind it than this. They assumed that the Gospels were not written until long after Christ's death and resurrection. Some extreme critics put them in the second century. This theory was started by the critics associated with Tübingen in Germany in 1833. They thought that miracles, including the resurrection, could not happen, so they thought that the Gospels were written long after, when romantic ideas had developed. They did not have all the archaeological evidence for Gospel accuracy that we have today, but their followers have been unwilling to change and yet they call themselves 'Modernists'!

For example, the Diocesan Certificate Course I have quoted before said: 'It is probably not possible to know who wrote the Gospel which is headed by the name of Matthew. Critics date it variously between 70 AD and 110 AD.'

These critics assume that they know better 1,900 years after the event than the early Church writers who lived in the times immediately after the apostles. Several of them tell us that Matthew was the first Gospel to be written, not Mark and Matthew took notes during Christ's ministry.

Resistance to Evidence

Unwillingness to give Bible believers the opportunity to pass on information was shown by all the book references given in that Certificate Course. For example, 11 books were recommended for reading. Practically all propagated the extreme critical theory. Not one book by a Bible-believing scholar was mentioned, yet the course is compulsory for any church person wanting to become a lay preacher.

Because the critics assume that the Gospels were not the products of eye-witnesses, they try to account for them in other ways. They actually disbelieve the statements by Luke and John. Luke says that his Gospel consisted of notes taken from eye-witnesses (Luke 1:2). St John said, 'He saw it happen and bare record . . . and his record is true' (John 19:35).

Not Cunning Myths

The apostle Peter says in 2 Peter 1:16: 'For we have not followed cunningly-devised myths when we made known to you the power and presence of our Lord Jesus Christ, but were eye-witnesses of his majesty.'

We have seen that scholars such as John Wenham, Professor F.F. Bruce, Dr B. Chilton, and J. Motyer, have shown that the Gospels were written early. Their evidence is that they were all written before the fall of Jerusalem in AD 70. Professor Bruce pointed out that Luke's Acts finishes before Paul's appearance before Nero in AD 62. As Acts was a sequel to Luke's Gospel, the Gospel must have been written earlier.

Aware of the lack of balance, one diocese asked me to write a brief corrective article. The following was what I submitted.

THE NEW/OLD SYNOPTIC SCENARIO

What is this new scenario? It takes seriously what the Bible says about itself, its origin and what the Gospels say of their origin. This is supported by the Early Fathers and many scholars who so far have not been mentioned in this course. As the four Gospels tell the history of our Lord Jesus Christ, let us start with them since it is central to our faith.

The Gospels declare that they are accounts given by true and honest men who endeavour to give an accurate record of the incarnate divine Son of God who fulfilled the Old Testament prophecies, who was sinless, worked great miracles, was crucified for our sins, buried, arose from the dead, ascended into heaven and is coming again to judge the world by his words, according to John 12:48. Those words, the three Synoptic Gospels tell us, 'will never pass away' (Mark 13:31).

Taking Luke Seriously

When were these words and works first written down? Luke tells us that it was by those who were eye-witnesses during the ministry of Christ. To translate the Greek of Luke 1:1,2 literally: Many before him, 'had taken it in hand to draw up a narrative' as 'eye-witnesses of the word', and 'it seemed good to me also to write'.

Note that the emphasis is upon writing, not upon oral tradition.

Who were these who had committed it to writing even before Luke? In reply, we shall also take seriously what the Early Fathers said. They lived much nearer the events than the Higher Critics of the last 200 years. They lived from AD 60 (the birth of Papias) and into the following centuries. We will also take seriously what has been discovered about the actual methods by which records were made in our Lord's time.

The critics of the Tübingen School of 1833 thought that nothing was written until AD 130. Later, during the twentieth century, this was moderated to about AD 85 for St Matthew's Greek Gospel and AD 75 for St Mark; but Luke declares that many 'had taken it in hand to **write** an orderly narrative' of our Lord's life **before** he himself did, and that they were eye-witnesses.

Who Were these Eye-witnesses?

The universal tradition of the Early Church Fathers (more than a dozen of them) is that Matthew wrote the first of our four Gospels. It has recently been argued that Mark came second in about AD 45; then came Luke's Gospel about AD 54, and finally St John's Gospel before AD 66, according to Bishop John Robinson. We shall look at the evidence for this.

Quite clearly, the statement by Luke that many eye-witnesses had committed the life of Christ to writing before him renders the succession of theories from Tübingen onwards irrelevant, i.e. Wellhausen, Form theory, Redaction, 'Q', Midrash, Hermeneutic, Structuralism. Some of these theories did not even allow for honest reporting, let alone inspiration for which the Lord Jesus said, 'The Holy Spirit will cause you to remember (*hupomnesei*) all that I have said.'

Furthermore, we can now see why Jesus called the customs officer of Capernaum's quayside tax office to follow him. The God who had foretold to 20 centuries of Old Testament prophets all the details about the coming Messiah was making sensible provision for the recording of its fulfilment.

Blomberg says that, for the last 20 years, a growing number of scholars have been taking seriously what Papias wrote while St John was still alive. He was quoted as saying that Matthew first wrote down the sayings of Jesus in Aramaic.

Without going into too much technical detail, let me first describe the scenario which this gives.

Rome's Strict Rules for Tax

As a trained tax collector of Rome, Matthew would continue his customary habit of taking down notes in the vernacular 'of all that Jesus began to do and to teach'. According to the Early Fathers, this was in Aramaic, the very language Jesus used.

Normally, when making tax reports, Matthew would then translate his notes into Greek and send them to Rome. It would, therefore be natural for him to translate his own notes taken during Christ's ministry into Greek after Pentecost when 'this gospel was to be preached in all the world' (Matthew 26:13).

The Early Fathers date it eight or ten years after the resurrection. This would be during the expansion beyond Samaria into the Greek world; Matthew would see the necessity as indicated in Matthew 28:19,20, 'Go therefore make disciples in all the nations . . . teaching them to observe all things whatever I gave to you in command.' So the remark in the Diocesan Certificate Course concerning Matthew's Greek Gospel: 'We shall probably never know who the author was. It may have been another Matthew' – looks to be wrong.

In 1996, Dr C. Thiede, a German papyrus expert, visited Magdalen College, Oxford, and identified fragments from Matthew's Gospel. He recognised a style of writing 'which had petered out' by AD 50. This is evidence for truth (reported in *The Times*) that the account was written by an eye-witness at the time of the events.

How would Matthew record what Jesus was saying or doing?

Shorthand Notes

It comes as a surprise to learn from Roman records that Matthew would be taking it all down in shorthand – a tax collector's shorthand script – then he would rewrite it in the vernacular (Aramaic), then translate it into a Greek report to Rome. Is that why we get the fullest records of Christ's brilliant preaching from Matthew?

Rome had a very elaborate and detailed tax system so that no one would escape. There were 111 categories of tax. As a tax collector, Levi (an appropriate name before he became a disciple) would have full particulars – long before he became Matthew – of every house and business in Capernaum. The names of Peter, James and John, and the size of their catches of fish at various dates and duty paid, would all be in his office.

Not only were there harbour dues, every person in the community was registered for poll-tax from the age of 14, and every trader would be vexed by road and bridge tolls.

As a customs house official, Matthew was the most hated type of tax collector. He did personal prying to collect and reported direct to Rome, not through middle men such as inferior tax men. Rome was regarded as the heathen power by the Jewish Targums (records). According to the Pharisees, even if Matthew's category repented, they could hardly be granted forgiveness. Evidence and details for this come from Wilcken of Leipzig, Deissmann, Edersheim, A. White, Goodspeed, Gundry and the Jewish Targums.

Tax Avoidance?

He would also investigate possible tax avoidance. Was Jesus avoiding tax by moving from one tax area in Nazareth to Levi's own area at Capernaum?

The report for tax assessment by the sons of Zebedee of a big miracle catch looks suspiciously like a late declaration of past unreported tax. Levi too was a captive hearer of Christ's pungent preaching opposite him at the quayside. Levi wouldn't like what he heard about 'You can't serve God and money'; 'Broad is the road that goes to hell'; 'Don't worry about food, clothes, or dwelling, trust in God'. Levi would have a nice house for retirement away from his unpopular job, not built on sand either – or was it!

One day, when Levi was softened up, Jesus looked in his tax window and said 'Follow me!' Jesus wanted one whose habit was to take notes in Aramaic and report them in Greek.

We learn that this was a time of very high literacy. All children were taught to read and write and *the practice of carrying note pads around was encouraged.*

Aramaic Behind the Greek Synoptics

Followers of Christ had access to Matthew's notes in Aramaic or even to Matthew's Gospel, just as Papias and others said. B. Chilton of Sheffield University and F.F. Bruce of Manchester University and others detect that an Aramaic script is behind the Greek translations of the material mutually contained in the three Synoptics. The individual word differences would arise through translation as they do in our various modern translations today.

'In many places where the Greek of these Gospels differs, it can be shown that one and the same Aramaic original underlies the variant Greek renderings' (Prof F.F. Bruce, p 30, *New Testament Documents*, IVP, 1979). Bruce quotes a number of scholars who agree on this. Principal W. F. Howard says 'Mark's Greek is the most Aramaic of the gospels.' J. Wenham points out that the small individual word differences for the same incident in the Synoptics, would have no point if they were copying each other; but they would make sense if they were making individual translations of the same Aramaic text (*Re-dating Matthew, Mark and Luke*, Hodder, 1991).

Blomberg says, 'Matthew preserves certain passages in forms which reproduce the original tradition more than Mark does.'

But what of the years between Matthew's notes and the Gospel of Mark? Papias' statement would apply here. Papias was born in AD 60 and became a disciple of St John. He said that 'every man translated Matthew's vernacular as best he could'. It would also justify Luke's prologue. 'Many have taken it in hand to draw up in order, a narrative of Christ's ministry.' These resources would supply the needs of the next five years until AD 45 when Mark wrote his Gospel.

Mark Next

Why AD 45? Because, from the records of the church in Rome, and matched with history, Peter's first visit to Rome was probably from AD 42 to 44. He went there after being delivered from prison by the angel (Acts 12). Evidence comes from Christian tombs in Rome which have the Angel of Peter depicted upon them.

'Peter would have left for "the other place" from Mark's home and Mark would have gone with him (and recorded Peter's teaching). This ties in with the witness of Papias, Irenaeus, the Anti-Marcionite Prologue, Clement of Alexandria and Origen' (J. Wenham p 169, *Re-dating Matthew, Mark and Luke*). Peter returned by AD 46 to Jerusalem when King Agrippa, who arrested him earlier, was dead.

But Mark had left Rome earlier in AD 44 or 45, having written his Gospel and been sent by Peter to found the church of Alexandria, according to Eusebius and the Apostolic Constitutions. After one or two years in Alexandria, Mark went to Jerusalem and then to Antioch with Paul and Barnabas. Mark had his Gospel already written, which would be the reason that he was invited to accompany Paul and Barnabas on their first missionary journey. It would be why Paul saw no reason to write a Gospel himself to leave with the first churches, but to have Mark with him would add authentication.

Luke Was the Next to Write his Gospel

John Wenham has pointed out that the gap of seven years in the 'we' passages of Acts 1:7–20:5 coincides with when Luke would be writing his Gospel about AD 54. This would give time for Luke's Gospel to become famed already so that Paul referred to him in 2 Corinthians 8:18 as the brother already 'famed for the gospel'. Several Early Fathers support this. Luke was no preacher. His fame would be in writing the third Gospel, not preaching it. It would be written well before his sequel, 'The Acts of the Apostles', in any case.

John Wenham was Vice-Principal of a theological college and Warden of Latimer House, Oxford. He is well known for his scholarly books, including one on Greek grammar. His theory that 'the brother famed for the gospel throughout all the churches' was Luke may not be quickly accepted, but in any case, Luke would be at work on his Gospel only three years later during Paul's first imprisonment at Caesarea where Peter outlined a life of Christ to the Roman garrison (Acts 10:34–43). It was near there that Luke spent a week with Philip and his four prophetic daughters, whom the Early Fathers say were famed resources of knowledge for Christ's life. As Professor C.H. Dodd said, concerning Paul's two weeks with Peter earlier, 'They would hardly be talking about the weather.'

That raises a much neglected question about Paul's 'mystic experience' as it is called. In his account of the Lord's Supper, he claims that he received this direct from Jesus. Compare 1 Corinthians 11:23 with 2 Corinthians 12:2–5. Is this what Paul is referring to when in two of his letters he refers to 'my gospel' (Romans 2:16; 16:25) which he received 'not from man' (Galatians 1:12), but he was three years in the desert after his conversion, then later he spent two weeks with Peter? Would none of this be passed on to Luke, his close companion?

The Terminal Date for All

The important question then is – when was Acts written? Acts would be written up to date while Paul was still awaiting to appear before Caesar Nero in AD 62. As F.F. Bruce says: 'The abrupt manner in which Acts closes can be best explained thus, that it was written up-to-date. As it is, after leading us up to the trial, we are left in ignorance of the trial itself' (*Acts of the Apostles Commentary*, Tyndale).

This could only happen if Acts was written before the outcome of the trial. That was in AD 62 when Paul was acquitted and released, according to history, but later re-arrested and beheaded. As Acts was obviously written before all this, the writing of Luke and all the other Synoptics must have been earlier, and within the fresh memories of eye-witnesses and their notes.

Luke adds a whole new section to his Gospel, namely chapter 9 verse 51 to chapter 18 verse 14. This would accord with his prologue that these additional accounts would be 'delivered to him by those who were eye-witnesses'. An important witness was Mary who would give him the birth accounts and songs, and also how the boy Jesus in the temple referred to God as his Father. Twice Mary expressed her private feelings that 'she stored all these things in her heart'. Personal details she could tell to a doctor.

It is evident that John's Gospel was written to supplement the three Synoptics. This is obvious from what John omits and what John adds.

Significance of John's Supplement to Matthew, Mark and Luke

From *Origin of the Bible* (Victor Pearce, *Hour of Revival*, 1989, pp 21–24).

Omission of prime events in Jesus' life such as the following:

a) The nativity stories: this is supplemented by the eternal aspect of the Incarnation in the prologue, 'The Word became flesh and dwelt among us'.
b) The call of the disciples is supplemented by the lovely domestic picture when some of them actually first met Jesus and were captivated by his message.
c) The Transfiguration is omitted (an incident of central importance).
d) Although the actual Last Supper is omitted, St John records five chapters of what Jesus said at the Last Supper and after it.

Secondly, certain **additions** are explained:
St John was closest to the Lord and is able to fill in with much personal information. Also, he had relatives at Jerusalem which gained him admissions (John 18:15) and interests in Judaea. Consequently, the larger part of his Gospel consists of Christ's visits and teaching in Judaea, when Jesus went up to the main festivals at Jerusalem. This also explains why the Lord's teaching to the sophisticated Judaeans needed to be more theological. But we also get a sample of it in Matthew's Gospel (11:27). St John tells us also that he selected from the Lord's teaching anything to give assurance of salvation. 'These are written, that you might believe that Jesus is the Christ, the Son of God, and that believing you might have life through his name' (John 20:31). Consequently, many have found 'the free gift of everlasting life' through the utterances of Jesus recorded here. Even in the prologue we are shown how to accept it. 'To as many as received Jesus by faith, to them gave he the right to become sons of God – those thus born again of God' (John 1:12).

A very old fragment of a copy of St John's Gospel called the Ryland Fragment is dated at about AD 120, and was found in Egypt. The former Director of the British Museum said that for copies to have time to migrate from

(Continued)

Ephesus to Egypt must mean that the Ryland's Fragment brings us almost to the time of John's actual writing. Incidentally, this includes a reference to 'The Pavement' in chapter 19.

Thirdly, the author can be detected by a **process of elimination.** We are told clearly that the writer (21:24) is 'The disciple whom Jesus loved' (21:20), that at the Last Supper he was next to Jesus closer even than Peter.

We know it must have been **one of the twelve**, because the other Gospels indicate that they were the only ones present. So the writer knew the real Jesus personally.

Who was this beloved disciple as close to Jesus as Peter? The evidence in the other Gospels is that on special occasions, Jesus took with him an Inner Three – Peter, James and John. Such occasions were the raising of Jairus' daughter, the transfiguration, and Gethsemane's vigil. This closeness correlates with other occasions in St John's Gospel when only the writer was closely associated with Peter; i.e. following Jesus to the high priest's court, and to the cross, and when they both ran to the empty tomb, and at the Lake of Galilee when Peter questioned Jesus about his close friend (21:21).

Thus the loved disciple must have been **one of the three**. It could not be Peter because in 13:24 and elsewhere, Peter is named separately. The only other possibility was James, who was John's brother – they were the sons of Zebedee mentioned together in the other Gospel as being among the seven at the resurrection appearance at the Lake of Galilee.

Fourthly, the writer could not be James because he was executed by King Herod quite early on (see Acts 12:2). So that leaves John only, as being the beloved disciple, the writer of the fourth Gospel.

Other processes of elimination give the same evidence; John was originally one of John the Baptist's disciples who joined Jesus in the informality of those earliest days of the ministry (1:40). As the writer's name was John, he had no need to add 'the Baptist' when referring to John the Baptist, as the other Gospel writers do (1:6,15).

He had first-hand knowledge of the geography of the Holy Land before the fall of Jerusalem, and was a Jew who knew the temple customs before the temple was destroyed, even though he may have written in Ephesus, where the holy mother, Mary, went to live in John's care as commissioned by Jesus.

And why did the dying Lord commit his mother into John's keeping? Not only because he was at the cross with her, not only because he was beloved and gentle, but because comparing Matthew 27:56 with John 19:25, it seems that John was a cousin.

As in the case of Luke's authorship of Acts, where the presence of the writer is only indicated by the word 'we', so John modestly hides under the pseudonym of 'beloved disciple'. There are also two 'we' passages, one of which is: 'We beheld his glory, as the only Son from the Father'.

Archbishop William Temple said (1943), 'I regard as self-condemned any theory about the origin of the gospel which fails to find a very close connection between it and John the son of Zebedee. The combination of internal and external evidence is overwhelming.'

BENEFITS OF THE NEW SCENARIO

The above then is a brief summary of the facts that have been discovered from Roman custom and history and the testimony of the Early Fathers living from AD 60 to the fourth century. It gives a different conclusion from that expressed by such remarks as 'We cannot, of course, guarantee that what we have are eye-witness accounts' or 'Where John got his ideas from is another area of dispute'.

Contrast this with John's statement in chapter 19 verse 35, 'He that saw it bares record and his record is true, and he knows that he speaks the truth that you might believe' or contrast critical agnosticism with the confidence of Luke's prologues:

Since many took it in hand to draw up in order a narrative concerning the matters which were fully carried out among us, even as delivered to us by those who were eye-witnesses from the beginning and attendants of the word, it seemed good to me also having investigated all things from their source accurately, to write them to you in order, most excellent Theophilus, that you might know the certainty of those things in which you were instructed.

Q What are the important points arising out of this New Scenario?

It can convince people that the Gospel accounts are not later church myths, but contain a translation of the actual words of Jesus. This we should expect, otherwise how could Jesus say, 'These words that I speak shall judge a man in the last day' (John 12:48); and, 'My words will never pass away' (Synoptic Gospels).

Advantages of this New Scenario

1. It gives a Christian strong faith.
2. Scepticism (reductionism) only gives the non-Christian a welcome excuse: it does not win them.
3. The Bible is used as a proof, not as a problem.
4. It is the scenario which the Bible gives, supported by archaeological and literary evidence.

Take the first point. A man in his early thirties wrote to me, 'If only your evidence had been available when I was 15, I would have stayed firm in my faith. I've spent 18 years re-finding the Lord.'

Another wrote from the West Midlands, 'Please send me a copy of Victor Pearce's *Origin of the Bible*, because one RE tutor at a college nearby . . . told his pupils that the Gospel of Luke was all lies.'

The second point illustrates this extract from the *Church of England Newspaper* editorial. It mentions a vicar who strongly declared his doubts about the resurrection on television. 'His congregation has dwindled to little over a dozen. Next door is a parish which will extend its building' to accommodate its congregation. The vicar there preaches that the Bible is true and accurate.

Thirdly, reductionism trains people to make a wrong use of God's Word. In searching for contradictions, it manufactures many of them, e.g., in the Bishop's Certification Course, two parables are taken, the Great Feast of Luke 14 and the Wedding Feast of Matthew 22, and then lists the supposed contradictions. But they are different parables told at different times. Luke's is during the Perean ministry told in a Pharisee's house and Matthew's is a public debate in the temple one year later. Besides, what preacher has not re-used an illustration with differences to suit the circumstances?

Another instance is the miraculous feeding. That of the 4,000 is regarded by some as a duplication of the 5,000, but Jesus refers to both later in Matthew and Mark and draws out a lesson from the two different instances, namely, 'Beware of the leaven of the Sadducees'. Critics refused to believe in miracles or resurrection and therefore rejected scriptures which taught it. Peter, Paul, Jude and John all warned that this reductionism would infiltrate the Church.

Wrong Assumptions Lead to Wrong Conclusions

Fourthly, Tübingen and Wellhausen started the whole trend off on wrong assumptions. They were subjective ones before the objective evidence from the ancient Near East was known. It is an attitude which has persisted and has not welcomed correction by factual discovery of those scholars whose works are now at long last being added to a Diocesan Certificate Course.

Commending them, Professor Kenneth Kitchen writes to me as follows:

The late F.F. Bruce was widely accepted internationally as a fair-minded scholar of the first rank – openly recognised by his being President of both SOTS and SNTS. Professor Wiseman is an Assyriologist and Semitist, with many decades of international standing. My colleague, Professor Alan Millard, is also an Assyriologist and Semitist of international standing. Both men are known for their restrained, moderate, factual presentation . . . on a basis of fact . . . I was always trained to go for facts, not merely party opinions . . . the same cannot be said of old-fashioned 'liberal' theory fashioned in a vacuum over a century ago and merely elaborated since.

SUMMARY

THE ENEMY WITHIN

Paul grieved that the snake of Eden would work in the Church (2 Cor 11:1–15).
- The snake put doubt upon God's Word. (Eve represented the church.)
- It would increase in the last days (2 Tim 3:1 and 4:3,4).

Jesus forewarned the disciples (Matt 16:6–12).
- 'Beware of the yeast of error.'
- Sadducees doubted miracles, resurrection, etc.
- Reductionist critics are in our main churches today.
- Courses for lay readers, etc. are full of it. Trains wrong attitudes (Is 66:2), wrong assumptions and wrong conclusions.

Disciples had the warning in mind and said:
- 'From among your own selves will arise men speaking perverse things' (Paul).
- 'The Spirit expressly says that in the last days many will depart from the faith' (Paul).
- 'They went out from us, but were not of us' (1 John 2:19).
- They deny the virgin birth (1 John 4:2).
- 'We did not follow cleverly devised myths' (Tübingen Critics said they did). 'There will be false teachers among you who will bring in secretly destructive heresies'. 'Scoffers will come in the last days' (2 Pet 1:16; 2:1; 3:3).

Critics manufacture their own contradictions:
- Jesus often told illustrations more than once, at different places, at different times. 'Behold I have told you before.'
- Critics take a parable in Luke told at an earlier time and contrast it with a similar one in Matthew told later, and say they were contradictions.
- Critics distract from the message and dwell on supposed contradiction.

17 THAT AMAZING BOOK

THE BIBLE'S CREDIBILITY

The Bible is the most remarkable book in the world, looked at from any angle. It is the oldest book in the world. It has survived down 40 centuries of human history. Other ancient records have perished and have been discovered only by archaeology, but the Bible as a book has been handed down the ages.

Why is this? It is because believers were told by God that its records were to lead to the Saviour of the world, that it must be preserved and handed down from Abraham to the apostles and from Adam to the second Adam.

The first section of holy Scripture was the Torah of Moses from Genesis to Deuteronomy, then to this God gave the prophets ever-increasing information to add. When the prophesied picture of the precious Saviour was complete in the Old Testament, the world waited 400 years until, 'In the fulfilment of time, God sent his Son'.

The living witnesses of Christ then wrote the New Testament. The canon of Scripture closed when the last witness died.

Because holy and honest men were inspired by the Holy Spirit (to use St Peter's words), those records were accurate and affirmed by many infallible proofs (to use Luke's words).

The Bible is remarkable because it has been the first book to be put into writing for a high percentage of the nations, and has been the foundation of their civilisation. When it has been neglected or disbelieved, that country has declined, as God said it would.

Miraculous Preservation

The Bible is also remarkable because it has been miraculously preserved by God.

More attempts have been made to destroy the Bible than any other book, yet it has survived with more extant copies than any other record made by man. Copies of God's Word have been burnt, attacked and despised. Believers in the Word have also been burnt, attacked and despised, yet today it has the widest circulation of any book. The words of Jesus have been proved true. 'Heaven and earth will pass away, but my words will never pass away . . . My words which I speak will judge you at the last day.'

In recent centuries, more subtle ways of attacking trust in God's

Word have been contrived by that snake who asked, 'Are you sure God said this? Did not God have ulterior motives?' (Genesis 3:1). That snake, 'which deceives the whole world', whose deception is so clever that he would deceive even the true elect if that were possible, brings to the unbeliever 'delusion and lawlessness' (2 Thessalonians 2).

Satan's time-tested strategy from creation to today's critics has been: Are you sure it is God's Word? Weren't there ulterior motives by God and his writers? Isn't it merely folklore?

THAT DANGEROUS BOOK

In Soweto, a woman was burnt to death for selling Bibles. Car tyres were put round her and set alight. 'We don't like what you are doing,' said the atheist agitators.

Now, what's so dangerous about the Bible, you may well exclaim. Everybody has had a go at banning it. They tried to ban it at various times down the centuries. In the first century, John the apostle was banished to the Isle of Patmos. He says in Revelation 1:9 that it was for the Word of God – that's the Bible isn't it – and the testimony of Jesus Christ. Did somebody feel threatened? Was it the Roman political power?

Later, at the beginning of the fourth century, Imperial Rome tried to destroy every copy of the Bible. Roman soldiers searched peoples' houses, and Christians were threatened if they tried to hide their precious copies. It is thought that Revelation 6:9 refers to this. It says: 'I saw under the altar the souls of them that were slain for the Word of God and the testimony of Jesus Christ.'

Jesus foretold this and put it down to Satan. Those who betrayed the Bible and gave it up to save their lives were called traitors by the Christians. That meant that, when the persecution was over, they were excommunicated.

Many centuries on, quite a different type started banning the Bible – religious people this time – church leaders in the Middle Ages. Tyndale was burnt to death for translating it. He had translated it so that the simplest ploughboy could read God's precious message for himself, but the church of that day didn't want him to read it for himself. Why? Was it dangerous? It was, because it exposed them, the church leaders, for they had added errors to God's Word.

A 'Con' Trick?

Later still, a more subtle attack was made upon the Bible. That started over 200 years ago and is still going on today. It started with the Rationalists and has now infiltrated into the churches. It was the accusation that the Bible was a fraud from beginning to end – yes, from beginning to end. There is nothing like making a thorough job of your accusations!

Moses wrote the first five books of the Bible, but they said this was a fraud – a pious fraud, they called it! But the Lord Jesus said, 'Moses wrote of me'. Also, the claim that Deuteronomy was written by Moses was a fraud, they said. It was a 'con' trick written in King Josiah's time, 700 years later than the book claims. To suggest that, shows that they have overlooked the fact that King Asa referred to Deuteronomy 200 years earlier than Josiah's time in 2 Kings 14:6.

They claim that the prophecy of Isaiah was another 'con' trick. It could not have been written by Isaiah, they said, because all the prophecies came true, so they must have been written after the events! The same was said of the prophecy of Daniel. This ignores the fact that there are still prophecies being fulfilled today.

The Gospels also were a fraud, they said. They must have been written a hundred years after the events, they say. The church had written many exaggerated stories which changed an ordinary prophet named Jesus into a miracle-working Christ. A TV programme still proclaimed this in 1992, and a Diocesan Course for church people only moderated it condescendingly as follows: 'As the result of such investigations, it seems reasonable to conclude that Jesus, like many of his contemporaries, performed miraculous actions'.

How is it that all types of people and philosophies have agreed either to ban or attack the Bible down the centuries? Was there something dangerous about it? Today, some countries still ban the Bible. People's houses are searched and the Scriptures are burnt. We get letters reporting this from those who have been converted through my radio broadcasts.

Whom Does the Bible Threaten?

The Bible is dangerous only to one person – Satan. It exposes him. It calls him, 'that old snake called the devil and Satan, who deceives the whole world' (Revelation 12:9). He gives power of propaganda, 'a mouth speaking great things and blasphemies against those who have the testimony of Jesus Christ' (Revelation 13:4–8). Why? Because he knows that he has only a short time left before Christ returns.

Propagandists have tried to tell you that the Bible is a fraud, written after the events that were prophesied. Could Jeremiah have foretold that Jesus would bring in the new covenant which would change believers' hearts?

Could Isaiah, writing even later, have foretold that God would become man? Could he have fully described Christ's suffering on the cross for your sins in chapter 53? Could King David – and we know when he reigned, it was over 900 years before Christ – have described Christ's suffering on the cross for your sins and described it detail by detail in Psalm 22? 'They pierced my hands and my feet.' Did anyone do that to David? Could King David have described Christ's resurrection and ascension and coming again to reign on earth in his psalms, unless God had told him. Indeed, Jesus said, 'David spoke by the Holy Spirit.' Could David have known, without that, that the Messiah would be his descendant who would make his throne – the throne of David – eternal?

And what about Daniel? If God had not told him his plans, could he have known that the Messiah was going to come to atone for sins in AD 30? In Daniel 9:24 we are given the actual length of time from a given event – that is the rebuilding of Jerusalem's walls, to the cross. It was to be 490 years. God told him. The rabbis of Christ's time had it all worked out. That is why all the Jews were expecting him, according to the New Testament.

A remarkable thing is the discovery in the Dead Sea Scrolls of a discussion amongst the rabbis. They said, 'The Messiah should have arrived by now. How is it that he has not come, that is except this fraud – the Nazarene!'

Oh yes, Satan tells you it is all a fraud, but the ironic thing is that the devil is the greatest fraud and liar that creation has ever known.

Don't let him deceive you. Listen to what 2 Corinthians 4:4 says. Satan, the devil 'has blinded the intellects of those who do not believe, in order to stop the light of the glorious gospel of Christ, who is the image of God, shining in their hearts'.

Beware of Imitations

The way God inspired his Word to be written is quite different from some conceptions. That Diocesan Course mentioned previously suggests divination as illustrating how Scripture originated.

Divination Is Different from Biblical Prophecy

Divination is strictly forbidden in Leviticus 19:31 and 20:6. The difference is set out in Deuteronomy 18:10–20:

> Let no one be found among you who sacrifices his son or daughter in the fire, who practises divination or sorcery, interprets omens, engages in witchcraft, or casts spells, or who is a medium or spiritist or who consults the dead. Anyone who does these things is detestable to the Lord, and because of these detestable practices, the Lord your God will drive out those nations before you. You must be blameless before the Lord your God . . . The nations you will dispossess listen to those who practise sorcery or divination. But as for you, the Lord your God has not permitted you to do so. The Lord your God will raise up for you a prophet like me from among your own brothers. You must listen to him. For this is what

An Arab Diviner at Work

(Extract from Guillaume, *Prophecy and Divination*, pp 118f.)

I was told the following by Abu-I-Hussain Ibn 'Ayyash:

I was informed by a trustworthy person that when Isma'il, the son of Bubul, was denounced by Sa'id, he kept to his house; and as he was expecting the birth of a child, ordered a Beduin Wizard to be fetched to take its horoscope. When he came, Isma'il asked him if he knew for what purpose he had been summoned. He looked about the apartments and said, 'To ask me about an unborn child'. Isma'il, who had given orders that the man should not be told the reason he was summoned, was astonished and asked whether it was a boy or girl. Again, the man glanced round the apartment and replied, 'A boy'.

Just then, a hornet flew on the head of Isma'il, which a slave flicked off, hitting it and killing it. The Beduin got up and said: 'By Allah! You have killed the vizier and are installed in his place; and I deserve a reward for announcing it.' He began to dance about, and Isma'il was trying to quiet him when a shout was heard announcing the birth.

Isma'il asked them to see the sex. When they replied, 'A boy', he was delighted with the success of the diviner and the hope he held out of the vizierate for himself and the destruction of Sa'id. So he dismissed the Beduin with a reward, and less than a month later, Muwaffaq sent for Isma'il, invested him with the vizierate and put Sa'id into his power.

Remembering the words of the Beduin, he sent for him and asked him, 'How was it that you said what you did on that day, seeing that you can have no knowledge of the unseen, and the matter was not one that was revealed in the stars?' He replied: 'All that we do is to note omens, to watch the flight of birds, and to divine from what we see. You began by asking me why I had been summoned. As I glanced around the room, my eye fell on a water-cooler with pots attached to it; I thought to myself, something carried, and said, "An unborn child". Then the hornet flew upon you, and that is girt at the waist as the Christians are girt with the Zonarion; further the hornet was an enemy which wanted to sting you; now Sa'id is by origin a Christian and your enemy. Therefore, I divined that the hornet meant your enemy, and as your slave killed it, I divined that you would kill him.'

Isma'il gave him a handsome present and dismissed him.

Guillaume cites this and other stories in order to demonstrate that divination was the result of emptying the mind so as to be receptive to people and events. He considers that both the stimulus of objects and a sensitivity to the people around the diviner, were important. How often the prognostication was right, and how often it was wrong, we cannot say – successes are generally remembered! However, the process, he claims, illuminates many prophetic oracles . . . or does the prophet mean something entirely different when he says: 'I saw in the night visions', and 'Thus says Yahweh'?

you asked of the Lord your God at Horeb on the day of the assembly when you said, 'Let us not hear the voice of the Lord our God nor see this great fire any more, or we will die.' The Lord said to me 'What they say is good. I will raise up for them a prophet like you from among their brothers; *I will put my words in his mouth,* and he will tell them everything I command him. If anyone does not listen to my words that the prophet speaks in my name, I myself will call him to account. But a prophet who presumes to speak in my name anything I have not commanded him to say, or a prophet who speaks in the name of other gods, must be put to death.' (NIV, my emphasis)

TRUE PROPHECY

The way in which God inspired his Word to be written is quite different. It is clearly stated in many places. To Moses, God spoke audibly and face to face. In Numbers 12, Miriam and Aaron said:

Has the Lord spoken only by Moses? . . . The Lord spoke suddenly to Moses, Miriam and Aaron and said, 'Come out you three.' . . . and the Lord came down in the pillar of the cloud and stood in the door of the tabernacle and called Miriam and Aaron, and he said, 'Hear now my words. If there is a prophet among you, I the Lord will make myself known unto him in a vision and will speak to him in a dream. My servant Moses is not so . . . with him I will speak mouth to mouth, even visibly and not in dark speeches and the likeness of the Lord he will behold. Why then were you not afraid to speak against my servant Moses?'

Audible Dictation

God not only spoke audibly to Moses, two-thirds of Exodus, Leviticus and Numbers are represented as written down as the *audible dictation of God.* Why then are so many not afraid to speak against God's servant Moses?

Look with me at some examples of how God spoke to the other prophets.

Isaiah heard an audible voice, 'I heard the voice of the Lord' (6:8). So did **Ezekiel**: 'The Lord said to me, "Son of Man, all my words that I shall speak to you receive in your heart, and hear with your ears" ' (3:10).

Daniel heard some of God's message in dreams and visions (2:19), but he also received audible messages. Gabriel the archangel was sent by God, 'and he informed me and talked with me' (9:22). So did the messenger in 12:8, 'I heard but understood not'. This makes it clear that they were not Daniel's ideas, but God's revelation.

The words in **Amos** 3:8 are explicit: 'Certainly, the Lord God will do nothing without revealing his secret to his servants, the prophets.'

The prophets were also told to write down what God had said. 'The Lord said to me [Isaiah], take a great scroll and write in it with a man's pen' (8:1). 'Now go, write it before them on a tablet and note it in a book, that it may be for the time to come for ever and ever' (30:8).

The word came to **Jeremiah** from the Lord saying, 'Thus speaks the Lord God of Israel, saying, write all the words that I have spoken to you in a book' for when Israel and Judah return to Palestine (30:2).

Ezekiel said, 'The Word of the Lord came to me saying, "Son of man, write the name of the day, even of this same day . . . and utter a parable to the rebellious house [of Judah] . . . I the Lord have spoken it. It shall come to pass' (24:2,3,14).

Some plans of God have a lengthy time schedule as we will see in Volume 3, so to impatient **Habakkuk**, the Lord answered and said, 'Write the vision and make it plain upon tablets that he may run who reads it, for the vision is for an appointed time, but at the end it will speak and not lie, even though it seems delayed, wait for it because it will certainly come' (2:2,3).

God's Timeless Word

It is because God's Word spans the ages that he says it will never perish. 'Heaven and earth will pass away,' said Jesus, 'but my words will never pass away.' 'For ever, O Lord, your word is settled in heaven.' 'All your commandments are true. Your testimonies I have known of old that you have founded them for ever.' 'Your word is true from the beginning, and every one of your righteous judgements endures for ever' (Psalm 119:89,152,160). 'The word of the Lord endures for ever,' said Peter in his first letter.

Sir Frederick Kenyon, former Director of the British Museum wrote in *The Bible and Ancient Manuscripts*: 'The Christian can take the whole Bible in his hand and say without fear or hesitation that he holds in it the true Word of God, handed down without essential loss from generation to generation throughout the centuries.'

Because his Word will judge us, as Jesus said, there are severe warnings against tampering with it. The Torah is not to be added to or subtracted from and the Bible ends with the same warning in Revelation 22:18–19. Jesus rebuked those who added church tradition to God's Word (Mark 7:7–13).

Jesus said that not one smallest letter or one comma will fail to be fulfilled and any teacher encouraging it will be called the least in the kingdom of heaven (Matthew 5:18,19).

The Attitude Required

For all these reasons, God states the right attitude required for us to approach his Word: 'To this one will I look, even to the one who is humble and of a contrite spirit, and trembles at my word' (Isaiah 66:2).

The proud intellectual doubter develops a mental blockage to truth which is 'revealed to babes', said Jesus (Matthew 11:25).

By way of summary, I quote Dr W.F. Albright of worldwide acclaim for his archaeology and knowledge of ancient scripts. He said, concerning destructive criticism of the reliability of Scripture: 'Those remarkable discoveries have dealt a final blow to such extreme critical views' (*Archaeology of Palestine*, Penguin, p 240). He draws distinction between 'well-trained philologians and empty pretenders to knowledge', who create sensations in the daily press (p 200).

Conclusions

I have given you evidence to help your faith in God's remarkable book, but 'you can lead a horse to water but you can't make him drink', the saying goes. It needs a change of attitude. That is what the word repentance means in the Greek. '*Metanoeite*' means 'change your mind, your thinking'. Paul wrote, 'We overthrow all reasonings and every proud thing that exalts itself against the knowledge of God and take captive every theory to the obedience of Christ.'

In the first Bible I bought after my conversion, I wrote in the fly-leaf (prophetically?):

We've travelled together, my Bible and I,
Through all kinds of weather, with smile and with sigh.
In sorrow or sunshine; in tempest or calm,
Thy friendship unchanging, my lamp and my psalm.

So now who shall part us, my Bible and I,
Shall 'isms' or 'schisms' or 'new lights', who try?
Shall shadow or substance, or stone for good bread,
Supplant thy sound wisdom, give folly instead?

Oh no, my dear Bible, exponent of light,
Thou sword of the Spirit, put error to flight.
And still through life's journey, until my last sigh,
We'll travel together, my Bible and I.
                              (Author unknown)

RELIABILITY OF OLD TESTAMENT RECORDS

Further Illustrated by Recent Discovery

Legal procedure
Sale of cave and field to Abraham (Genesis 23) is on Hittite legal terms practised in Abraham's time, 1900 BC. Archaeology verified this (K. A. Kitchen, Liverpool University).

Contemporary practice
In the time of Jacob, 1900 BC, Rachel took the family 'doll' or teraphim. The reason would not be known even to Moses. Archaeology reveals that the possession of the teraphim meant a right to a father-in-law's property.

Literary style
Ugarit tablets, 1400 BC, showed same style of poetry as in the Song of Miriam in Exodus 15. Independent dating methods agree with Bible dates and writing methods.

Educational methods
Gezer calendar, 1000 BC, is a schoolboy's exercise tablet. It gives the annual farming rotation, and reflects Old Testament scripts of David's time.

Parallel scripts
Samaritan Pentateuch (copies still exist) is found to be in the same style of script as the Siloam Inscription of Hezekiah's time, 721 BC, when the Samaritans were first taught the Torah.

Transmission accuracy
'The correct transmission of names is notoriously difficult.' Copies of Manetho's list of 140 Egyptian kings when compared with Egyptian monuments, has 63 of them unrecognisable in any single syllable. In contrast to this secular writer, 'the text in the Hebrew Bible has been transmitted with the most minute accuracy'. Dr J.W. Wenham, *Christ and the Bible* (Tyndale Press).

S U M M A R Y

THAT AMAZING BOOK

Oldest book in the world:
- 4,000 years back to Abraham; 3,400 years to Moses.
- Why? To prepare for Saviour (Gen 12).
- Prophecy ceased 400 BC to wait for Saviour.
- Other countries' histories only by archaeology.

Miraculous preservation:
- Attempts to destroy it and Christians.
- John imprisoned for writing 'Word of God' on Isle of Patmos actually enabled him to write Revelation.
- Roman persecution and traitors until 4th century.
- Medieval church because it exposed added errors.
- More subtle Rationalists by criticism.
- Satan says prophecies are fraudulent, but Satan is the big fraud (John 8:44, Rev 12:9).

Says how God inspired the prophets:
1. **By audible dictation** (not by divination – forbidden Lev 19:31; Deut 18:10–20).
   - **Moses:** Audibly and face to face (Num 12). 'I speak to Moses mouth to mouth and visibly'. Two-thirds of Ex, Lev and Num are written as dictated.
   - **Isaiah:** 'I heard the voice of the Lord'.
   - **Ezekiel:** 'Hear with your ears.'
   - **Daniel:** 'He talked with me.' 'I heard, but did not understand.' (So it was not his own ideas.)
2. **By vision usually with voice.**
3. **Told to write it down.**
   - **Isaiah** 8:1 'Write on a tablet and note in a book.'
   - **Jeremiah** 30:2. 'Write all the words I have spoken in a book.'
   - **Ezekiel** 24:2,3,14 'Write . . . I the Lord have spoken it. It will come to pass.'
   - **Habakkuk** 2:2,3. 'Write the vision. Make it plain.'

For all time:
- 'Heaven and earth will pass away but my words will never pass away,' said Jesus in all Synoptics (Mk 13:31).
- 'Your Word is forever' (Ps 119) 'Endures for ever' (1 Pet).
- 'Not one comma (you) will fail,' said Jesus. 'Any teacher teaching it will be called least' (Matt 5:18,19).

Scriptures claim:
- 'All scripture is given by inspiration of God' (2 Tim 3:16).
- 'Holy men spake as they were borne along by the Spirit of God' (2 Pet 1:21).
- 'David spoke by the Holy Spirit,' said Jesus (Mk 12:36).
- 'The Scripture cannot be broken' (John 10:35).
- 'Thy Word is truth' (John 17:17).
- 'Anyone adding or taking away from this book will have his place in the Holy City removed,' said God (Rev 22:19).

A SHORT BIBLIOGRAPHY

Albright, W.F., *From Stone Age to Christianity* (London: Doubleday, 1940).

Anderson and Coffin, *Fossils in Focus* (Zondervan, 1978).

Atkinson, Basil, *Valiant in Fight* (London: IVF, 1940).

Bimson, John, *Re-dating the Exodus and Conquest* (Sheffield: JSOT Press).

Bimson, John, *World of the Old Testament* (Milton Keynes: Scripture Union, 1988).

Blomberg, Craig, *Historic Reliability of the Gospels* (Leicester: IVP, 1987).

Bruce, F.F., *Acts* (Cambridge: Tyndale Press, 1965).

Bruce, F.F., *Second Thoughts on the Dead Sea Scrolls* (Carlisle: Paternoster, 1966).

Bruce, F.F., *Christian Origins Outside the New Testament* (Eerdman, 1974).

Bruce, F.F., *The New Testament Documents: Are They Reliable?* (Leicester: IVP).

Bruce, F.F., *The Real Jesus* (London: Hodder & Stoughton (The Jesus Library), 1981).

Cassuto, U., *Documentary Hypothesis* (Hebrew University, Jerusalem).

Conder, C.R., *The Teal Amarner Tablets* (Watts, 1887).

Daissman, Adolf, *Light from the Ancient East* (London: Hodder & Stoughton, 1927).

Davidson, F., *New Bible Commentary* (Leicester: IVP). Drane, John, Fact or Fancy (Oxford: Lion Publishing, 1990).

Edersheim, A., *Life and Times of Jesus the Messiah* (Harlow: Longman, 1920).

Evans-Pritchard, E., *Theories of Primitive Religion* (Oxford University Press, 1978).

'Excavating women: women scholars in European and Egyptian archaelogy', *J. Anthropological Institute*, Sept. 1999.

France, R.T., *The Evidence for Jesus* (London: Hodder & Stoughton (The Jesus Library), 1986).

Harrison, R.K., *Introduction to New Testament* (Leicester: IVP, 1977).

Harrison, R.K., *Introduction to Old Testament* (Leicester: IVP, 1977).

Haywood, A., *God's Truth* (London: Marshall, Morgan & Scott, 1973).

Kitchen, K.A., *The Bible in its World* (Carlisle: Paternoster, 1978).

Kitchen, K.A., *Pentateuchal Criticism and Interpretation* (Leicester: IVP, 1965).

Kitchen, K.A., *Ancient Orient and the Old Testament* (Cambridge: Tyndale).

Layard, A.B., *Nineveh and its Remains: an Expedition to Northern Iraq* (London: Murray, 1851).

Martin, W.J., *Stylistic Criteria and Analysis of Pentateuch* (Cambridge: Tyndale, 1955).

Millard and Wiseman, Essays on the Patriarchal Narratives (Leicester: IVP).

Mitchell, Terence, 'Ancient Aramaic Text form Egypt', *Faith and Thought*, Oct. 2002.

Monaghan and Boye, *Adventures in Reconciliation*, Eagle Press, 1998.

Morton, Harold C., *The Exodus and Modern Discovery*, Hammett & Co., Taunton.

Motyer, J.A., *The Pentateuch and Criticism* (Theological Students' Fellowship).

Packer, J., *Fundamentalism and the Word of God* (Leicester: IVP, 1996).

Packer, J., *Christ the Controversialist* (London: Hodder & Stoughton).

Ramsay, W.M., *St. Paul the Traveller and Roman* Citizen (London: Hodder & Stoughton, 1920).

Robinson, Donald, *Joshua's Reform and the Book of the Law* (Leicester: IVP, 1974).

Robinson, J.A.T., *Re-dating the New Testament* (London: SCM).

Rowley, H.H., *The Dead Sea Scrolls and the New Testament* (London: SPCK, 1957).

Sayes, Prof, *Archaeology of Cuneiform Inscriptions* (London: SPCK, 1906).

Stott, JW.R., *Basic Christianity* (London: Hodder & Stoughton).

Unger's Bible Dictionary (Chicago: Moody Press).

Wenham, John, *Re-dating Matthew, Mark and Luke* (London: Hodder & Stoughton, 1991).

Wright, N.T., *Who Was Jesus?* (London: SPCK, 1992).